Sally..

Thank-you for everyt[

Love
Sarah Jane McWeam.

Life What's the Point

SARAH JANE MELLVURN

authorHOUSE®

AuthorHouse™ UK Ltd.
500 Avebury Boulevard
Central Milton Keynes, MK9 2BE
www.authorhouse.co.uk
Phone: 08001974150

First published by AuthorHouse 2/13/2009

ISBN: 978-1-4389-2881-4 (sc)

Printed in the United States of America
Bloomington, Indiana

This book is printed on acid-free paper.

Prologue

I HAVE WANTED TO WRITE A BOOK FOR many years in the hope that it would help one person through their suffering and for them to seek help it is out there but You have to ask for it just remember that you're not the only ones this as happened to and you can survive the abuse and come through the other side and be a survivor.

Throughout this book my intention is to show that whatever you go through there is always a point to life and you can get through this. There is no shame in asking for help. The shame is not yours but the person that as done this to you.

There is always a point to life as I have found out. You're the only person that can ask for help no-one else can do this for you.

At least now you are believed but when I was going through the abuse you was not and it was very much swept under the carpet, For me abuse was not heard of like it is nowadays, it was not suppose to happen but it did and does far too often as I well know I suffered over eighteen years in total at the hands of different people as a child and also throughout most of my adult lief to, I have dealt with the abuse and slowly turned the guilt around. It has not been easy to do but I have done through counselling which as meant a lot of hard work but I could not got to where I am today if it was not for some very special people in my life and such close friends.

I have changed the names to protect the innocent..

God Bless you all

Chapter 1

I WAS EIGHTEEN MONTHS OLD WHEN MY PARENTS separated I had spent most of the time with my grandmother who was more of a mother to me than my own will ever be, through her I learnt to love and trust in people.

Life was not easy but the time I spent with my father was by far from an easy time more so when he re-married and the lady he married had four children from her previous marriage all girls I began to feel the odd one out even though I had an older brother which I never saw very much of once our dad got married again and even to this day I do not.

Family life can be quite strained at times but living through abuse afraid to tell anyone always feeling that it is your fault and being made to feel that what happens to you somehow you deserve abuse to happen but something deep down told me that this was wrong. I wonder if this had anything to do with what grandma had said to me about being careful of your dad and not to trust him as a daughter should, it began to get very scary I felt alone and very scared he was beginning to come in my room a lot more to start with he come in and ask me what I thought about his then new girlfriend and family and that point they seemed alright but I did not know them but I did say that I did not want to be with them or live them even though I did not really know them but something told me that it was not right but to say what I was thinking would have got me another beating maybe I should have said that I did not feel that it was right to say anything and I did not want another mother in my life and I did not need anyone else I had got my Grandma and as far as I was concerned that is all I wanted or needed apart from my mum of course.

I did not need another mother I had grandma and my mother as and when I saw her which was not that often not as often as it should have been.

We began to see more and more of his girlfriend and her family more and more and before long we would be moving in with them, we would have to move house I would have to move school leave all my friends and start all over I began to hate his new additional family and resent them.

I was already feeling pretty low and alone and soon he would be bringing more people into our home and it was already feeling that it was no longer our home but somebody's else home to, mind you the house were we living in was very cold our toilet was outside always full of rats especially in the mornings we lived very close to a river, I suppose it was expected to have rats and mice around when you are so close to a river. I hated having to go out there in the morning I hate rats and mice and one day my dad told me that it was about time I started to clear the rats away in the mornings and I was so young to and was frightened of them so I refused to do it so he took off his belt I was only in a thin nightdress he belted me until my back hurt so much that it was bleeding I had never known him to be like this before it was the first time he had ever hit me like this and this frightened me it was cold outside in the yard and the cobbles under feet was hurting my bare feet and I was crying he hit me some more and then from inside my oldest brother Peter came out to see what was going on he was about ten maybe eleven and I was four going into five. Somehow he stopped our dad and got me inside through the back door and into the kitchen which was very cold and bare we had no carpets or many things in the kitchen just the bare essentials Peter left me on one of the dining chairs and told me to wait then dad came in a short time later there was a big argument and a fight between dad and Peter and they were both hitting each other and I thought that they were going to kill each other and then Peter hit my dad so hard that he fell to the floor and was not moving and before long Peter was at my side trying to sort me out and calm me down he was comforting me and cuddling me and holding me gently in his arms, I was supposed to go to school that morning but I did not go I stayed at home for a while with Peter but he went out for a short while and then when Peter returned sometime later he brought my grandma round and saw me there she asked what had happened, Peter again told her that he has lost it I don't know maybe he had lost it before with Peter but if he had he was not saying but grandma was packing a few things for me and telling me to get what I want to take with me as I always took a few of my favourite things with me anything else I wanted was already at her place and I was going to spend some time with her how long I did not know but I knew that I was not going to school until I was alright again. I was already spending a lot of the time with my grandma, so spending some more time didn't seem strange to me I loved being my at my Grandma's and I loved her so much. I stayed with my grandma for about two weeks then I went back home and a few days later he was cooking tea he had some chips in the chip pan on the stove I asked for a drink he told me to get one for myself and he was too busy to get it for me so I had to get a chair and climb up to the kitchen sink and as I did I caught the chip pan with my jumper and crash everything went to the floor including me and the chip pan went all over me and he was furious and then he realised that I had hot fat all over me and it was burning my skin and the pain was unbearable and the worst part was that I was in woollen clothes which stuck to me and I had to go to hospital and was treated for burns to the whole of my left side I had second degree burns on my stomach, legs and arm but my face was alright they removed my clothing and dressed the burns and sent me home, a few hours later I had to go back to the hospital because the burns where bleeding and seeping through the dressings they re-dressed the burns and sent me home and I was pushed through the door into the living room which was a small dark room with only a small window in the room and a open fire along the wall to the right of the door and it was still glowing from being lit earlier and when we went into the room we was met with the warmth of the room. As I pushed through the door I tumbled and fell on to the floor flat on my stomach and I was in agony and again the burns were bleeding through the dressing and back to the hospital I had to go for the second time in a day so in the end they put plaster over the dressings so that it would protect them and save me even more pain it was uncomfortable but at least I was not banging the wounds all of the time or they were bleeding and me having to go back and forwards to the hospital so much and even though it was uncomfortable having plaster on my leg at least it was protected. It took several weeks for the wounds to start to heal which meant even more time off school.

When I finally went back to school a several weeks later I was glad to get back and I had missed my friends and being at school I just had not realised how much I had missed going to school but more so how much I had missed my friends. Everyone was asking why I had been off and when I told everyone, they told me I should be more careful in the future. It was not long after I went back to school that I would have to leave that school and my friends some whom I knew that I wouldn't be seeing again. We would be moving in with his girlfriend and daughters and I would have to move school and start all over again making new friends something that I did not want to do but I knew in time I would have to do.

I had always gone to church as a small child at first I went and sat beside my dad whilst he played the organ and he was fondling me throughout the service when he was not playing the organ when we were supposed to be saying our prayers, and told me that God would be watching me and making sure that I was being good and that I was obeying thy parent, and I would be judged on my own actions and I would be seriously punished if I said anything to anyone, he often said I would not see my mum or grandma again and that would be part of my punishment but God's punishment would be far greater than anyone else's punishment and I should be a good girl and keep quiet and not say anything to anyone or make sudden movement to let anyone know something was wrong, I began to cry inside very silent tears and tears that no-one knew that I was doing it was the only way I could cry.

When we got back to the house which was only a short distance from where we went to church and opposite the football ground but I hated that house I hated all the rats that came up from the river and I still hate them now I have not got over the fear of rats and will always fear them I do not think that this will ever go now either.

I was told that I had been a good girl in church and that I must now continue to being a good girl now that we were home. I was only three to four at this time. I could not understand why I was always being told to be a good girl as I was not a naughty child but I must have been a naughty girl to be constantly being told to be a good girl.

As time went on the Church became my way of escape from things for awhile but unfortunately that soon changed for me and the church was no longer an escape from things. It had become another place where I was no longer safe and another place where I started to fear, that something would happen and it did happen on several occasion. Not necessary at a service or on a Sunday I was slowly losing the specialness that I once felt in the church and the safety I felt there. Unfortunately that also had turned into another place that I dreaded being on my own with my dad. However I did still enjoyed the service and being part of the service once the service began this remained special to me. It still does today, but for completely different reasons

I was seeing so much of my Grandma and spending most of my days with her. She was kind, caring and so loving she was so special to me and always will be. She lived on the third floor of a high raised block of flats it was a two bed-roomed flat beautifully decorated and carpeted. She did not have much money but she got by. I was trying to read to my grandma but everytime I tried to say certain words I could not say them and she also noticed that there was other words I was struggling with and she knew something needed to be done to help me with this but she did not know what she could do or were to go where I could get the help. Grandma tried to talk to my dad about this as my speech was causing her concern and in the end it was my grandma that took me to the doctors to discuss this with the doctor and he told her that I had got a speech impairment but this could be corrected with a bit of help and I was referred to a speech therapist which came through within a few weeks to see someone, Grandma took me to the health centre the day of the appointment and my dad was convinced that it was a waste of time and it was just me playing up and being awkward and continuing to be a naughty girl and that I was attention seeking as usual my grandma stuck up for me and told him that she never as any problem with me. She told him that it must be something to do with your parenting skills than it was to do with your daughter, dad did not like this at all and slapped my grandma across her face her only response to him was that one day he would pay for what he had done to her and what he was doing and he was nothing special to this world. However as she walked away she was crying and saying things to herself none that I could understand what she was saying but I guess she was angry with him but we did not talk about this and I was told not to mention it again and out of respect for her I did not ever mention that day until now. I could not understand why a child would want to slap their parent or treat them like he had just done to his mother. I felt upset for grandma but felt angry at my dad how could he hurt the one person I love so much why did he after to hit her and hurt her. I was quiet on the way back to grandma's flat were she made a drink and made us lunch.

We were both quiet that night and I knew grandma was angry and upset but I just sat at the side of her cuddling her as she did me to. The love that we shared was so much deeper than I would ever know at the time it was a love that was unconditional love. A love that knew no boundaries was a special love.

I was due to go back to my dad's in a few days time something that I did not want to do but I knew that I would have to go back sooner or later, if I had my way I would not have gone back. I was scared to go back again I always was when the time came to go back to my dad's and grandma noticed it to and as always she reassured me that I would be coming to stay with her again as I always did.

I went to the speech therapy twice a week to start until eventually I went to weekly before going to monthly and eventually stopping and as always my grandma was there with me and helped me correct my speech as much as they possibly could do.

The next day I was going back to my dad's and I was screaming that I did not want to go back I wanted to stay with my grandma but knew deep down that I could not and the time had come for me to go back to what was supposed to be home but my home was with my grandma and that is where my heart was.

The day was fast approaching when I would have to say goodbye to my friends and leave the school where I was happy and the home that I knew, I was not sorry to get away from the rats though but I was having to start all over again not something I wanted to do but I did not have choice in that one.

We were beginning to spend a lot time at my dad's new girlfriend's house and her daughters I was told this was because they wanted us all to get a long and to get to know each other. The more I spent there the more I hated it the only advantage to being there was I was away from the rats and the outside toilet but apart from that there was no advantage to being there and it was a place I did not want to go to long term or ever if I could get my own way. We would spend several days there and then go back to our home but she often came with him to our home and I hated that it felt like she was watching me all of the time and she always followed me around the house and it did not matter where I went when I turned round she was there. I could not even go in to mine and my brothers room without her just walking in even my brother did not just walk in especially when the door was closed that either meant we were getting changed or we wanted sometime alone and some personal time and Peter and I respected that. It was a shame other people did not do that she felt she could do what she wanted and would do what she wanted she made that very clear that day that she would do what she wanted and go where she wanted and no-one was going to stop her. A few hours later she went back to her daughters and I was glad she had gone to. However I stayed in my room and sat on the floor in the corner of the room with my knees bent into my stomach and holding my knees into my stomach with my head on my knees and I was deep in thought and then I felt tears rolling down my face and I had not realised that I was crying before that, I was not bothered that I was I was more afraid of my dad seeing me cry because it was weak to cry and only weak people cried so I could not let my dad see me crying I knew what I would be in for if he did see me crying. I was sat in this corner for ages and I did not want to move and when things were bothering me I always sat like this it was my way of having space to think but my protective space and safe space that would not be invaded but that is what I thought and felt anyway I knew Peter would not have invaded this space he respected it the only thing Peter would have done would to offer me a cuddle when I was like this but did nothing until I nodded or said yes please. I sensed someone in my room and I knew it was not Peter as I had shut the door and I had not heard the door knocked but it could have been as I was in my own little safe world at this time, I looked up and saw my dad standing there with his arms folded and he looked so angry I jumped up from where I was and I wanted to run far from here but as I went to go pass my dad he grabbed my arm and gripped it very hard and just looked at me with the look he always used when I had been naughty but I did not know anything that I had done that could have been considered naughty however after a few minutes in occurred to me that the only thing I could think of was that I had been crying and I knew that was weak to do there was nothing else that I could think of. I was beginning to feel scared and I was starting to feel panicked and my stomach was doing somersaults I had to fight the tears from falling from my eyes. Dad then picked me up and threw me onto my bed and in doing so I banged my head on the wall, it hurt like hell and felt something wet run down my neck and when I put my hand across my neck to wipe it I saw that there was blood on my hand not a lot but even so my head was bleeding then everything went black. I don't know what had happened but when I woke up I was laying on my bed naked.

It was not long after this that I was told that we would all be moving soon and when I questioned how soon I was told within the next few weeks or so but I protested that I did not want to move this was our home and I was told to be quiet and do what I was told and my dad made a comment that I act more like an adult rather than of a child and for protesting I got a belt for answering him back and for questioning what he had told me after all I was brought up to respect my parents and my elders and at this point in time I was doing neither at this time and I was going to have to pay for this and I knew I would do to. I was surprised when my dad left the room after that without saying anything else to me. I was also surprised that he did not come back into my room that night, Peter was in the room for awhile on his own till I went up to bed which was always at 19:30pm and when I went into our room to get ready for bed he left for a few minutes whilst I got changed and called once I was changed and in bed which I seem to do faster each day and then Peter came back in we said our prayers together as we always did then he would tuck me up into bed and read a story to me sometimes he made stories up to tell me and I loved them sometimes they were sad and sometimes they were silly ones to make me laugh and there were times we just talked about things it was hard to believe that Peter was only seven years older than me. The way he acted he sometimes seemed much older than that. It did not matter to me if he was a few years older than me or many years he was my brother and I loved him so much. We always parted in the evening with a cuddle before he climbed into bed shortly afterwards after that as he always did it was our regular routine in the evening every evening without fail. It was great having my brother so close to me and having someone to protect me and to make me feel safe.

A few weeks later we were told that it is time to gather our things together as it was time to move on and supposedly to a better life and a better home but I was not convinced of this was the best thing for us and I was still not so sure that it was and I was crying as I did not want to move or leave my school and the few friends that I had. I found it difficult to make friends as I was often bullied because of my speech and the problems that I had with some words and other kids thought it was funny and that gave them an excuse to bully me but I still loved going to school and being with the few friends that I had. However before I left someone came up behind me and pushed me over and over I went and fell face first on the floor and split my chin open and I screamed and teachers and all the kids came running to the noise and when they saw it was me they were surprised that I was screaming as I was the one often sat in a corner with a couple of friends out of the way of all the other kids and had our own fun.

The day I left the school the small group of friends that I had we were all crying and promised that we would see each other again soon some of them I did but not for many years later and some I did not. It was a strange day, on my last day as everything seemed to go by so slowly as if we were in slow motion. Assembly was the time when they always said goodbye to anyone that was leaving and that did not matter if you were a member of staff or a pupil at the school they want you to feel special and that you would be missed from the school. It was hard for me to say goodbye and before the assembly was over I was crying uncontrollably and no-one could comfort me. The end of the day soon came and it was the first time I had been picked up from school since I could remember I do not ever remember being picked up from school before this day as I had always took myself to school and home again. It felt strange having my dad pick me up as this was not normal for me and I was scared that he had picked me up. Grandma picked me often when I was going to be staying with her but never my dad and Grandma did not pick me up that often I wished that she would pick me up more often but when she had it were special and a wonderful surprise when she did.

We were going to move into a small council house on a rundown estate with his new girlfriend and children, the house was too small for all of us but we would have to stay there for some time. It was a very small three bedroom house it was not decorated very well and the wall paper that was up, was coming off the walls it was decorated in oranges and browns in and the rooms felt very cold there was no heating just a small gas fire, her daughters were in one room my dad and his a girlfriend were in another and me and Peter was to be in the other. I hated that house I hated being there with all of them his girlfriend was becoming my step mum and trying to take over what I did or did not do she was the most cruellest of people and spiteful of all people I had met to date, and I did not need another mum I had already got one and I loved her so much. I loved my mum so much, I would have loved her more if she was not always letting me down but I tried to make out that I did not care that she was letting me down so much, as far as I was concerned she was my mum and was very important to me even though I did not see her very often. Which meant when I did see her it was even more special to me when I did see her.

My Grandma I adored and loved dearly in a lot of ways she was my mum, even though I knew I had my mum. The times I got to see my mum was becoming less frequent as weeks, months went by. I felt that she did not love me but I kept convincing myself that she did love me but something was stopping her coming to see me but I had no idea what this was.

Then the bomb shell came when my dad told me that they were going to get married and there was nothing that I could do about this, however they did tell us at the same time and all of us together were asked what we thought and I was the only one that objected to that my step sisters were over the moon that they had got a dad finally I was angry and crying saying I did not want this. Peter was not there he was out at the time but they had told quietly before he had gone out with his friends for a football training session as he did regular, so now she was going to become my legal step mum and four step sisters and on top of that I was expected to call her mum and if I did not call her mum I got hit with the belt but she was not my mum and never would be.

A few hours later there was a big argument between me and my step sisters and they were telling me that I am selfish and I am the only one that is spoiling things for them to have a chance of a happy home and family like they have always wanted. I just did not want to be part of this family they meant nothing to me and I did not want to be part of this family were all spiteful and cruel. I thought everything was going to calm down well they did leave my room and slammed the door a few seconds later I heard their door slam shut, I opened my door very slowly and very cautiously and crept out of my room and started to walk down the stairs I hear a creek behind me and the eldest step-sister Charlene and Donna were right behind me and then I felt them on my shoulders the next thing I knew I was tumbling down the stairs and when I reached the bottom of the stairs I sat a little dazed for a few moments then they were on at me punching and kicking me and somehow I manage to stand up and fight back they would not normally fight with me on their own as they were frightened of me I don't know why they were they just where. I had taken quite a lot of punches by this time so I retaliated and hit Donna and she soon backed away from me but Charlene did not she kept going at me and their mum started on me too saying I had no right to hit back at any one of her daughters and she gave me a very hard push were I went into the wall were my head banged hard on the wall at the same time Charlene was still kicking and punching me and whilst I was on the floor she was slapping me on my legs so hard and they were throbbing with pain and I was trying to protect my face from being hit any further but I wouldn't cry or scream or even shut out I just curled up in the corner and did not want to move but she kept going at me and now the two younger step sisters Marie and Rowena were now watching what was going on along with their mum and now dad was there to and not doing anything about what was happening to his own daughter he was stood there laughing at me but I still would not cry I was too scared to cry, Charlene was still slapping me and my leg was getting very sore and it was looking purple and now my step mum was joining in slapping my leg and she was leaving a hand mark now on my leg and with each slap hit was showing up more and more and my leg was stinging so much, Charlene was still slapping me and kicking me I swore to myself that one day I would get my own back for this and there was no way they would get away this and I was determined that they would pay for what they were doing to me. My step mum Karen was still slapping me and my skin was starting to break up now with each slap my leg was bleeding and stinging more and more and they did not let up, then I saw the front door open but they had not it was Peter coming in he was full of mud but he did not care he went absolutely crazy at all of them and told them they had no right to put their hands on me to this extent or any extent. He was more annoyed with Karen and my dad than he was with anyone else but I knew he would not let them get away with and like me somehow he would make them pay.

It was not long afterwards that Peter was at my side and picked me up off the floor and took me into the kitchen to clean me up and see what damage had been done my left thigh was in a mess but once the bruising had gone down and it had healed I would be ok but the pain was unbearable and it hurt to walk on it as each step a sharp pain shot up my leg. I hated them and being in this house with them so much.

Peter and I went to our room where I finally sat on my bed and cried it was ok to cry with Peter as he said it was ok to cry and after all he always cuddled me and comforted me. I loved Peter so much.

I went to stay with my Grandma that night once again and stayed for several weeks. I loved it there and I loved her and she loved me so much that was my family and the only family I wanted to be with at this time. Where I felt loved and wanted and more importantly I felt safe.

Their wedding came round very quickly. I already felt different and the odd one out and felt that I did not belong I did not feel that I should have been there and felt that I was very much in the way. Charlene, Marie and I were bridesmaids but my dress was different to theirs, mine was a brownie dress down to the ankles with flowers on it and theirs was a purple/lilac with very small flowers one of them had black hair and the other had reddish brown and mine was blonde and all the way down my back that day seemed to go on forever and friends and family went back to the house for something to eat which was only a buffet style food and finger food and the guest stayed until the early hours of the morning. I went to bed about half past ten I had enough by then and I just wanted to get out of the way and be on my own for a while. I felt that this was not my home or my family and I felt different to them, I stayed up till Grandma had left and then I was out of the way as far as I could see I had no reason to be up now Grandma had gone home. But that got me into trouble for going to bed whilst there was still guest in the house and was told that I was being very bad mannered and I would pay for it dearly later on. Once everyone had gone my step mum came into my room and told me that she was disappointed in me for not staying up longer and I had embarrassed her and my dad I could not see how I had done but she said that I will pay forever for that one and maybe she was right to she was shouting at me and saw was my dad. Then Peter came into the room and told her to leave us alone just because she had married our dad does not mean that she can start throwing her weight around she went out of out room crying the next thing dad was in the room having a go at Peter for speaking to our new mum the way he had done sometime later Peter went out of the room and out of the house and he did not come back again that night I don't know where he went but he did not come home to us. My dad came and sat down next to me on my bed and told me that I should not have left the celebration early and I should have at least waited till all the guest had gone, I waited till my grandma had gone but not everyone else as far as I was concerned she was the only family that I had that was there and once she had left I did not see the point of being up and being made to sit in a corner out of the way they did not really want me there but just to shove me in a corner out of their sight and out of their mind I was not needed or wanted for anything else he was not happy that I did not wait till her family had left to me they were nothing to me just more strangers that I had to accept and have them as part of my life if I liked it or not I had to get use to it. He was still in his suit from earlier I had thrown my bridesmaid dress on the back of the chair and he slapped me around the face and demanded that I should have respect for him and his wife and now my new mum and that I will respect that and respect what they have given me otherwise I will pay dearly for not doing so and so I did. I got another slap around the face and then he was cuddling me and saying he was sorry and then he started to kiss me and run is hands over me and told me that I will be good and that I will Obey them and honour thy mother and father I told him she is not my mother and there for I will not obey her, that was a mistake for me, he dragged me out of my bed and onto the floor and pulled my night clothes up and over my head I was lying face down on the floor I was now naked and he took his belt off me and I got ten lashings across my bare skin I cried out and he told me that Jesus did not cry out when he was being lashed so why should I, I was told that if God's son did not scream out then I should not and that I was weak and useless and then he pulled me back up with my hair and leant me on my bed and told me to stay as I was on pray to God for forgiveness for crying out when God's only son did not and ask God to forgive me for my weakness and to pray for forgiveness for disobeying a parent and bringing shame onto them and spoiling their special day and I would have to make it up to them somehow, How I did not know how I could make it up to them I did not see what I had done wrong just by going to bed before all their guest had left after all they were their guest not mine they did mean anything to me these people and I did not know them either.

We got up early the next day the sun was shining in through the bedroom window. We always got up early on Sunday morning for church at first we went as a family but within time that dwindled down to just a few of us going. We always went for the morning service and I always went for the evening service to, it meant a lot to me to be able to do this and develop my faith but in time it became a place where I could escape to and be safe well that is what I thought anyway. I soon found out that the church was not as safe as it was supposed to be and how much more the church and the scriptures that were used against me and in any form that was possible to do to and in many ways to and the effects of these are still having an effect on me now and finding it difficult to separate what was said and done and used out of contexts against me is hard to separate the two now for me but I am getting there slowly and realising how things are not as powerful as they were but losing this power is hard for me and it is only when something comes up from my past that I realise how power things are still today. I know I will get through this in time and I also know that my faith will be even stronger than it ever was before and be stronger than it as ever been and I feel that is getting there now.

I began to talk to the vicar at our church about how I was feeling and some of the things that was going on at home he was the first person I had ever told about what was going on he promised me that he would not tell a soul and that I could trust him I was not sure that I could but felt I had to try and trust someone else. It made it harder with the vicar at the church that we went to as a family betrayed my trust and told my dad what I had said ok he was a close friend to the family to which made it even harder to accept that someone would betray me the way I had been and to betray my trust you just do not accept that from someone who is a position of trust and not a friend of the family to but he was more of a friend to my dad than he was to me but even so he should never had betrayed my trust in the first place.

I was also betrayed by the church many years later and again my trust was broken by someone else's actions and breaking my trust and confidences but that is for another time and this was much later in my life.

My step mum was beginning to get very aggressive towards me she was hitting me for silly things sometimes I did not have to do anything wrong could be that I looked up at her and she did not like the way I looked up at her. On one occasion I had been at my grandma's and got back a few minutes later than I was expected to get back I was in the bath getting ready to see my mum and she came into the bathroom which was something that she had not before, but she started shouting at me and then she was hitting me in the face and then she was holding my head under water and not belong anywhere accept with my grandma but I knew she would not be around forever but thought she would be in another sense. My step mum made my nose bleed that day but that was not the worse she did but I do not know at this point how much more she was going to hit me and how bad it was going to get.

It was not long after this that we moved into a larger house it was great because I finally got my own room and I was so proud of having my own room that it was mine and I did not have to share with my step sisters I was so pleased about that.

Peter got his own room to.

Charlene, Donna, Marie Rowena had to share a room together then there was my dad's room which of course he shared with Karen our step mum, This house was so nice and it was better decorated throughout and we were not all over each other's feet all of the time the space for us all and plenty of room to.

Grandma was also to move out of the flat she was in as the hill that led up to her flat from the shops was very steep and was becoming too steep for her and she was falling over a lot more and hurting herself and it was decided that she should move to somewhere much more flatter for her, so in the end Grandma moved close to us which was great for me and she was only a ten minute walk from our home now, not that mattered as I was still spending so much time with her so it did not make any difference to me where she lived to me that she was closer she was to us the better it was but there was a down side to that my dad was checking up on me more and more and grandma told him that I am well behaved and good girl and I usually did what I was told for her she did not have to ask me more than once to do anything for her I adored my grandma she was my whole world to me. I loved her so much and cherished her and would always love her no matter what happened she was the one person that was always there for me and never judged me.

Chapter 2

AT THE SAME TIME MY MOTHER WAS ALSO seeing someone and I was not seeing her as much as I should have been seeing her which hurt me very much that I was not seeing her so much and when I did see her, which was not very often, she spent most of her time in the local pub I had not noticed this so much before that she was going out drinking but then she had not told me before she normally told me that she was going to see friends for awhile and would be back shortly. I was not suppose to know that she was seeing anyone and I only found out by accident but never said anything to my mum as she would not have told me anyway she use to say to me that I was too young to understand what happened between two people and if she explained it to me I would not understand. Little did she know I understood far more than she ever would know but then if she spent more time with me she would have known that I understood more than she expected me to understand for someone that was still so young.

I was excited that I was going to see my mum again it had been ages to since I had seen her and I could not wait to see her it was the first time in ages that I had something to smile about in that house but everyone else was trying their best to spoil it for me even to the point of threatening me that I would not be going to stay with my mum but I knew if she was really coming to pick me then there was no way that I would not be going with her.

About twenty minutes later my mum turned up as she promised me she would do. I was off to spend some time with her and I could not wait to run up to her when I saw her pull up in her car I thought that I was just going until Sunday but it was going to be longer than that and I did not know why when I shouted goodbye to everyone I will see you Sunday Mum smiled at me and said I was staying until Tuesday. I do not know why it was longer than usual but it was, she was driving a green cheviot, which was not the most reliable car as we broke down three times on the way to her place, she had a small flat, she did not have a lot of furniture but it was her little place and it felt so warm and welcoming but she could not afford much as she did not have a lot of money, but it was nice and homely and was fine for just her which it was most of the time apart from the times when I visited. It felt so cosy and comfortable there and safe even though mum did not have much it was beautifully decorated in soft pastel colours throughout and carpets throughout the flat which added to the warmth of her home but it was so perfect to me, and it was so special to time for me to be spending this special time with my mum. I felt so lucky spending time with her at least that is what I thought but I soon realised that was not the case but I still loved going to see her and she meant so much to be and apart from my grandma she was all I wanted to be with both of them meant so much to me and thought that it always would do.

However it was long before she was re-marring and before I knew it she would be having another baby and I felt left out and very rejected. I felt torn between my mum and dad there was no security or love shown by either of them all I ever wanted was a parents love and unconditional love but that was something that I never got from any of them.

My mum spoiled me that night and we had a take away and watched a video and we snuggled up together on the sofa and this was the first time we had done anything like this before and I felt so special and loved and this was the first time that I actually felt any love from her.

After the video had finished she asked if I had enjoyed it and I did and she then went very serious and the look on my face told me something was wrong and I started to feel very scared and tears were in my eyes and mum saw this and told me that there is nothing wrong but I thought that she was going to be the last time we were going to see each other but it was not the case. She was telling me that she was going to get married again, and she asked me how I feel and I said I didn't know because I did not know who the person was so I could not say but I did tell her as long as she was happy and that we would still see each other I didn't care she assured me that we would still be seeing each other and then she asked me if I would like to be there for her wedding and that they were going to be married on the Monday. Now I know why I was staying longer than I normally do and she wanted me at the wedding I felt happy for her but at the same time felt sad because it meant that there would be no more just me and her and things again was changing for me and there would now be someone else to in my life. I did not want anyone else in my life there was enough new people in my life as it was and I did not need anyone else. It was just a few hours later that her boyfriend came round to the flat and I was introduce to him he seem nice and friendly enough and tried to be a friend to me and to make me feel special but I just wanted my mum to myself for a while as I had not seen her in such a long time, but that was not going to happen, a little while later they went out for a drink and did not come back till late. Whilst they were out I was looking round the flat as I always did when I was at my mum's but I noticed that a lot of the usual things were no longer there and a lot of her things was in boxes she was leaving this flat I felt very frightened about that and thought that she was going away somewhere and did not want me anymore, as none of the things that I had there was packed so I thought she was going to abandon me and I was going to be left in the flat all alone.

It was late when she came back home and he came back with her I had noticed that he had some things here in the flat, I went into my mum and asked her why is she leaving me here and not bothered about me I was crying and in quite a state by this time and I was so tired to.

Mum looked shocked but she said to me that she was not leaving me and did care about me so much and then what was to be my first step-dad said that we were all moving into our new home together which apparently was happening over the weekend as they wanted everything in the new place before they got married so after they were married they could start in their new home, so I asked if we are all going how come none of my things have been packed and why did you not already move in and let me come to the new house in the first place they said it was so I was not frightened and that it was better for me to come to the flat first because it was what was familiar to me, I accepted their explanation to my question but I was not happy I still felt that I was being left and abandoned and un loved.

It was early the next morning and they were both up very early and Roland was making breakfast for us all and the smell of breakfast being cooked woke me up. Roland said that I could have whatever I wanted for breakfast so I asked if it was ok to have some orange juice as this was something that I could not have when I was with my dad as I was always told that it is too expensive and the response that I got was totally different to what I would have been told whilst I was with my dad, I was surprised with the response if that is what I wanted then I can have it and I was so thrilled to be able to have some orange juice this was total luxury for me and I was then asked what I would like for breakfast and I just asked for cereals and toast as this is what I always had and was not allowed anything else but my mum asked me if I would you not like some bacon for a change well that was luxury to me. This was rare for me and something I did not get very often and I knew this was expensive to and my eyes lit up with the thought of it and I asked are you sure this is ok for me to have as I was scared of saying yes please, Roland told me that it was ok for me to have this so I said yes please and I had the best breakfast that I had in such a long time and I felt so very special.

After breakfast the pots needed doing and I got up to do them and was told that I did not have to do them but I felt I should do them my mum was in the bathroom having a bath at this point and I went to help do the dishes and he raised his hand above me and not at me but I thought that he was going to hit me and I just screamed and my mum came running out of the bath with just a towel on to see what the matter was and I was crying and I ran to my mum and I clung to her she asked what had happened to make me so frighten and upset, I told her that I thought he was going to hit me and she looked at Roland and then back at me and she was cuddling me and Roland told her all he was going to do was to give me a hug but that was all. All I saw was his hand rising up towards me and I panicked. I was told to go to my room and I could hear them talking and her and Roland were talking and I could hear them quiet clearly they were saying something is not quite right in my head and mum just said that I have been through a lot of changes and I am not adjusting to them very well and a sudden movement must have frightened me as it was not like me to react like this. At this point mum did not know what was happening at home and I did not tell her for a long time because I did not understand what was going on in my life let alone telling anyone else anyway I did not want to be betrayed again.

We had a lovely day that day apart from that little incident earlier on in the day, we had been swimming and spent hours in the pool but I could not swim and was still wearing arm bands but even so I loved the pool and loved swimming it was a real family day something I had not experienced before.

It was later when we were getting changed that I was asked were had I got the bruises from on my back I just said that I had fell over and fell down the stairs and nothing more was said about that one again. I knew though she was not happy with my explanation but never questioned me again about it. I had forgotten the bruises on my back and had relaxed around her and Roland and it was a such a special time for me.

I heard them talking later about the bruises on my back and they were saying that things are not right somewhere along the way for me and something was happening at my dad's but they did not know what.

Sunday was a lovely day and it was the first time I had not gone to church in a long time but it was also nice not to go, but there was a lot to do with the wedding being the next day. We spent the day at the new house and everything had been taken there whilst we were swimming I was so surprised but there was something that I wanted from the flat and I was told that everything was here I told them that it was not as I had put something in a small box in the gap in the cupboard in my room so reluctantly they took me back to the flat and let me go and make sure that what I wanted was not there but it was just where I left it, when I was with my mum she did not believe in going to church and she did not like me wearing my cross so I put it in a box were I knew it was safe and I got it and was asked what was in there and I told them it is my cross and Roland said to me that I should wear it and not keep it in a box and I asked my mum if that was ok and she told me yes it was but tuck it inside my top I was happy to do that and I left the flat feeling happier that I had got permission to wear my cross something I thought that I would never have permission to do, and I had one last look around the now so empty and bear flat It was just a empty place but it meant so much to me and such a special place for me but that was no more everything I held dearly to me had now changed. I was told that I should not look so worried everything is going to be ok and that I will soon accept the new place as home and that this is strange for all of us but I felt that I could not accept anymore changes but I had to accept them as they had already changed.

The next day was the wedding it was quite a quiet day and a lovely service, which surprised me that it was a church service and I am not sure how they managed this one as I was always told that if you have been married before that you are not allowed to get married in church again. The church was a small country church and could not hold a lot of people not that there were that many people there, but it was friendly enough but felt strange to me but I did not know why it did, it had the usual smells of a church, cold and damp, bells and candles it felt strange being in this church and watching my mum get married but I felt part of the wedding day unlike when my dad got married I did not feel part of his.

So this felt very special to me, to feel so much part of the day they kept telling me it was my day as well as theirs I did not understand that it could be my day as well as their after all I am not the one getting married they are so how could it be my day to I do not know. It was a happy day and we all went out for a meal into a local pub to celebrate their wedding it was lovely and special day, we went back to the new house and I went straight to bed. The last few days had been so perfect for me and happier than I had been in ages. The next day I had to go home and I did not want to go back to them and the morning I protested and said that I do not want to go back if they made me go back I would run away, but I wanted to stay here with them but I was not allowed to as they were going away for the rest of the week but I could not understand why I could not go with them, I delayed going back to my dad's as much as I could, they promised me that I will be down with them soon, I hoped that they would keep this promise to me but it was weeks before I saw my mum again and I could not understand why.

My mum kept saying that she would be picking me up the next weekend and she did not come late that evening at that evening a telegram would arrive with some excuse or other that something had come up for her if she was not feeling very well and therefore it was not possible for her to come and collect me, but she reassured me that she loved me and would come and collect me very soon however this hurt me so much and I was looking forward to spending some time with her, she always let me down so why did I look forward to seeing her because she was my mum and I loved her.

Later that night after I had read the telegram, I threw it on the floor and ran to my room crying something I should not have done ran to my room and crying. I knew that only weak people cried and that I am now weak because I was crying it did not matter what had caused me to cry it was not allowed. I was weak and I knew it to. A few moments later, my dad came into my room and told me that I was weak and he and God was now ashamed of me for being weak. I was made to take all my clothes off and I knew what was coming now I was going to be hit just for crying because I missed my mum anyone would be upset if you were looking forward to something and it did not happen I missed my mum so much. After my dad had hit me with his belt a few times my step mum came into the room and said that she had only heard him hit me three maybe four times and I deserved a lot more than that but my dad said he had actually hit me more than fifteen times I had lost count of how many times he had hit me so she said that was ok and then left my room and shut the door behind her and she did not come back in my room again a few moments later my dad left the room but not for long he came back in with his bible in his hands and opened it on various passages He kept telling me that I was evil and that I am committing myself to a sinful course because I am so naughty and so disobedient to thy mother and thy father and God would not forgive me for this sinfulness that I was doing constantly but I did not understand what I was doing that was so wrong even if I asked for forgiveness it would not come to me he said as I was not worthy to be forgiven.

I was coming up to seven at this time, I feared my dad and the words he used but I feared God more and how he would punish me for being so naughty and sinful and God would punish me in his own time I was not sure what that meant or when I would receive my punishment. I was also told that every command that I was given by a parent had to be followed and it had to be obeyed.

It was not long before my dad was sitting next to be on my bed and said that he will not teach any more on the bible today as long I was to do what I was told from now onwards but I still could not understand why I was so naughty and what I had done wrong to deserve what I had just received. I was still naked and was unable to put on my night clothes as they were in the drawer behind were my dad was standing and I could not move to get to them I knew if I had moved my punishment would have been very severe.

He was sat by me and starring at me for what seemed ages, my middle of my back was hurting and sore but I did not dare complain about it and then my dad's arm went around my shoulder and pulled me close to him and his hands were wandering all over me he then kissed me and told me to get on my knees in front of him he then stood up and left my room and told me to pray for forgiveness and guidance I was not sure what all this meant but I did what I was told but I also prayed for other things to but I never told anyone what else I prayed for especially not my dad because he would have said that I was acting un-faithful to God. To me prayers are between yourself and God and no one needs to know what you are praying for well as far as I was concerned it was but my dad often asked me if had prayed for forgiveness and for God's guidance and I usually told them I had done but did not tell him any more about what I prayed about as I knew he would not approve because it was not what he wanted me to pray about it was what I felt I needed to pray for and not what he told me to pray for.

A few days after the telegram I had a letter from my mum saying she would not be picking me up but it would not be here but Roland would be doing and that I had to keep a look out for him to arrive as my dad and already forbidden my mum to let anyone else come to pick me up as long as I saw my mum I did not care who picked me up and the telegram told me that Roland was going to pick me up at 7.30pm on the Friday evening and that I was to be ready for that time and to keep a look out for him which I did, I saw his car pull up and he got out and waved and I was down the stairs and shouted bye, my mum is here and running along the path my dad came out and shouted he wanted a word with my mum but I pretended not to hear and jumped in the car and put my seat belt on and off we were. It was not long after that I was arriving to see my mum and she was in bed ill which was the real reason why she had not come to collect me the other weekend I ran to see her and give her a hug and she pushed me away but I did not understand why she was not pleased to see me. I was asked to go and play in my room for awhile as my mum was so tired and needed to rest about a hour later I went into my mum and asked her if she was going to die and she said "that she was not but she was just ill and that she will get better very soon and she was hoping to come with me to take me home on the Sunday."

The next morning she seemed a lot brighter than she had been the night before when I arrived I know she was not right though as I heard her being ill in the bathroom and I was worried for her but no one would tell me what was going on and what was wrong with her I was frightened I was going to lose my mum and she was dying and the more people didn't tell me the more I worried and the more I got frightened. My mum was up with us for most of the day but she was sat on the settee with her feet up but she did play a few board games with me which often did and we both enjoyed this special time together it was not long though that she was going to sleep and I played with my toys on my own for awhile and then she was awake again and not looking very well she asked me to fetch her a glass of water which I duly did and I heard Roland say to her we should tell her you know and she just said that she was not ready to tell me in case something went wrong I had not got a clue what they were talking about but it did make me more frightened that this was going to be the last time I saw her. We had our tea and mum did not eat much at all and she looked very ill and pale, which worried me even more I had not seen my mum like this before. Mum went to bed early that night as she said she was exhausted and asked me if I minded I just told her to go and get better soon. I was not up for too long after my mum had gone to bed I went to bed and read for awhile which I did often whenever I could do and I was still reading at 2 am when my mum got up to go to the bathroom and she came in to my room to knock my light out and was surprised that I was still awake and that I was still reading she thought that I would have been asleep by now which normally I would have been but I was concerned with what was wrong with my mum I just kept thinking that this would be the last time I would see her and I kept crying, and all I wanted to make the most of my time with her and I was going home that evening and I was scared that I would not see her again so the time I had left was not going to be that long to be with her so I wanted to make the most of the time I had with my mum. Mum told me not to worry and she promised to talk to me in the morning and to put my book down and go to sleep. So I said goodnight mum and I love you she just said goodnight to me and closed the door it was not long before I went to sleep and I slept well past 10am that morning that was late for me as I was not allowed to sleep past 8 am and that is if I was lucky to. I was surprised to be left to sleep till then and when I went down stairs my mum and Roland were already up and in the kitchen and having breakfast it was nice to see my mum up and about and looking better than she had done all weekend. They said that they wanted to talk to me and I was very scared because I thought that they were going to tell me they she was dying after all and this was something that I had feared all weekend, they asked me how I would feel if my mum was to have another baby a little brother or sister for me and at first I said that would be great and then I must have looked worried as I was asked what was wrong and I said does that mean you will not want me anymore if you have another baby and does that mean I will not be allowed to come and see you again they tried to reassure me that I was going to even more important to them and would need to come more often to help them, So I asked when does the baby come to the house and will I see it before I go home, then I was told they just wanted to ask me what I thought about it just in case that is what happened at some point. I felt disappointed about this I was sat in the kitchen looking at the back door waiting for the baby to come through the door but it did not happen, I turned round to my mum and said how come the stalk as not brought the baby yet? They both looked at each other and started laughing I could not understand what was so funny and then mum said that the stalk will not bring the baby for a long time I felt so confused and puzzled so I asked don't you want that then and they both said that they did but these things take time I felt even more confused than I already did. Nothing else was said about this for the rest of the afternoon and we all had a pleasant afternoon playing games laughing and joking with each other everything seemed so perfect and special but that changed as soon as I was told that it was time to take me home and the usual tears started and I kept saying I don't want to go home I want to stay here with you I ran into my room and sat with my back against the door and would not let them in I could not understand why I could not stay here with them, mum was knocking on the door gently trying to coax me out so she could talk to me but I did not want to come out unless she promised me that I could stay with her but she could not make me that promise. That I did not have to go back it was something she could not do and I did not want to come out of my room unless I could stay with her but that was not possible but in the end I did come out of my room crying and feeling very sad I wished that I did not have to go back to my dad's I felt that was so unfair but I had to. I knew if I was late home there would be trouble. We stopped on the way back to my dad's for something for tea and I took my time eating as I Did not want to go back to my dad's I wanted my mum. My mum just kept saying that I will see her again soon but would not commit when that would be she just said it depends how well she feels I was still worried that she was going to die but no-one would talk to me about important things I was told that I was too young to understand adults things and not to worry about anything because everything will be ok I did not believe them I had no reason to believe them they had not given me any reason to believe them but somehow I forced myself into believing them because I had nothing else to believe but I knew something was wrong. Don't know how I did but I just knew something was wrong.

Mum came with us to take me home and my dad had serious words with her and told her never let anyone else come and get me and it would be better if she could not come for me that no-one did come for me but I thought that it was better to have someone pick me up was better than not seeing her but my dad was having none of it and he told her if she was to send anyone in the future he would make sure she did not see me again I was crying at this point I did not care who got me as long as someone did, the weekend was now ruined thanks to my dad I was told to go inside and I did and went straight to my room. A huge argument had broken was not allowed to even give my mum a hug.

They did not get on with each other at the best of times they could barely stand being in the same area as each other let alone speaking to each other they had been like this for as long as I could remember there was also a lot of competition between them to see who I loved most and who I would rather be with this went on for a number of years.

There were constant battles between them custody battles which went on for many years I was supposed to spend every other weekend with my mum and half of the school holidays which did not happen very often I was often left feeling disappointed and let down and very alone.

I felt very alone and rejected and I could not understand why she would not want to see me.

However her letting me down gave him an excuse to come into my room. The worse part about it she let me down more and more and that meant he came into my room more and more. His excuse was to see if I was all right but what excuse can you give for foundling me and rubbing himself against me there is not one that I could think of. This was just the beginning of what was to happen to me things got much worse later on in my life. I felt very scared did not know what to do or which way to turn.

So I began to runaway just to escape what was happening I needed to be on my own away from everyone I did not know where to go I just wanted to get as far away as possible. So the next day I went to school as usual but decide to go from there I had no money or food to take with me but I just knew that I had to go and to get away from him and his new family he got them he did not want me really he had got everything that he wanted at what expense?

I had already decided were to go and the best way for me to get there I had been planning it all day and I did not care how it made anyone else feel as long as I was away from them my only worry was how would my Grandma take this and how worried she would have been. I was scared and probably very stubborn at the time but I was determined that I would not be going back into that house again if I was to get my may.

In my stubborn anger I walked out of school and thought to myself I will show them. I was not sure how I was going to show them but I knew somehow I would do.

The weather changed and cloud was now above me and I thought it is going to be a cold and wet night and perhaps some storms and it was the middle of June to and the day had been muggy and hot so having rain and storms would not have surprised me and it had been so hot for almost three weeks now. So a bit of rain would do things some good and hopefully cool things down a bit.

I knew the area well and all the streets and the best ones to use and the ones I should avoid because I did not want to walk into any of my step sister or my step mum because I knew they would have questioned me on where I was going why I was not going straight home I did not feel I had a home well I had but not what you would call a proper home.

Not to me anyway. The only true home I had was the home I had with my Grandma it was the only home where I felt loved, wanted and safe, I did not with my mum but not the same as I did when I was with my Grandma.

I was coming up to seven at this time and my hair was blonde and all the way down my back down to my waist and I thought I should have tied it up this morning because it was now irritating me and getting into my face I hated my hair when it was in my face but my hair was my pride and joy and I would not let anyone touch it let alone cut it.

As I was walking I started to feel a few drops of rain on my face so I quicken my pace until I was running. Tears began to stream down my face. I said to myself dam them dam the lot of them.

I stopped in Ginall (*jitty, or alleyway*) and ducked behind a wall as I saw one of my step sisters and I remember thinking what is she doing here, she is not where I expected her to be and she is going in the wrong direction to what she should have been but then again so was I, so I had to rethink the way I needed to go and quick so I backed up a little bit and took a off shoot to the back of some house and I knew a few people down there so I knew if I had to I could have gone through their garden but thankfully I did not have to I went down a Ginall between two of the houses and out onto the street in front of where my step sister was and somehow I managed to avoid her and I hurried past just in case she did see me because I know that she would have gone home and told them that she had seen me going this way and they would have known something was wrong and I wanted them to suffer as much as possible like they had made me suffer. I knew I had to be at a certain point before this weather got much worse otherwise I was going to get completely soaked. So again I started to run and I was running very fast at this time and the rain was beginning to get heavier and heavier to. So I ran as fast as I could I went through a couple of housing estates and along a number of very long roads some of them were surrounded with trees and plants that were in full bloom and this looked so peaceful and beautiful I stopped to look at this beauty and I was standing there in the rain looking at what was so peaceful and beautiful something so undisturbed. I stood there for a few moments and I was beginning to feel very wet and cold but I stood there to admire such beauty and peaceful atmosphere and all of a sudden I jumped there was this sudden loud bang and I realised that it was now thundering and a few moments later there was a flash of lightening and I started to run again I had to get to the woods and I was nowhere near where I wanted to be at this point because I knew that I had to get off the streets before they started looking for me I knew they would, once they realised that I was not at home and not home when they expected me to be coming back but then again maybe they would not even miss me I did not think or feel that they would have done or if they cared for me or not, I knew deep down that they did not otherwise they would not have done to me what they had done. A few minutes later I was approaching the woods and I knew my best plan was to go deep into the woods and that way I would have a better chance of being dry well that is what I thought.

I went into the woods I was not afraid and it was nice and peaceful there and it did not seem to take me long to get there from school but I knew that it had done. Then again I did not do the direct route I could not afford to I had to go the way I did, I had no idea what the time was and I did not really care what the time was either. The only thing I was scared of was if there were mice or rats there but thankfully I had not seen any.

I stayed in the woods for some time it was raining and I was cold, I had not been in these woods since the middle of winter, so I started walking around walked all the way through the woods and came out. I was wondering around the fields ahead of me for some time and I knew that I needed to go and find somewhere that was quite dry so that I could get some shelter and away from the weather. I knew it would not be long before they had informed police and they would soon be looking for me. I kept walking around when I came onto a farmer's field that I was familiar with and I had played in here before and I recalled that there was an old tin barn that was no longer used that much so I headed for there and kept a look out for anyone that may be around as I did not want anyone to see me, I was soaked and very cold and I had now started to shiver I found this barn at the other side of the hill I had forgotten that it was as far as it was I went into the barn and climbed up some very rickety steps and to my surprised there was still some hay left up there and I spread it around and covered myself in it and I just hoped and prayed that there was no rats or mice in here as that is the only thing that would have made me scream and draw attention to myself. As I was getting towards the barn I looked back and noticed that there was some police in the field below me and in the field just to the left of me, so I assumed they were looking for me because I thought that by now they would have called them as I had not gone home from school I hoped that they had not even missed me as yet but then they would have done as they would no-one to fetch and carry for them and do everything they requested of me. I had no intention of going back to them either, never would be better for me and as far as I was concerned I was not going back and I was determined that I was not going back to them but I knew that deep down that eventually I was going to have no choice with this one. I was determined that I was going to stay here and then move on to somewhere else in the morning well that is what my thoughts were at the time but then I started to think about school and grandma and how worried she would be if he had told her I doubted he would have told her because I knew if he had she would have questioned him about what was going on there and what had caused me to run away in the first place. I started to cry at first it was only the odd tear and then I was crying uncontrollably and I kept having to tell myself that I had to stop being weak and being strong and God would not approve of this weakness and he would not forgive me for this weakness either well that is what I believed anyway and it had been said to me so much that I actually believed that this was true. I laid there completely still and afraid to move I could hear voices outside who I assumed that they were police outside and they were getting closer to me it seemed strange that there was so many police about they cannot be looking for me I thought it was too soon to have so many police looking for me. Even so I laid perfectly still afraid to move. It felt ages that I lay there but it was probably only a few minutes or so but felt a lot more. I eventually got up and moved and went down the steps and out of the old barn. I went very cautiously down the side of the barn and I could not see anyone around which I was grateful for. I ran down the hill as fast as my legs would carry me and over the road and down a short dark path and into another field the rain had started to ease somewhat, which I was pleased about I came to an old railway station waiting room and I wondered if this was still opened and thought that it would be a good place to stay here the door was locked but there was a was a small window where I could just climb inside it was still warm in there from where the heater had been on in there during that day . I began to think about them and thought how they were feeling not that I was not really bothered I was glad to get away from them all for awhile I did not really want to go back to any of them. The fire was still warm and there was heat still coming from it and I was beginning to feel warmth so I thought that this would be a good place to sleep that night so I curled up and got comfy and went to sleep when I awoke it was morning what time in the morning I had no idea I was awoken with the sun's rays beaming in through the window so I got up and started to walk the way I had come from the streets were busy, there was a lot of traffic about and people on the streets business as usual I asked someone what the time was and they told me that it was eight-thirty I thanked them and went on my way. It was another warm morning so the rain and storm that we had last night did not do anything to cool the weather down it was going to be another warm day. I was beginning to feel very hungry and I was getting stomach ache, I had no money to buy anything and there was a greengrocer's ahead of me I walked passed and took an apple and started eating it and went towards school I intended to go to school. When I walked through the gates they were their speaking to my teachers I walked back out of the gate and waited in Side Street until they had gone. The teachers asked me why I was late and said that they will have to inform my parents of my late attendance so I thought that they would be back for me in a instance I was glad to be in school at least I knew if I stayed there all day that I could get a meal inside of me we were on free school meals. As the day came to an end I knew that they would be there to pick up the rest of them and there was no way that I was going back with them. So I stayed in school until everyone had gone or at least I thought that they had but I was wrong no there was no parents but some teachers and a policeman but I did not know that until I left school and walked out of the gate and then they came up to me and asked where I was going I told them it was none of their business but they said it was I had been reported as missing so they told me that they would take me home just to make sure that I got home all right. They stayed for quite some time and it was not until after they had gone that they started laying into me first it was shouting at me and then they stripped me down so that I was naked and then they took the belt to me everyone hit me and I was hurting so much and I wanted to cry but afraid to cry, I felt isolated and very much alone I was sore from the belting I had just taken, they were pushing me and laughing at me and calling me names horrible names they kept calling me ugly, a tramp and a worthless piece of crap and they were saying that I was Devils spawn, this went on for some time and eventually I was then sent to my room and told to go to bed, so I did and thought that things could not get much worse for me but I was so wrong and it was not long before he was there standing in my room and tut tut tutting at me telling me that I only got what I deserved. I did not really deserve what I had just got or did I, I don't know anymore, I was crying he came over to me I was still naked I was very sore he sat on my bed rubbing his hand over my hair telling me that I should be a good girl then from now on then, and what had happened down stairs would not have to be repeated again, but what was the reason for him rubbing his hands over me up and down my body between my legs and very lightly rubbing over my pubic area, then he left my room but before he went he said that grandma is very cross with me for what I had done and she did not want to see me for a while, that broke my heart I loved grandma so much I could not believe that she did not want to see me. That night I did not sleep all that much, wondering what grandma was going to say to me next time I saw her. I was in pain and very uncomfortable I was up early the next morning and out of the door before anybody else was up and at grandma's just as she was getting up, "she asked me what I was doing there so early in the morning" I said to her that I did not think that you wanted to see me she could not understand what had put that idea into my head when I told her what had happened and what I did she said that would not stop her from wanting to see me so he had lied to me and he knew what would hurt me and he did he knew how close we were, and what would hurt me psychologically I also told her how they had hit me and how my back was hurting so much she looked at it and cleaned it up and then we started talking about school and general things all of a sudden I looked at the clock and it was almost nine-thirty I felt panicked I was late for school grandma must have seen my response because she asked if everything was all right when I told her that I was late for school she said if you think that you're going to school in that state I had another thing coming there was no way that she was going to let me go we had breakfast together we had toast and tea I became very tired all of a sudden she said your bed is always made up go and lie on it. It did not seem that long before grandma came to my room and woke me up. She told me that it was the middle of the afternoon and she felt that if I did not wake up then, then I would not sleep that night, she also informed that I would be staying with her indefinitely she had already told my dad and she said that she did not care what happened to him as long as I was all right. She was furious with him for what he had done to me I was with her for my seventh birthday it was the best birthday that I had had. He came round to see me first to wish me happy birthday and said that he wanted me back home with them I was quite happy staying were I was with the one person who was always there for me and loved me for who I was and not for what she wanted me to be.

There was a huge argument between grandma and my dad he slapped my grandma and this was not the first time he had slapped his mum, and she told him that over her dead body would she let me go back to that house, she fought tooth and nail for me and there ended up being another custody battle which was scheduled in a few weeks time and she was going to put in a proposal for custody of me and she did, and she won on the condition that she would allow me access to both my parents if that was my wish or until she could no longer look after me.

She abided by all the conditions of her getting custody of me I did see both my parents on a much more regular basis I even saw more of my mum a lot more which was to my delight. I also saw my dad and his new family however they felt strangers to me to.

Sometime much later I noticed that grandma did not look well, but she insisted that she was fine I got the feeling that she was not and that my time with her was going to come to an end and sooner than I wanted it to do to. I felt frightened for her I know she was seeing the doctor regular but I did not know why.

I know that my step sisters had been spending time at their aunties so that dad and Karen could spend time together and make sure that her parents and Grandma was ok not that they came to see Grandma when I was there.

Whilst they were all at their aunties Grandma had arranged for me to see my mum but she had not told me about this surprise. I was so pleased when there was a knock on the door and I opened it and standing there was my mum and I was going to be seeing my mum it had been ages since I saw her and I was excited about this surprise to see her again I could not believe that it was her standing in front of me, tears rolled down my face I was so pleased to see her and Grandma invited her in. It seemed ages since I had seen her.

Chapter 3

WHEN I SAW HER PROPERLY FOR THE FIRST time in a months after she had been so ill the last time I had seen her. and I still did not know what had been wrong with her, I said to her you look fat, your belly is huge and she laughed at what I had just said to her I thought she going to angry with me but she said that she was not fat but having a baby and it was going to be my little brother or sister I was thrilled with the news she had not told me before because she thought that I would have been upset and she said you remember the last time you saw me I was being ill and you were worried it was because I was in the early stages of pregnancy. She began to involve me in the baby and we talked lots about it. It was the school holidays so I was spending some time with her, Grandma had asked if she could keep me for longer than a week because she was not sure how long my dad was going to be away for as she was not well, and she felt that she could no longer keep looking after me I had the feeling for several weeks now but Grandma never said anything to me and asked my mum not to say anything to me as Grandma did not want me to worry or to be upset she always had my best interest at heart and I knew that she had to she was the one person that had never let me down and who loved me, but she mentioned it to me whilst I was there she told me that it may not be long before I would after go back to live with my dad permanently I had been expecting this for some time but did not want to admit it to myself or really accept this. I was more worried that once I went back to my dad's that my mum would not want to see me again once I was back with them. However mum did her best to reassure me that she would still want to see me I doubted that she would see me as often as she had been doing since I had been with my Grandma. I stayed with my mum for almost two weeks it was great no school going everywhere with her to the hospital when she had to and shopping everything seemed fantastic I believed that it was it was a happy time and that she wanted me to be there. She even let me buy a small toy for the new baby and a small outfit to it was sweetest little outfit I had ever seen not that I had seen many outfits for babies as I had not been round that many and to me one baby was she like all the others except this one because this one was going to be so much more special than all the others as this one was mine.

The time with my mum went by far too quickly and it did not seem like I had been with her for that long but it had been for two weeks I wanted to stay longer but I was not allowed to I don't know why I was not but I was not as far as I was concerned it was the school holidays so why couldn't I stay longer, I started to cry because I was going back I wanted to be with my mum so much and I wanted to be with her for when she had the baby which was in a few weeks time. I could not wait till the baby came I was really looking forward to it.

It was soon time for me to go back home; I thought that I was going back to Grandma's that was the plan anyway and were mum took me back to however when I got there my dad was waiting there for us, he told us that Grandma was in hospital after a bad fall and she was to stay in hospital to recuperate, which will be for several more days I was crying and asked to be taken to my Grandma and begged my mum to take me and I was clinging to mum and she was pushing me away and dad kept telling me to stop being so weak. I did not want to go home with him I wanted to go back with my mum but dad told me that if I went back with him he would take me to see my Grandma in a few hours time. I reluctantly went home with him, I began to cry again and he started shouting at me to shut up or I would not be able to see my Grandma so I stopped crying and went home with him.

Mum said that she would see me soon kissed me goodbye and left I hoped that I would see her very soon.

We went back to their house and it seemed to be taking forever for him to take me to see my Grandma and was told that if I ask again I would not be able to see her, I asked which hospital she was in and which ward I was told that she had been admitted to the Blackburn Royal he told me the ward but I could not remember which ward it was and I had decided that if he did not take me to see her soon then I would go on my own to see her, I knew were the hospital was and would not think twice about walking to the hospital to see her. Almost three hours later dad called up to me to say it was time to go and see my Grandma I came down the stairs so fast I almost fell down them all. When we finally got to the hospital Grandma she was so pleased to see me, as I was her. I was frightened by the way my Grandma looked and how frail she suddenly looked I knew this was more than just a fall I don't know how but something deep inside me told me this was more than a fall. I had no idea how bad she was or how long she was going to be in hospital, I hope that she would be better soon and would be able to come again very soon. I prayed for her a lot that night and whilst I was at the hospital she was cuddling me as I sat on the edge of her bed and at one point she pulled me into her and I was laying down in the warmth of her arms, Before she went into hospital I was spending less time with my Grandma than I had been I felt Grandma did not want me anymore I did not know that she was so ill. I was frightened by the way Grandma looked and no-one would tell me what was wrong or how long she would be in hospital for. The car journey on the way home I was quiet and I was crying inside afraid to show this to anyone on the outside afraid of being belted for being weak.

My dad was coming into my room and this was becoming more and more frequent than it had been before he was expecting more and more from me. The bible was used so much against me but he said it was his teachings to help me be a better person and a better follower of Christ this was being said more and more to me and my behaviour was being unfaithful to God and I was being sinful to God with my behaviour. He also said to me that if I went to church every day all day God would not forgive for my sinful and unfaithness. I would have to suffer and pay for in later life. He told me for disobeying him and therefore I had disobeyed the Lord and therefore I deserved to be cursed and have a terrible time and I did not deserve to be even in this house with him and his family and I was lucky that Karen and the girls had agreed to take me back in. I did not want to be in that house anyway but that did not make me feel any better, he was saying things out of the bible from the top of his head and I could not understand how he could do that or how he had managed to remember so much as he did. He told me that I would be judge by God for all my actions in time. The next minute he was pulling me into him and he was all over me and he was not in my room for too long only a few minutes that night as he said I was not worthy to be in the same room as him or as God. As he left he told me that I had a lot to think about and the last thing he said to me as he left was that it was my fault that Grandma was in hospital and had that fall if I had been a good girl then she would not have been in hospital but I was at my mum's when this had occurred so why was it my fault I loved Grandma and I did not want her to be in hospital I wanted her home with me.

I prayed hard that night and for a long time to I could not understand why I was such a naughty child as I did not think that I was and I could not understand why my dad would think that I was then God would be too if what my dad was saying was right but I thought that he must have been right and it was wrong of me to question this.

I decided to go to sleep but I was not going to be sleep in this bed for some time to come. I did not sleep much that night as I was thinking were I was going to go and how I would get there.

I was up early the next morning and before anyone else was up but that was not unusual for me to be up before the rest of the household that often happened. I made sure that I was up extra early on this particular morning because I wanted to take a few things out of the cupboards with me and if anyone else was up they would have firstly told dad and their mum and secondly they would have stopped me taking anything out of the house so I was having to be extra quiet and careful. I was about eight at this time and I was determined that I would not be coming back in to that house again I hated being there I hated all of them in that house.

I headed for the hospital as I wanted to see my Grandma and make sure she was ok, at first I did not think that the nurses would have let me on the ward so early in the morning but they did and Grandma looked up as I approached her bed and smiled when she saw me but was surprised to see me this early in the morning and straight away she asked me what had happened for me to be visiting her so early in the morning, I did not have to say anything what was wrong the look in my face must have said it all and she then asked me what as my son done to you now. I was crying again and she cuddled me and I told her I love her and I missed her being at home. She looked at me then slapped me around the face and told me that she loved me and always would do but it was time that I left to go to school. She kissed me and hugged me and said goodbye to me, I was crying as I left the ward a nurse came up to me as she had seen what had just happened and told me to take that to heart as old people who are ill do that to the ones that they are closer to so when they do go the hurt is not so hard and you should not miss them as much. I was crying even more now and asked where she was going to be going I did not want her to go anywhere and I told her she is not old she is my Grandma and I loved her.

A short while later I left the hospital I was still crying but I had seen my Grandma and that was important to me that I had done this. I walked out of the hospital and crossed the main road and I headed towards school in Mill Hill and walked passed my school and headed for the railway lines which was only a few minutes away from the school and I knew these so well as I often went on them and along the embankments they were easy to walk along and there was plenty of trees were I could stay out of the way and not be seen by anyone, it was so peaceful here and there was no-body to bother me, just me and my thoughts I wanted to get as far as I could as fast as I could and out of this area so I started walking very fast I was almost running the sun was shining but there was plenty of cloud around so I knew that it would not stay fine all day. I wanted to go to my mum but I was not sure how to get to her and I knew that it would probably take me days to get there but I was going to try to get there if I did or not I thought was a different matter. I was not sure how far I would get before they realised that I was missing and not gone to school I wonder how long it would have been before they reported me to the police as missing, and how long it would before they were searching for me but they would have thought that I had gone to school and would not think anything else of it till I was due home well that is what I hoped anyway so with any luck it would give me the whole day to get as far as I could and as quickly as I could.

At least before I left the house I managed to pick up some biscuits and some crisp and a bottle which I filled with squash before I left which I was carrying in my satchel I wanted them to think that I had gone to school I just hope that is what they were thinking only time will tell on that one I suppose.

I also knew what I had picked up would not last me for very long, so I was going to have to be careful with the little bit of food and the drink that I had brought with me I knew I could easily get my bottle refilled with water if I needed it to be filled up but I knew I would have to be careful with the bits of food that I had got I knew it was not much but I made sure that I had breakfast before I left the house I was hoping that I would make my breakfast last until nearer lunchtime and that is what I was going to have to do. I knew somehow I had to make what I got last me till I got to my mum's which is where I was heading I was not sure that it would last me until I got to my mum's but I had to be careful with what I had got and I did not take much as it would have raised suspicion very early on and I did not want them to think that something was out of place or anything was wrong.

I walked along the side of the railway lines for what seemed ages and I only came off them when I was coming near to a station or for when there was too much shrubbery in the way that was blocking my way through. However there were times when I actually walked along the lines to continue on my way but I knew that I was ok for me to go along the lines but as I could not feel any vibration in the tracks I knew there was no trains coming at least for the next few minutes, However I ran through as fast as I could in case I was wrong, I went under a bridge and kept to the wall as much as I could It was difficult under foot as it was dark and it went on for ages but I took my time as I did not want to rush in case I slipped and I had misinterpreted that silence and lack of vibration that I had not felt on the line and it seemed to take me ages to get through to the other side. When I finally came out at the other side and I quickly went back on the embankment and kept out of the way as much as I could I had been walking for hours and I was beginning to get hungry and thirsty. So I decided to sit and hide out of the way amongst some trees and have a drink and a biscuit I did not want to have too much as I knew that this had got to last me for some time yet.

I know I sat down between the trees and the sun was shining and I laid down for a while just to enjoy the peace and rest for awhile I closed my eyes just to enjoy the peace and the sun shine for awhile but I must have fell to sleep as I awoken suddenly with water coming down on my face and I realised that it had started to rain and I must have been there for ages as when I got up the sun had moved quite away round to what it was when I sat down so I thought that it must have been around three in the afternoon by now and I was annoyed with myself for laying down and going to sleep, I got up and started to run I had lost enough time now and I wanted to get a move on before the night was to set in and I also had to find somewhere safe to go to sleep and I had no idea where that was going to go be but when I was ready to go to sleep I would find somewhere but right now I am not ready to think about this.

I was thinking about them and was wondering if they had realised that I had not gone to school yet? If they had realised that I had been gone all day? I suspect that by now they would have known school probably would have contacted them as I went to the same school as them and they would have been asked what was wrong with me today and if I was ill and I know they would have said that I was up and gone to school before they were up. they were picked up from school and I would usually have seen them in school at some point and they would not wait to tell anyone that I had not gone to school and they would have thought that they were going to be getting one over on me and knew that it would have got me into trouble and they loved causing trouble for me which they did often.

My thoughts quickly came back to where I was, and where I was heading to and I thought I don't care what they did or did not do all's I knew that I was not going back to that house well not if I had anything to do with it I was not. But something deep inside of me told me that I would be going back to them at some point. I felt that maybe I would have to go back but I did not want to. I continued along the path I was on until I could not continue along this path for quiet sometime but occasionally I had to change course to avoid towns and when there more trains and I could have easily been spotted but I knew where I was going and were I had to get to and that is all I was concerned about.

In the distance I heard some church bells ringing and the chimes from a clock sounding out and it was five' o'clock I so surprised that it was so late and I still had a long way to go before I would rest up for the evening.

I walked up the embankment and started walking on top of the wall and I walked along the wall for quite some time as the drop on the other side was very steep so there was no way for me to get down at this stage so I had to continue longer than I would have liked to have done, I was walking along this wall which seemed ages before I was able to get down and walk along the path. I was walking along the path and climbing up a very steep hill but it was the only way that I could go that got me through to where I need to be. I came to the town that by now I was hoping that it was disserted and that there would not be that many people around well that is what I had hoped anyway. As soon as I could be I would be back on the tracks and walking on the embankments again at least I felt that I was out of the way and no-one would see me and I knew I was well out of the way and out of sight from anyone. I just kept telling myself that I have to keep going. I was getting hungry and tired now and I knew that the time would soon come for me to have to find somewhere to stop and sleep for the night. However I wanted to continue for a while and I wanted to get a lot further on yet and to be as far as I could before I called it a night. However I was beginning to get tired and hungry. So I thought that it was time to find somewhere to sleep and rest for the night. I seemed to walking around for ages before I found somewhere to sleep. I came across a very old waiting room at a disused station no trains had stopped here in ages so I knew that it should be a safe place for me to stop it was warm in there from where the sun had come in through the window during the day and there was a small electric fire in there and I hoped that it was still working and to my amazement it was so I turned it low just to give me some light and to keep me warm during the night. I had some more biscuits and some more of my drink I was trying to be careful how much I had to drink, but I was so thirsty and drank more than I should have done I had not realised that I was as thirsty as I was and I just hoped that I could fill it again during the next day but I had saved some for the morning. I wondered if the toilets were still in reasonable condition and if the still had water running through them. I was wondering around whilst there was still some light and found the toilets and I was relieved to know that there was still water running through them at least it meant that I could get some water in the morning and I could also freshen up the next morning.

I was woken that morning with the suns raze coming through the window, it was nice and warm were I was and I took my time getting up. I was aching from sleeping on the floor I could have gone to sleep on the bench that was in there but decided to settle in front of the fire to keep me warm.

I got up and had a small drink and the crisp and a biscuit I was trying to make these last till I got to my mum's place. I knew I still had a fair way to go yet but I was still determined to get to her place if I could get there without anyone picking me up I knew that I didn't want to go back there ever again but somehow I did not think that I would have much of a choice in that one I knew I would have to go back to them eventually. After I had a drink and the crisp and biscuit I went into the toilets hoping that there was a tap with drinking water in there and there was if nothing else I could have a drink. I began to freshen myself up when I heard I noise but I hoped that there was no-one out there or worse looking for me. I hurried with the wash that I was having even though the water was ice cold it was all I had and I knew I had to make the most of this. I quickly left the toilet area picked up my satchel and hurried back on way.

I carried on along the tracks for sometime I think and hoped that I was well over half way but I was not sure and I also knew that I would not be able to stay on the tracks for much longer as I knew that I was going to have to go by road very soon I did not want to but I knew I would have no choice and that came unto me sooner than I thought which meant I was further than I thought I was I was pleased with the progress that I had made the previous day. I was not sure I suspected that I still had a long way to walk but I knew I had come along way so far and even if they found me now and took me back to them I would have achieved much more than I expected to do.

It was now round mid morning and I was having to come off the tracks I was fast approaching Preston and Knew I could not stay on the tracks passed here I had to get off them very quickly as I knew how

Preston station was laid out and there was no way I could continue the way I was going for the time being. however I did continue to head for Preston station along the paths rather than the tracks and I knew that I had to take a great risk going on there but it was a risk I had to take if I wanted to get to my mum I walked into the station and I was lucky that there was another family going into the station so I attached myself to them so no suspicions would be aroused and lucky for me they were going to the same platform that I needed to go to, I looked at the screens to see what time the next train to Manchester was leaving I discovered that there was one due in within the next five minutes or so and it was not long before the train came into the station and stopped right where I was standing so I sneaked onto that train and avoided as many people as I could do, I sat quietly and amongst other children and families that were on the train with the hope that I would not be picked out as not supposed to be there or that I was on my own. I listened carefully to the announcements to what station we were approaching when I heard over the speakers that we were now approaching Manchester. I got up with a lot of other people and was ready to get off Manchester. As I left the station I was amazed that I had gotten this far without any questions being asked or anyone stopping me. My next task was that I had to now make my way to Bury which was miles away, but I knew somehow that I had to get there if I wanted to get to my mum's but I was beginning to doubt that I would get there as I knew at some point I would have been stopped to see where I was going and who I should have been with. Thankfully I had got this far without being stopped and I hoped and prayed that I would get all the way to my mum's and more than anything I hoped that she was going to be in even she did not know that I was on my way to her.

My next task was how I was going to get to from Manchester to Bury without any money. I found the bus stop were I needed to get the bus from. I did not have a clue how I was going to get on the bus but I thought that I would worry about that when the bus came in. I stood waiting for almost a hour before the bus arrived and I felt nervous standing there and I felt that everyone was staring at me and looking me up and down and the look on people's faces was saying to me what is a child doing alone at a bus stop, I heard one pass by say that her parents want stringing up for leaving her there alone. I thought to myself what do you know about my parents and what right have you got to criticize them you don't know them so how can you say this about them. The bus finally came in sometime later and I went to get on the bus and the driver asked me where I was going and he told me the fare, I looked at him for what seemed a life time and he asked me again for the fare I said to him I beg your pardon he told me the fare again and I was surprised how much he had said he asked me for £1.40. I started to cry and told him I have not got any money but I am trying to get to my mum she had my ticket but I lost her and I think that she went on the last bus, he looked at me for awhile and I felt even more scared and I did not know what I was going to do. He told me no fare no ride and asked me to leave the bus. I was crying saying I wanted to get home and mum would be worrying about me he still refused to let me take the bus home I was now crying uncontrollably but he still refused to let me on, as I was about to get off the bus one of the passengers came forward to pay my fare for me. I was so pleased and I thanked her so much and her reply to me was that she could not leave me here stranded in a city that I did not know. If only she knew what I had done to get to where I was today I thought. So I had managed to get on the bus that was going the way I needed to go. It was nice to be on the bus and heading towards my mum's finally. The lady that had paid for my bus ticket sat across from me and asked me if I was alright and how far from getting into Bury was it to my mum's house I told her that it was only a few minutes' walk and would not take me to long once we got into Bury she was not convinced about what I had said as I could see it in her face but I did not know what else to say to her, I was thinking to myself what if she says something to someone after she gets off the bus? I hoped that she would not but I could not be sure anymore about anything or anyone. At this point I also thought about my Grandma and I hoped that she was ok and making a good recovery from her fall and that she would be home again soon. It seemed to take ages on the bus and when we finally arrived in Bury we had been on the bus for around forty five minutes the lady that had paid for my ticket had got off before we got into Bury but I was still worried that she would have said something to someone but what could she tell them I thought. I was still not sure how I was going to get there once I got into Bury town centre but I knew it was not far to walk from there if I had to, I felt pleased with myself that I had got this far. I got off the bus and started walking towards my mum's place but it was all main roads so I had no-where to hide so I was walking and sometimes running and I hoped that any one passing by would have just thought that I was a child playing outside. However I kept going and when I finally turned up at my mum's place there was no-one there and I had not noticed straight away that the house was empty. I was so disappointed she had moved again and not told me where she had moved to. I was devastated that I had come all this way to her and she was gone I would have gone to her new home if I had known were that was. Why had she not told me that she was moving? I sat on her doorstep and started to cry I did not know now what to do now.

One of her neighbours came out whom I knew very well and she told me that they had moved out of there over three weeks ago, and she was surprised that she had not told me that they were moving However mum had given her phone number in case she should need it. She offered to ring her if I wanted her to do this for me. Or if I wanted to do so I could ring her. She asked me if which did I prefer me or her to ring her I asked her if she would mind ringing her again she asked me if I was sure that was what I wanted and I said that I was and thanked her. so she did ring her and she allowed me to speak to my mum and as soon as I heard my mum's voice I started to cry however mum was not to happy with me for going to her home without permission and she told me off for going all that way on my own and for not telling her she then told me that I was naughty girl, What upset me more was when she told me that she did not want to see me at the moment and that she would be in touch with me as soon as she as settled into her new home and was prepared to see me. She told me that I have go back home where I belonged but when I insisted that I wanted to be with her and did not want to go back she told me to stop being so selfish and a naughty girl and accept that is the way things are and there was nothing I could do about it. I then said goodbye to her and told her that I loved her but she slammed the phone down on me I felt very upset and very hurt by this.

How could she do this to me I thought, she was more bothered about herself than she was about me and how I had got there in the first place. I felt that she should have been more concerned about me than she was about herself. I felt that she could have been more concerned and happy that I was alright and safe rather than telling me off like she just had done. I was in tears and I did not know what to do next, the neighbour put her arms around me and then made me something to eat and after about a hour she said that she had to go out for awhile but she wanted to make sure I was going to be ok first I said I would be. I sat outside my mum's old place crying after my mum's neighbour had left I did not know what to do now. I just sat there for ages and then it began to rain. I did not move I just sat in the rain crying.

I had been sat there for ages and the night was drawing in fast and it was getting dark and it got dark early that night but then it had been raining for some time and there was a storm now over head.

I saw some headlights coming up the street and I hoped that it was my mum coming to pick me up that was wishful thinking that my mum had cared enough to come and get me but it was not it was a police car and I just sat there and did not move and I hope that they would not have been coming for me but they were, they called me by name and at first I ignored them hoping that they would go away but as they came close to me and said my name again but this time I answered them and they tried to persuaded me to go back with them it took them some doing though as I did not want to go back. I asked them if they could make me they informed that if I do not go back to them they would have to find me somewhere else to go, I told them that I was not going anywhere with them and I stood up at first very slowly and turned towards them and at first stepped a few steps with them and turned away and ran down the drive and through the back garden and I hid in the gap that I had often hid in when mum use to call me in and when I wanted to be on my own unfortunately for me they saw were I went and was quickly were I was, I began to shiver as I was wet through and cold and started to cough and I was hungry and thirsty to. They persuaded me to go back to the station with them at least I could have something to eat and a hot drink to warm me up and give myself a chance to dry out. Eventually I agreed to go back to the station with them. Once back at the police station where they got me several hot drinks and something warm to eat and wrapped me in several blankets to get me warm as I started to dry out and finally stopped shivering. After sometime they told me that they would have to take me back home. I said want my mum. They told me that I would have to go back home and they said they were very worried about me I doubted that they were, but when they told me my Grandma was worried about me I started to cry that I had worried her. In the end I agreed to go back home if you could call it that but it was the only home I had at that time. Before we went back they asked me how I got there and I would not tell them, they asked me a lot of questions all of which I refused to answer after all who would believe me?

I curled up on the back seat of the car on the way home and they put a blanket over me as I began to shiver again it did not take me long to fall asleep, it was not long before we were arriving at my dad's house. They woke me up as we approached my dad's house and all the lights were on in the house so I knew everyone was up and I was scared and I asked them to take me to see my Grandma but they said they could not do that they had to take me back to my dad's as he was the one that reported me missing and that is what they did took me back to his house with her and her kids.

The time it took us to walk up the path seemed to take forever and I was walking behind the police officers and I turned to run but they were too quick for me they pulled me back and told me that I had to go home but I did not want to. They knocked on the door and my dad answered and he said "was she there did you find her and is she safe". To all his questions they said yes she was and we have brought her home for you. Is it ok for us to come in and of course he said, "It was". They went in and sat down in the front room and they were chattering to them and saying that I had been through enough and it would be better if I was to be left alone and allowed to go to bed as it had been along few days and quite an ordeal for me, even the police said "that they were surprised how far I had gone and how I got there they still did not know" My dad asked how did I managed to get there without anyone noticing that I was alone. All the police could say was that a child alone is not that unusual. The police officers were very nice and they had a cup of tea and then left shortly afterwards I followed them to the door to see them out as I wanted to get out of the front room as quick as I could do. I saw the police officers out and they said to me "don't do something like that again I could have be killed" I just shoved my shoulders I was not bothered if I had been killed it would have been better than were I was living with at that time. I shut the front door and started to walk upstairs to my room, I managed to get up a couple of steps before they shouted at me to come back into the front room I did not want to go and went to go up another step and was called back in again, I knew that I was in trouble and I also knew the longer I left it the worst it was going to be for me so I reluctantly went into the front room. As I opened the door they said, "too me what have you got to say for yourself young lady?" I did not say anything and I looked out of the window and could still the police car there. They were shouting but I was not really listening what they were saying I did not care what they had to say they did not mean anything to me anymore. The only ones in the room were my dad and step mum and I. My stepsisters were in bed when I got back but I knew they were listening they always did and then made fun of me later on.

Then my dad started saying all sorts of things but it was when he started using the scriptures that he got my attention, he said to me " are you not speaking because you know you have been sinful", with what I have done. He also said "he said to be as a child I am unclean." And I should feel guilty for what I had done. He told me for being so sinful there would be penalty for the sin I had committed. I was not sure what sins I had committed maybe running away was my sins but I was not sure. with what I have done. He also said "he said to be as a child I am unclean." And I should feel guilty for what I had done. He told me for being so sinful there would be penalty for the sin I had committed. I was not sure what sins I had committed maybe running away was my sins but I was not sure. He told me that I had been unfaithful to the Lord and to him and that was my sin. I was not sure what he meant but I thought that he must have been right.

Then my step-mum started shouting at my dad and saying to him what good is that going to do as she is nothing but evil and evil alone was sinful. She deserves her punishment and it was time I paid my price she started slapping me and then took my dad's belt off him and went to strike me with it and he turned to her and said only he is allowed to use that on me. The next thing my top was up and my trousers were down and he was hitting me with the strap part of the belt and she told him

I deserve more pain and more punishment so after a while he turned it round and hit me with the buckle end and that did not half sting and hurt I cringe with every lash of it and bit my bottom lip until it bled but I did not dare move and after another three or four more hits from the belt I was told to go to my room and get into bed.

I heard her say that he lets me get away with too much and to easily.

I thought well it is not her that is being belted with a belt and the buckle end at that I was hurting and crying as I went up the stairs I started to cry one tear at first then the tears were streaming down my face and Marie was at the top of the stairs and said it was nice that I was back home and if I was ok and then all of a sudden Charlene and Donna out of their room and saw me crying and then they shouted down stairs that I was crying and being weak, I just glared at them and thinking if you had just been hit the way I had been hit then they would have been crying. I did not go straight into my room I went into the toilet and then the bathroom and I locked the bathroom door and I decided to run myself a bath which I was not allowed to do without permission but I did not care I just wanted to wash and clean myself and wash some of the sin away that I had committed not sure thought that was possible though. A few moments later I was getting into the bath and just about to sit down in the bath, there was a knock on the door and I was told to open it and I ignored them and just laid down in the bath to wash my back and help to ease the soreness the next minute the bathroom door was being forced opened and he was standing in the bathroom tut, tutting at me and he was then pushing the door to and now raising his voice and shouting at me for having a bath without permission that was a no, no when I was growing up we had to ask for everything we use. His shouting was to cover up him foundling me in the bath. I just wanted to get out but he would not let me, eventually I got out and got a towel round me and went into my room and started to dry myself off and he was not long before he came into my room behind me and he just stood there watching me. As I moved the towel to dry myself he was just watching me but as soon as I went to put the towel around me again he stopped me and he sat me down on my bed and I had stay where I sat and how I sat down then he moved his hand over me and pushed my legs opened and told me that now I am his and I will not be anyone else's and he told me that God would be pleased with me for the way I looked and he was pleased with what he was looking at and told me that this pleased him, I was feeling very frightened and worried and then he got me my nightie and helped me put it on I was beginning to shiver and he said he did not want me to catch a cold. I was already coughing a lot. He soon left me afterwards and I thought peace at last. If only that was the case, I was just settling into bed and that night I prayed but I had not kneeled down beside my bed and a few moments later my dad was back in the room and told me that I could not have finished praying already as there was a lot I had to ask for forgiveness for. I told him that I had prayed and asked God to forgive me he told me he did not believe that I had prayed that much so quickly as he had only been out of the room for just over fifteen minutes which was not long enough to ask for that much forgiveness and I should have prayed for at least a hour for every sin I had committed against God and against my family. I would have been up all night if I was to do that and it was already late as it was.

He walked across my room towards me again and I thought that I was going to get belting as he did not think that I had prayed enough for what I had done. However he was soon sat down on my bed next to me and he was foundling me, and pulling my hand towards him and he wanted me to touch him I felt dirty and frightened and not sure what I could do to stop it. He seemed to be in my room for ages that night well when I looked briefly at my clock it was almost three in the morning and he was still in my room and touching me and kissing me. A little while later my step mum came into the room and she asked him if he was going to get into bed or was he going to sit up with me all night he told her that he was making sure that I did not get up and go off again. She told him to come to bed and to stop worrying about me as I was not worth it, as there were others in the house that needed his attention besides me.

So a few minutes later he left my room and finally I had some space and some peace so I could get some sleep at last.

The next morning when I got up things had changed for me for the worse I was going to be punished forever for what I had done and with it being a weekend it was even worse I went downstairs just after nine thirty which was not that late but my dad and step mum said that was to late with all the jobs I had to do and there was a lot of them my first job was to get the back boiler going and it was a horrible job to do and a dirty job I had to go and fetch the coal in and get the wood and make sure that it was the right size to go into the boiler, I lit that and got it going very quickly as this was the only way we could get hot water into the house, as I used the hot water last night I had to make sure that there was enough hot water for the rest of the day which meant I had to keep putting coal on it to keep it lit all day. After that I was going to have to do all the pots on my own and then clean the kitchen floor they kept making me do more and more all day long and I could not go out as I was not worthy to go out and be with my friends I hated it more and more there and I just wanted to get out of there as fast as I could but I knew I could not but I would abide my time and I would get out when I could.

I kept asking how my Grandma was and if she was home yet and the only response that I got was what do I care what happens to her if I did I would not have gone off the way I did. Could not understand why they treated me this way and why they would not listen what I wanted.

I wanted to go to bed early that night I was very tired and very sore but I was not allowed to they said they had not finished with me yet there was more that they wanted me to do before I went to bed I started to feel like a slave in that house or more like Cinderella I did not get any time for myself even when I did go to bed I was got up just to go to the shop to get them something and I had a time limit to get there and back which was ten minutes and that did not include having to queue in the shop I was hoping that by the time I went to the shop that there would not be a queue but there was and when I got back in I was three minutes late and I was in so much trouble and I said it was not my fault that there was a queue and I had to wait they told me that was my problem not theirs I felt that they were being unfair and unreasonable but I did not dare say that to them. They were both shouting at me and told me that I could not be trusted to do anything right or do what I was told.

I soon went to my room out of the way and to be on my own I was sat on my bed looking out of the window and I was crying and he came into my room and he saw me crying and told me how weak I was to cry and that I should know better. He was soon sitting next to me and at first he was giving me a hug but I knew it would not stay as a hug. I always hoped that it would but I knew that it would not he was soon putting his hand up my top and touching my skin and I got a shiver down my spine as he did this another mistake for me because he said I should be able to bear his hands on my skin, I would have done if it was not for what he was doing it was not long before he was going up my skirt I wanted to scream but something stopped me from doing this and I don't know what maybe because I knew there was no point in screaming as no-one would do anything to stop him or no-one would come running to my aid if I had done well apart from Peter but he was not there he was never there these days. He told me that I deserve everything that I got and everything that happened to me if I was not so evil then maybe good things would come my way and I had to stop being so sinful all of the time otherwise God was never going to forgive me for my sins. As they were to severe to forgive me I could not understand what I had done that was so severe that I could not ask God to forgive me for I always believed that God would forgive anything if you was to ask God to forgive you maybe I was wrong on that one to I did not know anymore. His hands were still all over me and he was holding my hand on him and that made me feel even more uncomfortable. This went on for what seemed ages and when he finally left my room I felt so violated but was not sure why I felt this way. He came back into my room briefly a few minutes later and I asked him again "if I could go to my Grandma's for a while" and to my surprise he told me I could go and that was what he was going to tell me when he came back in my room.

The next morning I was soon off my bed and getting ready to go and see my Grandma I could not wait to get out of that house. What he did not know I had a key for her place and I was told not to tell anyone and if I did not have my key on me I knew where there was another one so I could always get into her flat but that was our secret. I could not understand why he seemed pleased that I was going to my Grandma's but maybe pleased was the wrong word the look on his face told me he was pleased I was going but there was something else there but I could not work it out what it was. When I got to my Grandma's she was not in which was a surprise to me because she was always in especially in the mornings and it was early morning and I had let myself in with my key as I always did and I felt so disappointed that she was not there but I knew there would be a note somewhere for me as she always left me a note when she went out even if it was a few minutes so I knew there would be a note there for me and I knew something was not right as her post was still on the floor so I went looking for the note and I found one where I always found one in my room on my pillar in the usual place in the same coloured envelopes she always used for me. She told me that if I was reading this and she was not there then she knew my dad had not told me where she had gone she was in the Isle of Man until the Tuesday afternoon of that week and I suddenly realise why my dad had let me go so easily and why he was smiling when he said I could go he just wanted me to be hurt even more. I stayed in Grandma's for a while and I saw my dad come towards the flat but I stayed still and then I saw the look on his face and he looked worried but I was not going to move I stayed perfectly still so he could not see me through the window once he left. I decided to leave to and I was back at the house before he was I knew a slightly quicker way to go and it was and I was sitting in my bedroom window when I saw him coming up the path and I heard him tell my step mum that I had ran away again and she told him that I had not and that I was in my room and had been for some time.

He asked me how my Grandma was and I told him she was not in and you knew she was not in and this was one of the first and only time that I had spoke to him like that he was not pleased at all but I did not care there was no more he could do to me that he had not done before. I felt so angry with him for not telling me my Grandma was away and she would not be back for a few more days but he did not know that I knew that she was away and also did not know I had a key for her house. If he had he would have took it off me. Something else he would have said that I did not deserve to have.

I was still seeing my mum from time to time but she was more interested in drinking and her new family than she was in me. She hardly kept to her arrangement for her to collect me like she should have done the strange thing was at that time I worshipped her adored her I still felt so much love for her even though she let me down a lot I always made excuses for her regardless to her reasons for coming to collect me. Deep down I believed that she loved me in her own way weather she did or not I will never know. She got a new family now she did not need me well that's what I thought and felt anyway.

Chapter 4

I BEGAN TO SEE MY GRANDMOTHER LESS AND less apart from weekends from spending almost every day with her I had to start living with him and her as well as her children.

At this time my mother was trying to get custody of me. Even though I was still spending a fair bit of time with them I hated it I was very unhappy and felt an outsider I was beginning to spend more and more time with them and less and less with my Grandma.

One afternoon he would not let me go to her like I was supposed to do and Grandma came to his house to collect me he refused to let me go she took me with her anyway even though I was in my nightie she was not bothered I was in my coat and shoes were on and we were almost out of the door and Grandma was almost out with me when he slapped her around the face. This upset me and Grandma was furious, when we got back to her place she told me not to worry about what had just occurred but to watch out for my dad cause you do not know what will happen and most importantly do not trust him, I was not sure what she meant at this time after all I was only eight and half years old. I loved the time that I spent with Grandma it was so special to me and even now still means a lot to me her teachings meant and mean so much to me.

A few months later my Grandma began to get ill and she was not able to look after me like she had been able to do before, so I was spending more and more time with them and only seeing Grandma a few times a week and some weekends. That's when my life as I knew began to change for the worse. I was grateful that I had my own room and that I did not have to share with any of them at least I could have some space of my own but that left me wide opened for what happened in that room. If only life was this simple as I was about to find out how my life was about to change at that point I had not realised just how my life would change or what was wrong with my Grandma as no-one would tell me, and how what was happening was going to affect me so much as I got older.

I could not understand why I could not go and see my Grandma as much as I was doing I felt that she didn't love me anymore so I began to runaway a lot and Grandma got more ill, I was then blamed for her illness that if I had not run away she would not have got so ill. At this time I did not know what was wrong with her but my Grandma was suffering with cancer but I did not find out this too much later on in my life. I began to blame myself for her illness but it did not stop me running away. I could not stand it in that house I could not bear to be away from my Grandma but I was not allowed to see her but that did not stop me going to see her as I often sneaked in to see her and she always asked me why I had not been to see her I told her that dad had told me that I could not and that you did not want to see me anymore. I was so angry when I found out that she did want to see me and that it was my dad who was trying to stop me seeing her and who blamed me for her illness. She again said to me that I have to be very careful of him and whatever you do don't trust him, I could not understand what she was trying to warn me of, but I do now. But back then I had not got a clue.

I had gone to see my Grandma at her flat and when I went into the flat I was calling her Grandma where are you? Grandma, when I got into the living room she was laying on the floor in her night clothes and she was so cold I don't know why but I gave out a very loud scream and I was shouting for help I did not know what to do I had left the front door opened when I came in and when the postman came I was still screaming for help and I was in tears, I was sat on the floor beside my Grandma and I was holding her saying please don't die I love you, I had heard the postman coming up the path so again I shouted for help and he called into us and asked if everything was ok and I just screamed again and this time he came into the flat and saw me now kneeling next to my Grandma and crying and I was still saying Grandma please don't leave me please don't die, He looked at us dropped his bag and ran out of the flat I did not know where he had gone but a short time later he was back and there was an ambulance coming and they were there within a few minutes but it seemed I had been with her a lot longer than that I was very frightened that I had somehow done this to Grandma regardless of what Grandma had said to me, somehow I knew that it was all my fault and no-one would be able to tell me anything different. The ambulance Crewe were asking me loads of questions some of which I could not answer as I did not have a clue what they were talking about, they were soon attending to my Grandma and when they told me that she was still alive I cried even more and I could hear myself saying thank God that she was ok but I was crying again. I found myself asking was this my fault did I cause this, I was told that I was not to blame for this as they think she may have had a stroke and I felt even more confused to what I already did so I asked what is a stroke? They told me that is was something to do with her brain but Grandma was old and this was common in elderly people I found myself saying that she was not old she is someone very special to me she is MY GRANDMA!! A few moments later they took her away in the ambulance and said that someone would have to contact my dad to let them know to late someone had already contacted him as they put Grandma in the ambulance he was there and asking me what I had done to her now, and was shouting at me. He was told to calm down and it was possible that she had had a stroke and this was nothing to do with anyone else no-one could have done anything to cause this. He then turned round to me to get back home. I did go home but to the home where I loved being Grandma's home I went back into the flat and locked all the doors behind me. I was shocked about what had happened to someone I loved and I just wanted to be around her and near her and the only place I could do that was to be in her home, our home. I stayed in Grandma's flat all day and when the evening night was turning I saw dad looking in through the window and calling me, Katrina, Katrina are you in there we are worried about you, I ignored him I did not want to see him or speak to him I certainly did not want him to blame me for this one too which I knew he would do I was so still in Grandma's you would not be able to tell that I was there at one point my dad looked straight ahead at me and I actually thought that he had seen me but if he had done he would not

61

have left. He left a few minutes later and I watched him drive off. I stayed in the flat all night on my own and for one night I did not have anyone coming into my room and no-one touched me, I had the peaceful night's sleep that I ever recall having. I was awoken with the morning light coming in through the window, I got up and had my wash and got dressed as I had got plenty of clothes at my Grandma's, I made myself some breakfast and cleared my pots up and something made me look out of the window and I saw my dad parked outside I wondered if he had been there all night I did not recall seeing him when I got into bed last night or did he really know that I was there? Was he waiting for me to leave? I sat near the window looking out and he was looking towards the flat. I was sure he had seen me. I stayed watching him for awhile and I was wondering how I was going to get out of Grandma's without him seeing me I hope that he would leave before I did but something told me that he was there to stay till I went out. I made the decision to leave the flat but I was not going round the front of the flat and with the entrance being on the side of the house I knew I could get out and through the back and if necessary I could go through the back of the gardens and out at the top of the road were my dad could not see me and he would never know that I had left. I decided that now was as good as any time to leave and just as I was about to go out of the door he was coming to the door he opened the letter box and called my name, Katrina are you there? Katrina please open the door I am not angry with you. I still did not answer a few seconds later he put a note through the door which I thought that strange as he knew his mum was in hospital. When it fell to the floor it was not for Grandma but for me. I picked it very carefully as I was worried that he was still outside and he was listening for me to walk along the hall but I was already sitting behind the door I picked the note up and crawled very carefully and slowly back to my room and it was there I opened this note. I read Katrina you have done nothing wrong and I am sorry how I spoke to you when they took Grandma away she is asking for you please come home we all love and miss you. We will see you at home in a little while. I thought there is no way I am going home to them yet. I sneaked out of the door and round the back of the flat and through a couple of gardens and out onto the road ahead of were my dad was sitting in the car. I walked as if I had not seen him there and my first point of call was going to go and see my Grandma I needed to see for myself that she was ok but I was scared that when I got to the hospital that I would not be able to find her and I did not know what ward she was on or which hospital she was in I assumed that she would have been in the Blackburn Royal Infirmary but that was just guess and when I got there which took me a good twenty minutes to walk there I went straight to the ward were she was last time I don't know why I had done but something inside me told me that is were I need to be. It was around half past ten now and I was not sure if they would let me into see her, this early. I was surprised that when I got to the ward the doors were opened and I walked straight down this long ward as I did I could feel my legs shaking they felt like jelly I had not noticed the tears that I started to let go at first or I did not want to acknowledge that I was crying because I knew that it was wrong to do this. As I came to another set of doors and was in the processed of walking through them a nurse asked me who I was looking for and I told her that I had come to see my Grandma she asked for my Grandma's name and I told her it was Sally Woodly an she checked the board to see were she was and said that she is very poorly and may not want to see me I told them she will see me and surely enough she did. As I approached her bed I could see her face light up and change and the first thing I did when I saw her was give her the biggest hug I had ever done and I did not want to let her go. I was crying but happy tears as I had still got my Grandma and she still got me. I was told not to stay to long and not to let Grandma get too tired. I promised that I would not let her get too tired. I was sat next to her on the bed and she pulled me into her as frail as she was she could still pull me into her for me to cuddle up with her so we could have a proper cuddle I was now laying down beside her and this felt so special for me and I was wondering how many more times we would be abe to do this. We were talking about all sorts of things and then I just sat up for a moment and I told her how very sorry I was that I had put you in here again. She smiled and told me that it was not my fault but these things happen and she loved me so much I then layed back down beside her and that is were I remained for quite some time I remember a nurse coming to see if she was ok and had not noticed that I was there at first I heard Grandma say she was fine she had everything she needed just here andthen the nurse saw me and she looked at me and smiled a little while later I was being covered with a blanket. I looked up and the nurse smiled and said it is ok just stay were you are. I smiled and put my head back down and I knew my Grandma was asleep and I was still laying down with her the warmth and love I felt that day is undiscribable but it was one of those special moments that did not come along very often for me. I snuggled back up with my Grandma and went back to sleep with her. I was still asleep with me Grandma when my dad came to visit her and was asked by the nursing staff not to disturb my Grandma or me he was shocked when he saw me there but I felt warmth and safe snuggled up with my Grandma.

When I awoke he was sitting there in the chair with his arms folded across his chest but he did not look very happy at all. As soon as I was awake he dragged me off the bed with my hair and told me that I had got no respect for my Grandma and how sick she was I was a selfish and evil and he quoted "oh what a great sin you have committed" I shall not be forgiven for this sin. Grandma now to was awake and was quite sharp with him and told him in no uncertain words that I had done anything wrong and that I hd not committed any sins against her or him and he should stop quoting things from the Bible to me as he was being very unfair to me. Grandma told him that I was one of the most gentle and kind child and she is so loved by me. No-one would stop her loving me.

I wanted to laugh at him but did not dare do this as I knew the consequnecs if had done and that was not worth thinking about. However I got this nervous feeling as time was getting on it would soon be time to go home and I was not looking forward to going back and I knew now he was here that I would not have much choice about going back with him either. The time came to quickly for us to say to goodbye to my Grandma and on the way out dad had the nerve to ask the nurses not to let me again they told him it was a pleasure to have me on the ward and I was as good as gold. I was so pleased to hear someone say that I was good as I was always hearing that I a naughty girl. I walked off the ward smiling and we got back home I went straight back to my room and hoped that I would have some peace. I was amazed that night I was left alone without any disturbances and it was good that I was.

I was visiting Grandma in hospital and she was getting worse and the only time I saw her for the next few months was at the hospital a few days later I went to see her she was in a bad way I could see that I was frightened she slapped me round the face but I don't know why a nurse said "to me that they usually lash out at the ones they love just before they go." The next day I ran away again because I was blaming myself for the way she was however I did not go very far just to Grandma's flat as least I was warm and safe there and no-one could get into me without me letting them in. I t was lovely to be surrounded by her things the flat was small but very cosy and beautifully decorated and carpet and her cupboards were always well stocked I stayed there for a couple of days and I was surprised that my dad had not been down to look for me maybe he knew were I was or maybe he did not care, the following day I went to see my Grandma and she could not recognise me. I went home feeling very sad and the last time Grandma had spoke with me was the day she had slapped me a few hours later he came in and said that he had to talk to me I knew with the expression on his face that she was gone he did not have to tell me anything I knew, I looked up at him and I asked if she gone to heaven now and when he nodded I just started screaming and crying and I did not care if anyone said I was weak and no-one could comfort me all I wanted was her but she was not there anymore, Auntie Sammy took me to her place for the night more than anything to spend some time with them and to try and comfort me. The next day when I returned My life, The house, felt empty I was missing my friend my Grandma the one who loved me the most the one who was my mother, who had always been there for me and she give me so much support I still felt that it was all my fault and it was said to me as soon as we walked through the front door I felt so guilty because I felt somehow that it must have been even though I did not know how it was. I was eight and ten months by this time. The day of the funeral soon came I went to the funeral I do not know why I wanted to go but I just did I felt that I had to and to say good bye to the one person I cherished and loved so much it broke my heart that day I was afraid to cry at the funeral but I looked up and saw my dad crying and I remember thinking to myself that it was ok for him to cry and not be weak but not me. I then to began to cry and as soon as I let one tear go there were many moretears soon followed no-one out there arms around me to say that everything would be ok and it was ok for me to cry. I stood alone and felt very isolated. Meanwhile back at the house after the funeral I sat in a corner curled up with my knees pulled up to my chest and my head resting on my knees I felt so numb and did not know what to do or who to turn to. I began to shut myself away from everyone and keeping myself isolated from everyone else I did not want anyone near me I did not feel worthy of being with anyone else as I felt and thought that I was evil. I often felt my Grandma's presence in my room and often felt her in my bed at the side of me at times I felt her next to me holding me more so when my dad had been in the room I felt her there more so and when he belted me it felt that they were not as hard as they had been before as if someone was stopping him. I know that Grandma was still with me in a different way it felt like she was still trying to protect me. When I first felt her there it frightened me. She always promised me that she would always be there for me and feeling her presence told me that she was still there for me. I just didn't know at that stage just how much my life was going to change and not for the better. Grandma had tried to warn me to be careful of my dad that he was dangerous but I did not know what she meant it seemed odd that someone I loved so much was telling me to be careful of my dad her son but she wouldn't say why I had to be careful it was not apparent until a few years ago. I did not understand what she really meant at the time.

Even after everything that was happening to me with my dad and step mum things had changed so much since my Grandma had died. I miss her terribly and all I want to do was be near her and I began spending a lot of time by her grave and when things got more difficult at home I began sleeping at the side of her grave it was my escape from everything and everyone it was where I felt safe being near to her.

The one good thing about being with my dad and step mum was I did not have to share a room with my step sisters I got a room to myself but that was a bad thing for me in a lot of ways, because that give my dad the chance to come to my room and then there was no chance of him being disturbed he was free to do what he wanted and he usually came into my room was usually to tell me off or belt me one or something else. I would be belted if I did not do what he wanted or I would not give him a goodnight hug I would get a belt for it and he used is belt whenever he felt he had to sometimes I did not have to do anything wrong. Then he would say to me that now I need to make it up to him for being a naughty girl. So I had to give him a hug, every time he belted me I always

66

had to undress and stand in front of him naked it was embarrassing and cold. The house was a very cold house. The rooms were cold and damp. Whilst I was stood in front of him naked he would belt me with his belt sometimes just with the strap and sometimes with the buckle end and if I scream or cried I got hit even more he said to me that he had to make an example of me to make sure I turned out the way he and God wanted me to turn out. HE would say you know that God wants you to obey your mother and your father. Remember the bible tells you to honour thy parents he used to say to me. There were other scriptures he would use on me just to get what he wanted. This particular night I had not long got back in from being at my Grandma's grave and I said I did not want to look after Marie and Rowena on my own again as I was doing this most days at the moment and I was only just coming up to ten years of age. That was my mistake that night saying I did not want to do this again and his reply was it is my duty to do what he said and that God is going to be very angry with me for not doing what thy father had asked of me. It had been just over a year since I lost my Grandma and it was a difficult year for me it was a year that so much had changed and so much I had lost. During the year I had not seen my mum very much and was letting me down more and more I did not have any idea why she kept doing this to me.

He made me strip down and stand in front of him naked. He turned me round and took his belt off and started to belt me with it I had to bite my lip to stop myself screaming and crying unfortunately for me when he turned me round I was crying and he told me only weak people cry and because I was weak I deserve what was going to come next.

I was only ten and I had already developed and my body was already changing he said I would never be a good person or make a good wife if I am not to do what he wants and do what I am told. That night things change for the worse for me things had been bad before that but they got even worse after that night I was terrified of God being angry with me and not doing what God expected me to do and be a good child to a the parent. At first I pushed his hand away but he just kept saying to me what would God think of what I was doing to thy parent and not honouring them and I was not being a faithful child. By being good to thy father, God would love me more and then good things would happen

67

to me. He sat me down on my bed I was still naked and feeling very frightened. He brushed his hands across my face and down my chest and over my stomach and down towards my legs. My back was hurting from where he had hit me not so long ago. He began to kiss me at first on the cheek then onto my lips he grabbed my hair and pulled it back and told me to kiss him so I gave him a peck on the cheek like I always did he told me that was not the kiss he wanted so he kissed me on my lips again and told me this time that I had better respond to him they way he expected me to and if I didn't God would not forgive me for dishonouring my family. I felt so frightened of upsetting God that I allowed him to do what he did. His hands was between my legs and brushing my legs and gradually moving up and he told me to accept what he was doing and God would be pleased that I was doing what was expected from me and being a loyal child. I felt very frightened and not sure if God wanted me to allow this or not but he said that it was what God had wanted me to do to please him. He was in my room for a very long time and then he took my hand and made me touch him and feel what a good girl was doing to him I did not like what I felt and was unsure what I was feeling at the time I was frightened and was wishing that he would leave my room and soon. Once I held my hand where he held it over the top of his trousers he started to kiss me again first at my lips and then down onto my chest and his hand was moving up to the pubic area on me and brushing over the pubic area. He was pushing my legs further apart and wanting to see what God had given me and I had please him so I don't make God angry. He was moving his hand further up my legs and touching me I did not feel comfortable with my dad doing what he was doing something did not feel right about what was happening. My Grandma warned me not to trust him and to be very careful of him, maybe this is what she meant I thought but I was not sure I felt very confused with what my Grandma had said and what was happening at the time and what I thought God wanted me to do. I did not know what God really wanted me to, was I in the wrong or was my dad in the wrong and who was God going to punish? I felt unsure of what had just happened but also felt very confused of what all this meant for me.

As always before I went to bed I knelt down the side of my bed and put my hands together in prayer and asked God to forgive me for being a naughty girl and disobeying thy father and for not honouring them. I also asked for guidance on what was right and what was wrong.

I also asked God to help me be a good girl and do what he wants me to do the work he wants me to do and to help me be a good child. I also asked for his forgiveness in all I do that is wrong and all that I do that angers the Lord our Father.

Chapter 5

My Birthday was hard that year and I had been given a present that my Grandma had bought whilst she was in the Isle of Man she often bought me something back from the Isle of Man for my birthday that year she brought me a teddy bear and there was a small simple note with it and it said " My dear Grand-daughter, I love you forever and always" and then at the bottom of the note there was a few more lines which said that when you receive this I will be gone and it was bought for you, to give to you love always remember I love you dear child and that you are a special child and don't let anyone tell you are not. I cried so hard that day when I read what she had said, my dad tried to take it from me I just held onto it and would not let it go Peter was around and he stopped my dad taking it off me and told our dad that our Grandma wanted me to have that and what she wrote was for me and special to me and always would be and Peter threatened my dad that he ever took it off me there would be so much trouble for him. Peter was being serious to and my dad did not look very pleased that he had been threatened in his own house and by his son. A few minutes later he snatched my teddy bear from me and I was in tears as this meant so much to me and the next thing I knew Peter was giving me back the teddy bear and Peter and my dad were fighting not just verbally fighting but physically fighting I know Peter was trying to do right by me and protect me but at what cost he ended up being hurt and I ended up getting a belting and him in my room punishing me because of what had just happened and said see what evil I am to turn son against father but what I saw it was father going against son, and in a away I was pleased that someone had stuck up to my dad and that he was getting a bit of his own medicine and he was the one being hurt for a change. Peter came into my room whilst my dad was with me just as he put his hands on me and Peter did not take kindly to what he saw and told my dad that he was nothing but a pervert but as I did not know, what he meant and they started to fight again and Peter was not going to leave it be and he wanted to make our dad pay and told him that he would kill for what he had just saw and I thought that he would have done to he was so angry at our dad for doing what he was doing to me and my dad promised him that nothing like that would happen again but the problem was Peter did no longer live with us all of the time and only spent the odd day there he hated living at the house almost as much as I did but the only difference was that he could leave the house as he was old enough to do so but I was not and I had no were to go apart from my mum's and she did not seem to want me either. Peter came into my room after he had finished fighting and he looked a mess and he had several cuts on his face which were bleeding I would not like to think what had happened but I was scared that I was going to get the punishment for this if not now at some point. My dad popped his head round the room and saw Peter there and I looked up and Peter saw the fear that was there in me and he told him to get out and our dad said he was just coming to say good night to me which he did from a distance he would not dare come into my room whilst Peter was there, Peter was cuddling me and just holding me in his arms it was the first time since my Grandma had died he had done this and it felt so warm and so safe and my brother stayed with me all night he watch me sleep and I woke briefly to some noise but I cannot remember what was going on but Peter just said to me it is ok go back to sleep your safe. So I turned over and went back to sleep it was the most peaceful night's sleep that I had in such a long time. When I awoke the next morning the sun was gleaming in through my window but with it being the winter months it was low in the sky but even so it was still nice. And I turned over and Peter was asleep on the floor so I stayed very still so not to wake him but he must have sensed that I was awake as he sat up quickly asking me what was wrong I just told him nothing as I had just woken up. It was very early in the morning and the house was still and quiet which was so nice, I asked Peter if he would like a cup of tea and he said he would love one so I went down stairs to make us both a cup of tea I was in the cold kitchen making us a drink and I was deep in thought when I turned round my dad was standing there watching me and I screamed as he had made me jump and had frightened me I had not realised that he had got up and come down the stairs which was unusual because you always heard people coming down the stairs in that house I had dropped the cups with boiling water onto the floor and broke the cups and I was in trouble for breaking the cups and he was telling me off but on hearing me scream Peter was down the stairs and at my side within moments of me screaming he thought my dad was doing something to me again but when he realised that I had dropped the cups and our dad was having a go at me for breaking them well Peter told him that he should not creep up on people and should not be telling me off for breaking cups he should be more concerned about whether I am hurt and not about a couple of cups. I started again to make the drinks for me and my brother but this time Peter carried the cups and I went off in front of him there was words exchanged between Peter and dad and my dad said you will not always be here and he will wait until he was gone to punish me and I would be punished severally once he got the chance and I knew it to. It was great having my brother there for a while but I was dreading the time coming to him having to go and I knew that time would come very soon and it would come sooner than I would like to.

A few days later Peter gave me his home telephone number and told me not to give it to any one and if I needed him or he did anything to me again I had to ring him no matter what the time of day it would be and he would be straight over I hoped what he was saying was correct but I was not sure that he would be but then again he may as well live back with us because if I was to call him every-time he was to do something to me then he would be spending a lot of time with us but the thought of that pleased me but I knew he had his own life to lead and he could not always be there for me as much as he said he would be but at least he cared about me and wanted me to be safe.

Peter was with us for almost four weeks in the end as our dad kept making threats to me and saying that I will be punished because I was be so defiant and sinful not just to him but to God to and God would want me to be punished for this and it was my dad's duty to carry out this punishment. Peter was having none of it and told him what he could do with his words and supposedly God's words because Peter told him that he was not saying things correctly and he did not believe in what was being said and never would. I was amazed that Peter said these things and I felt more confused than I was already about things and especially about God and the bible and the church.

A few days later Peter had to go and I clung to him and I did not want him to go and I cried so much that day but It got me a slap around the face for being so weak and that was in front of my brother to and Peter told him that I was not weak but a child who as just lost someone very special to me and who I loved so much and who loved me more than anyone ever could and loved me as the child that I was and not something that I was not again dad did not like being told what to do or how to treat me. I was sent inside by Peter but I went into my bedroom and opened my window and climbed onto the shelf outside my window and I watched them both at first they were just stirring at each other and none of them saying anything to each other than our dad just went to punch Peter in the face but my brother blocked the punched and retaliated and another fight broke out between them and I started to cry again and I began shouting at them to stop it was only then that they realised that I was watching them but it did not stop them fighting it just got worse but I did not want my brother to go but I knew he would be doing as soon as this was over this fight seemed to go on forever but it was probably only for a few minutes but it felt and seemed a lot longer than it was. It began to rain but I just sat outside my window crying and I did not want to go back into my room as I knew that I was going to be in trouble and get my punishment for the last month and I knew that it was not going to be pleasant for me and I was beginning to get even more scared as I saw Peter start to walk away from the house and I started to shout out to him to come back but he turned waved at me and told me that he loved me and then he was gone round the corner and out of sight I just stood there and shouted out to him to come back but he did not and I just sat on the ledge in the rain getting wet and cold and I did not want to go back into the house and I was not going to do if I had my way either and I was determined to get my way.

About a hour later I was still sat there crying when my dad came into my room and saw that I was still outside in the rain he ordered me back in and I refused he told ordered me back in again and I still refused he told me that he would give me one more chance and if I still refused then I would be there all night which I did refused and I was there for most of the night I was wet and cold and Marie sneaked into my room and opened the window and let me in but they said that I would have to be back out there by the time morning broke so I climbed into the window and got warm about six in the morning I heard movement and I jumped out of bed and back out of the window and curled up on the ledge and closed my eyes a few seconds earlier I heard my bedroom door open and he was at the window and told me to come back inside and I was not going to do what he had told me I was scared and confused of him and not sure what he was going to do next and it was getting cold out there but then again it was coming up to the middle of December and it was so cold and I was coughing again and I knew that I was going to be ill if I was not careful eventually I did go back into my room whilst he was still in my room and I began to tremble all over and cry and I was terrified about what was going to happen next I knew deep down what was going to happen but I was beginning to fear it and him more and more but I could not understand why maybe it was because of everything that had happen in the last month whilst Peter was there maybe it was a lot of other things who knows.

It was now two weeks to Christmas and I had not seen my mum now in almost six weeks but this was getting a regular occurrence with her now and I did not expect anything else from her and reside myself to the fact that she did not care and did not want me or love me but it did not stop me being hurt and loving her which I still did and so much to and that hurt me so much the way she treated me and was not there for her daughter unless it was to her benefit or that is how it felt to me.

I was still in my room and so was my dad and he was looking at me and stirring at me and he told me that I had be foolish and unfaithful to him and God and I am evil and wicked and being so wicked I will be brought down for my wickedness.

I was trembling at his words and afraid of God now and afraid of what he would and will do to me.

The next minute I was standing naked in front of my dad and being belted with his belt and his hands but is hands did not hurt me so much but it was his hands were doing that bothered me more and I kept going over the words that my brother used on him in my head and when he pushed me so I fell onto my bed and his hands was between my legs were I got the strength from and the courage to say it I do not know but I called him a pervert not that I knew what I was saying or what it meant but I regretted it the moment I said it because it made my dad so angry he just started laying into me and touching me more and more and I began to feel dirty for what was happening but I still did not understand this or why I felt the way I did but I just did. He was in my room for ages that night and doing what he was doing and he was becoming even more forceful than he had before and hurt me so much more and not just by the beating I was taking but the way he was holding me and touching me he was no longer being gentle like he been before things changed that night for me and for the worse to up to now he had always held me hand on top of his trousers but that night was different he took his trousers and underwear down then changed his mind and left my room and came back in a few moments later in his dressing gown and nothing else underneath it I did not know that when he came back into the room I was embarrassed seeing him in his dressing gown as I had not done before and it did not feel right that I should be doing now. He sat down on my bed next to me and grabbed my hand and opened his dressing gown so I could see his naked body it frightened me seeing him like this and I was still naked from the beating I had just took and from him just leaving my room to get changed into his dressing gown. He was saying things to me but I refused to listen and refused to accept that he was really in my room but I knew that he was and he was not going anywhere for awhile he told me that I had nothing to be afraid of and it is something that I would see a lot more as I got older I was ten at this time and only just gone ten at that and I was missing my Grandma so much and now Peter to. I just kept wishing that Peter would come back in now but that was not going to happen I knew he would not be back unless I called him and I was not in a position to be able to call him at this time and there was no-way my dad was going to let me go out of the house at the moment. I kept telling myself that this was not happening to me that it was someone else there and not me but it was me and I was so scared and I did not know what to do and I was afraid of what would happen now this was all new to me as this had not happened like this before this day he was always dressed but for some reason things had changed that night but I did not know what or why things had changed. He kept telling me, that I was wicked and wickedness had to be punched and this was not punishment for me as such but I did not know what this was and it was something that I did not know about and this frightened me so much. I started to cry and again I was told I was weak but this was nothing to be afraid of but something that is so natural between two people. I did not feel that this was natural at all and that I feared. I kept pulling my hand away from him and he was not at all pleased by this so he left my hand alone for a while and his hands was going across my face down over my chest and over my stomach and down towards my pubic area I kept trying to push him away but again I made him angry he told me to honour him or God's vengeance would be severer. I already felt God was going to punish me because I had not honoured thy father and I was afraid of this but I still kept trying to push him off me I do not know where this courage had come from as I had not done this before and then he threatened me with further lashes of the belt if I did not honour and obeyed him and in time I stopped pushing his hand off me why I did I don't know but I did. His hands were now free and wondering all over I was so frightened and his hand was now between my legs and over my pubic areas and touching me and he was kissing my breast and kissing me and trying to get me to kiss him back and kiss him on his lips and I could not I kept fighting this one it felt horrible to kiss him on his lips. However he kept pushing me and kissing me and pulling my hair and pushing my head so that our lips were touching and he was kissing me hard and it hurt me he let go of my hair and took my hand and held it in his for some time and then he pulled my hand towards him at first it was on his stomach then he pushed it down to his pubic area and I felt uncomfortable and afraid and I did not like what I was feeling and what he was getting me to touch it did not seem natural to me but he kept telling me that it was natural but it did not feel natural to me it felt horrible and so unnatural to me and I was too young to understand what was happening and why it was I kept thinking that this is what I deserved. He held my hand over his pubic area and what I felt I did not like or understand what I was touching and why this felt different from the rest of him he held my hand on him and put his hand over the top of mine it frightened me. I knew men and women were different but I was not sure how they were and I knew that night how they were but it was still frightening for me he started moving his hand over the top of mine and this felt strange to me and I did not understand what was happening with his other hand he was still touching me over my pubic area and this was beginning to feel very uncomfortable to me and I was scared of what was going to happen next. He was still rubbing my hand over him and I tried to pull my hand away and he told me that I better not because it is giving him pleasure and that it would not be long before this was all over but I did not have a clue what he meant and then I felt this sticky stuff all over my side and on my arm. I was frightened and shaking I thought that I had done something wrong and he told me that is what I do for him and how much he was turned on by me I still was not at all sure what he was talking about but he said that he was pleased with me and that God would soon forgive me for doing that and obeying my father and God would forgive me in time for my unfaithfulness and sinful ways.

Two weeks to Christmas and I was dreading it and I did not want to be here for Christmas the next morning when I got up I packed a few things into my satchel and I knew by now there was others up so I climbed out of my bedroom window onto the ledge and I dropped down onto my neighbours garden so I would not be seen and I went over the back wall and onto the lane it was cold and icy that morning I had no idea where I was going to go but I knew that I had to get away even if it was for only a short time, this time I headed for my Grandma's grave I felt that was the safest place to be but as I was walking I came across a phone box so I tried to ring Peter but there was no answer I was so disappointed that he was not in so continued walking towards the cemetery and to be near my Grandma it was so peaceful there and I knew where I could hide if I had to. Near to were my Grandma was buried there was a large Oak tree but I also knew that if I got over the hedge beside this tree that I could hide there for ages if I had to and I had done on many occasions. I had put a small blanket in my satchel I knew I was going to need it as the night came in but that was hours away yet. I knelt down at first next to my Grandma's grave and then eventually I

78

sat down but I sat on the blanket to help keep me warm as I could stay, it was a bitter cold day and I was at my Grandma's grave side talking to her and crying and telling her everything that was happening I wish that she could have spoke to me and hold me like she always did but I knew she could not but maybe in another way she could but I was not sure how she could and whilst I was talking to her I suddenly felt the warmth around me and the feeling that someone was there and close to me but I knew there was no-one there but it did not prevent me from looking around just to make sure that there was no-one there. All of a sudden I felt safe and protected once again and it felt like my Grandma was there with me and comforting me and telling me to get out of that house as soon as I can and be safe but I got the feeling of warmth and love like I always did with my Grandma. It felt strange feeling this but it also felt nice to. It felt as if my Grandma was there with me but not in a way that I could see her but in spirit and something also told me to go back and face what was happening to me and I can remember saying in a little while as I want to stay here with you. I felt that she said to me ok but only for a little while. I laid down next to her and I felt the blanket move over me but there was no-one there and then I felt my hair being stroked like she always did I was not sure what this meant or what I was feeling but I knew it was special to me and would always be a bond between Grandma and me and a bond that nobody could or would break this was a special bond and one I would always treasure for years to come and I knew I would do to. I fell asleep at the side of my Grandma's grave and felt safe there being so close to her there was a lot of noise in the back ground all of a sudden which woke me up with a start there was loads of people arriving at the cemetery it was late and unusual for so many people to be arriving at the time of day it was it was well into the late afternoon by now the weather had turned colder and I had not realised how cold it had gone and it had been snowing whilst I was asleep but not a lot but even so there was a light covering of snow on the ground which was expected for the time of year and it had been forecasted for days now but I did not think that we would have got any so soon. This group of people were getting closer to me and they were all dressed in dark clothes I could not make out who they were at first but as they got closer to me I could see that there was a couple of police officers and my dad, mum were there I was surprised to see my mum there and it was her who I focused on everyone else did not matter and she was not the first one to get to me it was dad and a police man and I pushed him away and told him to stay away from me I want my mum and within moments my mum was at my side and giving me a love and saying how much she had missed me. So I asked her why she had not been to see me and she told me that my dad would not let her see me and was told to stay away from me. I hated my dad for trying to keep my mum away from me he had no right to do that. I told her that I did not want to go back to his house I wanted to come back with her and to my surprise she took me back to her place and it would be great to see my little brother I had not seen him for almost six months he was now two and a half, my mum took me back to her place and the police agreed that it would be a good idea for me to spend some time with my mum as it was obvious that I did not want to go back with my dad.

It took us ages to get to my mum's as she was now living in Leicestershire and I had not seen her since she moved there I was surprised to find that she owned a shop and a huge back garden and it was a nice little shop and the people around were very friendly but they all thought that I was in boarding school. With me not being there very much and that is what my mum had told them I suppose it made things easier for her. What I did not know was that I was not going back to my dad's until after Christmas that made my day spending a Christmas with my mum and she told me a few days after I was with her for that I was spending Christmas with her I was delighted that would mean all most three weeks with her. I loved it in the shop and even though I should not have done I was working in the shop for a couple of hours a day and I loved it but what I loved most was spending time with Mark going for walks and taking him to the park even though it was cold and winter it was still good fun and Mark enjoyed it to, but my mum was glad of someone to take him off her hands for a while and for her to have some peace it was nice to start with but it started to become more and more and days became evenings and then all nights to whilst I was there I became his sole carer which should not have happened. Our mum should have been the one to care for us but it was me and I noticed that she was drinking more and more and spending more and more time out. She was very friendly with the next door neighbours and he was spending a lot of time at the house my step dad that was then did not like it and objected regular about it but they all went drinking together so I thought that things must have been ok.

Christmas soon came round and I was sad on Christmas morning as it was the first Christmas without my Grandma and I missed her so much. I was still blaming myself for her death to. My mum told me that it does not matter that she is not here as long as she is always in my heart and memories then she is always with me and I cheered up a bit after that but even so that Christmas was very hard for me and I missed my Grandma so much.

I felt guilty for her death and I was blamed for her death because I had ran away and had caused her to become ill, I missed her so much and daily I ask God to forgive me for killing my Grandma and I believed that I had done. I believed this for many, many years to come.

I was dreading the time when I had to go back to my dad's and I knew that I would have to sooner or later but I did not want to and I knew that I would not be there for much longer as I had already been there for just over three weeks and if it was how the arrangements that were made before then I had to be back for New Year's Eve otherwise he would be onto her for not having me back to share one or the other with him and my mum left it till the last minute to take me back as well she took me back for around 10pm on New Year's Eve and she stayed around for while and she was still there when the new year came in and that was so nice to have her there. She kissed me and said goodbye and that she would see me in a few weeks time and I hoped that I would have done to. The atmosphere changed after she had gone and my dad was not very pleasant to me and told me that I need to be punished for what I did before my mum took me away for those three weeks I was hoping that he would have calmed down by now and maybe forgotten about that but he had not and I was already hating be back there and I had only been back a couple of hours as well and I knew that the next few weeks were going to be even harder than I thought that they would have been.

Things were no easier at the house and things were still continuing. Without my Grandma I had no one who loved me like she did and I knew I would never again.

The weeks since I seen my mum seemed to take forever to go by and my dad was in my room most nights by now and I was scared of him again and I did not contact Peter either and I know I should have done but I was not sure what he could have done to stop him because I knew nothing was going to stop him.

A few weeks later I was supposed to be going to see my mum but it did not happen but at least she had let me know this time and a few days before which was unusual for her she normally left it till it was too late and I was upset but this time she told me that she could not come and collect me as there was a lot happening in her life I did not have an idea what was going on for her but at least she told me she loved me which was something she did not say maybe it was to cover up her guilt I was not so sure about anything anymore. I did not know whom to believe any more either.

The days seem to come and go so quickly these last few weeks and I still had not seen anything of my mum but I was hoping that it would be soon but I could not understand what could have happened to keep her from coming back for me but then again I should have been use to it by now she always let me down and made promises she could not keep.

Time was going by very quickly and the time I saw my mum was becoming less often and when I had given up that I would see her again she was at the door coming to collect me and apologised for mot getting to see me sooner but I did not feel that she was being sincere with her apology she said it too often and without feeling. The journey to my mum's was a long slow journey and it felt like we had be travelling for hours well we had but it felt a lot longer and I was tired and hungry by the time we got back to shop, Mark was already in bed and fast asleep and he was going to be surprised to see me there in the morning. I was made something to eat and a hot drink and my mum told me that she was no longer with Mark's father and there was someone else in her life but I would meet him sometime over the next few days and I had to be nice to him as in the past I had not been the only person I could think of that I had not been nice to was the bloke that lived next door and I did not like him at all. She told me to go to bed and that she would lock the door as she was going over to the pub for the last orders which meant she would not be back till late and she did not come back alone either she brought someone back with her but that was up to her. The next morning my little brother awoke and I heard him ask why is my bedroom door shut and my mum said go on in and find out and the next minute the door of my bedroom door was flung open and Mark came bounding in with a huge grin on his face and when he realised it was me he ran full power to me and was jumping all over me and giving me hugs and kisses and I just hugged him and he went and fetched his favourite story and asked me to read it to him as he loved it when I read to him so he sat down on my bed with my arms around him I read him the story and he was just smiling when I had finished I said lets go and have some breakfast and he came down stairs gladly with me and I made his breakfast and my mum said she cannot get him to come down and have breakfast without the battles she could not understand how come I could get him to eat breakfast without any problem and she could not. I was not sure either but I think it had something to do with how I was with him and the love and affection I gave him and the time after all mum was only bothered about her next relationship and drinking everyone else did not seem to matter.

For some reason that day mum asked me if I would like to come and live with her and I told her that I did and I asked her if that was going to be possible well she said "she was going to go and get custody of me" and was hoping that this time she would be successful. That was all I ever wanted to be with my mum. I hoped that I could at last come to live with her but I was not sure that I would be able to but only time would tell on that one. Later that day I was in the living room with my mum and little brother when Mark asked if he could have a drink of coke and my mum said he could and he was pouring himself one, I was talking to my mum and then for some reason I turned round and saw that my brother was drinking port that was in a lemonade bottle and not coke I turned to my mum and asked her why is there coke in a lemonade bottle and she told me that it was not coke but Port that she had taken out of the box in the shop to get rid of the box and put a new one out and she had forgotten that was in the fridge and had not realised how much Mark had drank until I asked how much was in the bottle she said "it was full" which meant he had drank almost ¾ of a bottle of port and for his young age that was dangerous she then began to panic and then called the doctor and was advised to make him sick to get it out of him as fast as possible which she did and then put him to bed and once he was in the bed she told me off for not making sure he got the right drink in the first place I told her she should not have had it in the fridge were a child can get to things like that and she should have known better and then she was shouting at me and told me that I am only a child and I don't know what I was talking about obviously I knew what I was talking about more than she did by the way she just responded to me and then she raised her hand and slapped me across my face and told me that if anything happen to Mark it was all my fault for not watching him more closely. That night I sat by the side of his bed all night watching him sleep I was scared that he was going to die and I could not cope with someone else's death on my conscious and I watched him all night long and praying for him to be ok to, and when he woke at about five thirty in the morning he was not very well and looking very pale and green but he was smiling again and I just sat there and cried. I was so happy that he was ok I just cried for ages then my mum came running into the room asking me what has happened and when she saw her son was ok she too started to cry. Then she went back to bed and then I went to bed but it was not long before Mark was coming into my room and wanting a story but I said I would read him one in a bit but come and have a hug from me and he did he laid down next to me and I just held him and it was not long before we were both asleep and we stayed that way until almost lunch time I was surprised no-one had woke us up.

When we went down stairs there was no one around which surprised me, and the shop and been shut early to which was unusual to. I went into the living area and found a note from mum saying she left us to sleep because we needed it but she would not be back till late that day and to make sure me and Mark got some food and she had left us some money to get a take away in for tea. She had never done anything like this before and was surprised she had now maybe she was feeling guilty about what had happened and so she should have been feeling guilty to I thought but I was pleased that she had left some money for a take away later on but there was plenty in that I could cook and I did I made us a sandwich for lunch and something hot for tea and I had done all the pots by the time they got in that night which was passed midnight. I wanted to make the most of my time there as I was going to have to go back to my dad's soon and I did not want to but I knew I had to. The time to go back to my dad's came round so fast and the next morning I was going to go back to my dad's and I did not want to go back but I knew for the time being that I had to.

As always my mum dropped me off as late as she could do which did not please my dad as he said she has got school in the morning and needs to be in bed well before now my mum just told him that whilst I am on her time she would bring me back when she feels fit to do so. They had heated words for several minutes and he turned and slammed the door in her face and I was waving to her from my bedroom window.

I was also surprised to see that Peter had moved back into his old room for a while but apparently not stopping there for many nights but at least he was back but when he was there he kept himself out of the way and in his room but I could knock his door and he would let me in but anyone else got a lot of verbal abuse from him I never did.

I thought that I would be safe now my brother was home and to a point I was my dad was scared of Peter and he did not seem to be scared of anyone if he was he did not show it.

I found it hard being back with my dad and my step mum and her daughters I felt I did not belong with them and they did not want me there. Things were hard there and I could not see them getting any easier as time went on.

I was seeing my mum a lot more now than I had been before but then again she had applied to the courts to get custody of me and when my dad got the paperwork through he was furious and said there would be no way on this earth that they would allow me to go with her on a long term basis. He decided to take us all to school and he was worried that my mum was going to collect me from school without his knowledge he was panicking that he was going to lose me so he was a constant shadow around me and it drove me mad being constantly watched I always felt that I had done something wrong even when I had not done. I had to do more and more around the house to and there was no freedom for me at all. There was always someone on my back.

My dad was taking us all to school in his car he was proud of his car and we all squeezed into the back of it and I was near to the door and this particular day I was leaning on the door and the door came opened and I was hanging out of the door and my head was scrapping along the road and my step-sisters were screaming at my dad to stop but he did not seem to take much notice of them he thought that they were just playing up like they usually did as we went to school but it was not till the step-sister that was sitting in the front turned round and saw me hanging out of the door with my head scrapping along the floor and she pulled my dad's handbrake on my dad went mad at her and told her not to do anything like that ever again but she turned round and said "well how else could we get your attention they had all been telling you that there was a problem but you chose to ignore what was being said" and when he realised what had happened he looked pale and frightened but I felt that he did not care and he wanted me to get hurt even die. He shouted at me for not getting his attention quicker but I could not do anything all I could do was hanging on to whatever I could hold on to. When we got to school he let the others out of the car and kept me in the car and he asked me if I was ok and I told him that I felt fine but my head had a cut on it and was bleeding but I had not noticed it and I felt fine well that was until I got out of the car and stood up and fell straight to the floor. Several people were standing over me including a couple of teachers and they said "I should go home and not be in school for today" my dad explained what happened and told them that he will be taking me to see a doctor immediately and I was surprised that he did to. It was just a bad bang on the head with a small cut and I had got mild concussion and that I should be kept an eye on and allowed to rest I laughed at that point and the doctor reinforced that I had to rest and not do anything for at least twenty four hours and my dad "told the doctor that I would not do anything" I did not believe that for one minute. He took me home and sent me straight to my bed and told me to stay there for the day and he brought me a drink and some biscuits up which surprised me maybe he was feeling guilty for not listening to the others when they were telling him to stop, it was not long after that he got rid of the car and said he could not take that chance again of something similar happening to anyone else.

He was not at work that day and he kept coming up to see if I was ok and I was ok considering, as the day went on he was spending more and more time in my room and started sitting next to me and putting his hands over me and it was not long before he was going under my clothes and touching me I began to hate him and dreaded him coming into my room because he only came in to do something to me these days. He was not coming in my room out of care or duty unless it was for what he wanted and nothing else.

Easter came and went and I had seen my mum over four times in the last month she was actually keeping to her promises which made a change and she kept saying to me that she had applied to get custody of me and she was checking that I still wanted to be with her that was what I wanted more than anything and where I wanted to be more than anything. I hope that I would get to live with her this time but I was not sure that I would do but then things had changed since my Grandma had died as she now no longer had custody of me and it was now reverted back to my dad which gave him so much more power and he used it to his advantage over and over again.

It seemed to take ages to get a court date for the custody hearing and this was the first one that I had been to and was asked by the judge who I wanted to live with I told him that I love both my parents but it is my mum I want to be with but my wishes were not taken into consideration when it came to deciding it was felt because of having step-sisters and a "stable Life" were I was and the fact that I had lost my Grandma just over a year it was felt that I would be better staying were I was. When I was told I asked, "better for whom" because it was not better for me and it was not what I wanted. I was so angry about not being able to go and live with my mum; maybe the court liaison officer picked up on something at my mum's that I did not know about. Who knows I saw her briefly before she went back home she told me that it was my fault why I was now not coming home with her but I did not understand why it was my fault that I was not going home with her. Maybe it was my fault but I am not so sure that it was but maybe it had something to do with what I did say that the outcome was the way it turned out. I did not know what I could have done or why it was my fault but for some reason it was.

That night my dad was in my room saying that it is a good job that I did not go with her as if I did he would not have wanted to see me again as I belong to him and no-one else and he told me that even if the courts had decided that I could live with my mum he was not going to let me go.

I was very down and had been for a long time and I was getting fed up of everyone in that house I did not want to be there and I did not want to live I felt and thought that I would be better off dead no-one would miss me or care that I was not there anymore.

That year went by very quickly and another Christmas came and went and not without any problems or more abuse but at least I was seeing my mum a lot more and she was selling the shop as she said "that it was not her dream but Mark's dad's dream to have the shop" she was seeing the neighbour a lot and he was practically living with my mum and Mark I did not like him and I did not always get on with him but I tried to for the sake of my mum and because I had been asked to make the effect with him. I put up with him I did not like him but I had to accept him if I was going to keep coming down to see them, it did not give me much choice really. After all I wanted to be with my mum. Each time I came to my mum's I always refused to go back but this time was different as they were having problems with their car and it would not get us back to my dad's and them back home again and it was getting late so my mum put me on the train to make the journey on my own back to my dad's this was the first time I had travelled anywhere like this on my own since I had gone to my mum's on my own in Bury sometime ago but this distance was longer and I had to change trains twice as there was not one that went straight through it was a very frightening experience for me and it was late at night. I had to Change at Crewe and Preston to get the connection at Blackburn, it was very scary doing this journey on my own for the first time. I arrived in Preston at 12.05am and my connection to Blackburn was at 01.05 and this was the last train to get me home, I was sat on the train when a police officer came on to the train and asked me to come off the train but held the train up whilst he was talking to me, he asked me where I had travelled from and where I was going and why I was on such a late train and travelling on my own. I told the police officer that I was travelling back from Hinckley in Leicestershire and I was going back home to my dad's and I had just seen my mum and I was on such a late train because my mum's car had broken down and this was the next best thing to getting me home and that my mum could not come back with me as she had Mark to look after and my dad should be meeting me at the station. The police officer said to me "that if I was lying I would be picked up at the other end and be treated as a runaway. I was then allowed to get back on the train and I started to cry and there was a nice lady on the train who knew my dad but I did not know her I did not think who comforted me and sat with me till we got to Blackburn and waited with me until my dad arrived which was only a few minutes and they had a conversation for a few minutes and then they went their separate ways. My dad was very angry with me for being on the train and for coming back on my own and he told me that I needed to be punished for this and on the way home he pulled in at the side of the road and started to take his belt off and he hit me with it and then he was cuddling me and touching me and I felt so uncomfortable with him now and I was feeling very self conscious to and I was becoming ashamed of my body for allowing him to do what he was doing and felt that I had done something so wrong to get this sort of punishment but I did not understand things anymore and why I was being punished the way I was and so frequently to.

I knew that God would not forgive me for my foolishness and unfaithfulness and my dad told me that he would not and that God wanted him to punish me, and God would in time to.

His hands was all over me and touching me at first I tried to push him away but there was no point and I knew it because I only got the belt and more words from the bible about me not honouring thy father and obeying what he wanted from me and that God would not approve of my sinfulness and being unfaithful to God. His hands were now under my clothes and he told me to get undress and I refused and that got me another belt. I did not undress that night I did not feel right and we were still in his works van at this time and what he was doing was bad enough without having to be naked in front of him and I was extremely self conscious now to. He had undone my bra strap and said that it was better for him now that was undone I felt scared and embarrassed about what he was doing then his hands were going up my skirt and he was pulling my underwear to one side and he was touching me in the pubic area and I felt tears coming into my eyes but afraid to let them go so I started to pray and I asked God to stop this and to punish me in another way this just did not feel right and why would God what to punish me this way then I started asking myself was it because God was this way to but I did not think that he was and it was not what I believed God to be. I believed God to be much more and very different to how God was being betrayed to me at this time. I started to pray that he would get his punishment but maybe I still needed punishing but I was not sure why I did. I prayed for forgiveness all the time and prayed for God's guidance and for him to help me. I was not sure if that was the right thing to do either but it felt right to me.

We had not long got back home when I received, belting because I had not obeyed thy father and would not do what he wanted and that I would have to be punished severally when the time comes.

We had in the last eighteen months or so had a new vicar to the church and I got on very well with him but more his daughter and I was often going round there it was nice and one day the vicar said to me if there was anything I wanted to talk about then I could do, I thought I would be safe talking to him and I asked him if he ever touches his daughter and he said of course he did but he had not realised what I was asking him at the point he said both parents touch their children by giving them a hug, a kiss. He then asked me why I looked so puzzled with what he said at first I did not say anything and he asked me again. Eventually I said to him" so you only touch your daughter on top of her clothes then" he now looked puzzled and he then shut his office door he said it was better to talk with the door shut and no-one else could hear what was being said as he felt that what we were starting to talk about was not for the rest of his household to hear. He asked me " to tell him more about what I meant with what I had said about you only touch your daughter on top of her clothes, I found it hard to explain to him but I trusted him and felt it was ok to talk to him and to trust him after all he was doing God's work or that is what I thought so I asked him was it right for a father to touch their daughter and under their clothes he replied it depends so I asked him on what. He then said "if it is on their arm or on their back whilst wearing a t-shirt for instance that would be ok but he said if it what I seemed to be saying then no it was not alright.

90

So asked him who would be unfaithful and sinful to God then he said that was difficult to answer with not knowing what I meant we seemed to be talking for hours but I was not really saying much he looked at his watched and said it was time I went home and we would have another chat next time I was round which was very often and he asked me if I was coming round the next night and that I could sleep if I wanted to do and I said yes please if that was ok with you, he told me that he would clear it with my dad and he did and the next night I stayed round at his place it was so different to being at home and so nice and loving, when I was watching them all having fun I started to cry and I was asked why I was crying and I could not answer that one, and then I was apologises for being weak and for crying he told me that it is not weak to cry and that it is natural to do. He said we could go into his office and talk if you want to which we did. I was asked why I thought that it was weak to cry and I told him that I had been told that it was and Jesus did not cry so crying was a sign of weakness I was then told that it was a natural human emotion and that does not mean it is weak just means I have got feelings I found that hard to accept because I had been told for so long that it was weak to cry and the beltings I had taken because I had cried and I believed that this was a weakness I was not convinced what I was now being told was correct but it did put doubt in my mind. Then there was a bit of general conversation and then we started to talk about my dad how we got to talking about my dad he asked me how I felt still to be living with my dad and when I told him that I wanted to be with my mum and I hated him I hated him for keep coming in my room he replied to me that it is natural for a dad to come in my room and to tuck me in at night and I told him it was not just tucking me in. He looked puzzled and confused with what I was saying and I was constantly being told that my dad was a good man and I should be proud of him I told him it is what he wants everyone to believe but I knew differently. He started to ask me more questions and at first I told him to mind his own business and he promised me that whatever I said to him would stay with him because of the work he did he was not allowed to discuss anything with anyone else and I believed him to I wished that I had not, but I did open up to him and I did tell him what had happened and he asked me time and time again if I was with what I was I was telling him I told him I was. What I had forgot about was how close friends my dad and he was but even so

91

I did not expect him to go and tell my dad what I had said, he dropped me back at home and asked me to go and see if my dad was in and he was I said to him that the vicar wanted a word with you and he asked me if I had been a naughty girl again I told him that I had not and he told me off for not bringing him straight away but the vicar did not want to come in as I had already asked him in. I went upstairs to my room and gently opened my bedroom window and I could hear them talking and it was quietly to and I heard him tell my dad what I had said and of course my dad denied this and said he had no idea what he was talking about. The vicar just said that I would not say things like that as it was not like me. My dad told him he does not know me very well. Their friendship suffered and they did not see each other very often after that. After the vicar had gone my dad came running upstairs and swung my bedroom door opened and told me that I had no right to tell anyone anything and that I had just ruined a very special friendship and I would be punished for that one and I was, not just by the belt but I suffered in other ways to not just that night either for days and weeks to come. I felt scared and betrayed both by a family friend and the vicar who also meant the church to and that stayed with me for many years to come to.

A few weeks after I had spoken to the vicar he was doing a sermon in the morning service about weakness and he used what I had said about it was weak to cry and how different people saw this and how the church saw this I was furious about this he had no right to say any of this and after a few minutes I switched off from listening to what he was saying I was just so mad at him, it was not long after that service that he announced that he was going to be leaving the parish after the next choir Sunday which was in about four and a half months. That time soon came round and I had not really spoken to him since that day but I still went round to see his daughter and I was dreading them going because I was going to lose one of the closest friend that I had ever had. It was a long and hard few months for me and I was seeing loads of my mum and she was planning to get married again but no date or anything like that had been set as far as I know well if they had I was not being told about it. I did not expect to go to another wedding of hers as I knew he wanted a low-key wedding. I was not bothered anyway. I spent that Christmas with my mum, Mark and step-dad to be it was a hard Christmas on me as they were drinking a lot and I was the one looking after everything and I had enough of that when I was with my dad do this and do that. It was different to compared to other Christmas's it was not nice and no longer pleasant being there but mum kept saying it was my fault but I did not know how it could be. I thought it must be because of me and I was a evil and as wicked as my dad and told me for years but I was not sure that I was but I was beginning to believe that I was. I had stayed throughout the New year to that year why I did I do not know but I did, it was nice seeing my mum and spending so much time with her and Mark but something did not feel right.

Later that night I heard them talking and he said something is not right with me I seem more withdrawn than I had been before and subdued but I had not got a clue what he meant or what he was saying all my mum said was she noticed that I was quiet but nothing untoward about me she said that she did not know what she would have done without me over the time I had been down there and I had given her the freedom to be able to do what she wanted, it started to get a bit heated and she said she is my daughter and she would know if something was wrong with me. He just said ok fair enough but something is not right.

In the morning I needed to go to the shop for some personal items and I tried to ask my mum for some money discreetly and she started to shout at me for wanting some money to buy what I needed from the shop ashe was yelling at me saying that everything I needed was in the house but it was not and she did not seem to understand what I was asking for or she was not listening and she told me that she had not got time to argue with me as she was going to be late for work. It was always what she wanted or needed not about what her family needed or wanted.

I thought that they were both out when I came back down stairs with my bedding but he was in and he asked me why I was bringing my bedding down and putting it in the wash so soon I told him it did not matter and it was nothing to do with him and then he asked me what personal things I needed from the shop I told him it was none of his business and it should be my mum here helping me not you. He suddenly realised why I needed money because he saw my bedding I was embarrassed that he had seen my bedding and more so that I had a period at my mum's I had been having them for nearly three years now but it was the first one I had whist I was at my mum's she had not got a clue that this was happening for me and I felt dirty about it to and felt that it was un natural to, I got my bedding into the washing machine and he gave me some money to go and get what I needed which I did and when I returned he was waiting for me and he said to me that he had not realised what a beautiful young woman I was becoming and that I would make someone very happy one day but that day would become sooner than I would think to but I did not take much noticed of what he said as I thought that he was just messing around or trying to pay me a complement but I was not sure that it was either it frightened me. I went down to get my bedding out of the machine and put it on the line to dry it was a cold but windy day and the sun was shining and it did not take long to dry and I was just taking it off the line by the time my mum got in from work and asked why I washing my bedding I told her it did not matter. She then went and asked my step-dad why I had washed my bedding and he said leave it for now I will tell you in a bit and they had a few crossed words and said that he better not be getting any ideas about me and left it at that. I went back upstairs to make my bed and my mum came up a few minutes later and said to me why did I not tell her and she would have given me some money and I told her that I tried to that morning and you were not listening and she thought that it was the first time for me and she was surprised that I had been having periods for nearly three years now and that she started to tell me that now I am a woman that I could now get pregnant but I was so naïve I just said but the stoke brings a baby for you and she just laughed and told me that I had a lot to learn but the time is not right for me to know about that yet. I found that conversation strange and puzzling for me. She soon left my room and as she left she said to me that in future I had to me more specific what I needed or wanted in the future I felt embarrassed by that I had to ask in more detail with her.

It was soon time for me to go back home and I was now going to and from my mum's by train on a regular basis and we always tried to get a straight through train for my sake more than anything every-time now and more often than not I did get straight through train it did not bother me anymore going by train it was actually nice being that little bit more independent but more so having some time on my own without any one hassling me. It was a long journey to be doing on my own but it was good for me and for a lot of reasons to.

When I arrived at the station my dad was usually there to meet me but there were times that he was not and I was kept waiting round the station for ages sometimes up to a hour before he came to pick me and sometimes I had walked back home faster than he had picked me up and on a number of occasions I had actually walked in to the house before he was even getting ready to come and collect me walking through the town at night and along the streets did not bother me after all it was not the dark that could hurt me but only people in it my Grandma told me that many times so I was not afraid of being alone at night and I had slept in the dark many times on my own. This particular night whilst I was walking back I was running home normally I would take my time but It was cold and it was raining heavily and there was the start of a storm and the one thing I hated and frightened me was a thunder storm I don't know why it did but it did. As I approached the back door of the house there was a clap of thunder and a flash of light and I screamed and ran through the back door and slammed it behind me but by doing this I broke a window my dad came running into the kitchen wondering what had happened and he saw me on the floor crying I had got hurt from the glass as it broke, I thought that I was going to get a belting for this but I did not he just said that it was an accident and these things happen I had a cut on my left wrist and a cut on my shoulder to. They were bleeding quiet badly and I had to go the hospital to make sure that everything was ok there was a lot of questions how I did it but when they realised that I had shut the door with the glass panel rather than the frame and I was afraid of the storm they seemed to accept that and sorted me out lucky for me there was no glass in my shoulder or my wrist I had some steri-strips put onto the wounds and sent home. I was only frightened of a storm because I was told so often that it was God's anger that made a storm and he was coming to punish me for being unfaithful and sinful and for not honouring thy father and I believed that this was true and I was so afraid that I was going to be punished by God for everything I did that was wrong, sinful or unfaithful to him and my parents.

When I got back in from the hospital I went straight to bed and my dad left me alone that night which surprised me so much as he very rarely left me alone he was always in my room these days and sometimes all night so I was relieved but surprised that he was not in my room that night.

I was at school the next day and for the rest of the week and I had came home from school with a letter regarding the school I wanted to be attending I had already tick my preference but I knew I would not be allowed to go and I was going to have to go to the same school as my step-sisters which is something that I did not want to do but I had no choice and I hated that choice it was not what I wanted and I felt that it was unfair as they had a choice which school to go to but I did not and I felt that was so unfair. I tried to purposely fail the entrance exams so I did not have to go to that school but even that did not work as they called me back to do them again and told me that they knew that I had deliberately tried to fail them because of the way I answered things and my dad told me that I had to answer them properly this time or else I would be in trouble and I did and unfortunately for me I got into that school and I hated it there, I hated everything about that school, the uniform, the people, the teachers there was nothing I liked about it. I was dreading the September coming round but that was still almost seven months away.

That year was a busy year for us all with one thing and another but it did not make me feel any better about things.

By the end of February the Choir Sunday came round and I found that so hard that so hard that year because the day came that I was going to lose my friend and I was in tears by the end of the day and she could not understand why I was so upset as we would be in touch. I was not sorry to see her dad go the vicar because I felt he had let me down but someone said to me and it was a close friend of his that he could not stay because of something that had happened and they knew no more than that and I just assumed it was because of what I told him and his actions afterwards but I don't know that one if it is right or not but I assumed that it was.

It seemed strange not having them around and I found it hard going past the vicarage and not seeing them there I missed my friend so much and they had been gone for almost two months now and I had not heard anything from them and my dad said he had not heard from them either and that was my fault for ruining a perfectly good friendship but I did not understand why it was my fault but I felt that it must have been somehow I was finding a lot of things difficult to understand at this time and felt that I must be the reason why so many bad things happened. It felt that it must have been something about me that made bad things happen. I had spent that Easter with my mum and brother but there was no sign of the neighbour there and she had moved again every-time I went it felt like she was into a different place and I was seeing her in different houses all of the time and that was very unsettling for me and especially not knowing where she was from week to week but she told me that things would settle down for her once she gets things sorted out. It was always the same when she got things sorted out she would have me more often and she would be able to do more things with me I just felt they were empty promises and nothing more. I had hoped that they were not but that is how I felt.

Times with my mum were getting less and less it was a difficult year for me it was a year and so much had changed and so much I had lost. During the year I had not seen my mum very much and was letting me down more and more I did not have any idea why she kept doing this to me.

Whilst I was with her she was not spending much time with us but spending more and more time drinking I just thought that she was making the most of it whilst I was there because it gave her break from her responsibilities and nothing more, I still wanted to live with her and the older I got the worse that became and the more I wanted it.

Every-time I returned home the harder it was for me to go back there. The more I dreaded it to.

I was looking forward to the long holidays as I was going to be spending a lot of it with my mum and she was meant to be taking me away I was not sure that she would have done but neither the less I was going to spend a lot of it with her.

The other part of it I was spending it with my dad and step-mum and stepsisters. As far as I was aware we were not going anywhere we were lucky if we got a holiday with my dad they had a week without me the first week I was with my mum and my stepsisters were boasting that my dad took them away and not me and that they meant more to my dad than I did but I already felt that anyway even so it still hurt and upset me. I felt that is what they intended to do.

I had four weeks with my mum so when I came back I had to go and get my school uniform I hated that uniform but at least it was warm but it was not pleasant to wear and everyone was in the same it was a strict school uniform and not many people liked it either but we put up with it. I found the school hard and found mixing with other children difficult and I was jealous at times that they had both their parents with them and they seemed to be loved and happy and they talked fondly about their parents I tried not to talk about my parents because I did not feel right doing so and I missed my mum so much and she was so far away from me I know it was not that far but it felt like she was so far away I suppose in a way she was far away. I did become friendly with a couple of girls who travelled to this school but it was only half a hour on the bus but it was still a distance for someone to travel to school well at the time I thought that it was, and as the school year progressed we became quiet close and she began to tell me some of her secrets but I was wary about telling her anything about me I was afraid to trust her but in time I did trust her to a certain point and she was always there for me as I was her.

I had seen my mum a few times throughout that school year but she was becoming less reliable again I was getting use to that. As for my dad he had not changed he was constantly in my room at night and his hands were all over me and touching me and wanting me to respond to him and kiss him back he was still using the Bible against me to get what he wanted but not as often as he use to do I am not sure why he did not use the Bible as much maybe I was beginning to understand the Bible better as I got older he still did from time to time and it still had the same effect on me as it did when I was younger I suppose it was his way of getting what he wanted but I did not know that at the time.

The following school year soon came round and it was a hard year but I was being bullied at school for different reasons one for being different, another because I had no mum that lived with me and they thought that was so wrong. And for coming from a poor background and not being able to do a lot of the things they could do but I did not see things that way I felt everything was my fault and some reason I even deserve what I was getting at school to as well as at home. The second school year was almost half way through and I hated that school I kept asking my dad to let me change school but he would not let me and he asked Charlene and Donna if they had noticed that I was being picked on at school and they said they thought that I was but they was not sure and they said they would try and keep a look out for me and in their own way they did.

This particular night I did not go straight home from school I went into town first as Christmas was coming up and I wanted to have a look round I loved the lights and everything to do with Christmas but I was afraid that I would lose the meaning of Christmas even though we did not get a lot for Christmas I still loved to look around and enjoy the Christmas atmosphere that was in the town centre and as I was walking through the town centre the Salvation Army was there and I remembered going there with my Grandma and she told me always stop and listen to them when they are in the town singing as there was something special about it and she was right to and whilst I was stood there listening I started to cry as I could still hear my Grandma amongst them and for a brief moment I thought I saw her standing amongst them and smiling at me for stopping and watching and listening it was such a magical feeling for me and I felt Grandma was still with me and still a part of me and I am not sure why I went to town that day something just told me that I should and I did maybe it was a feeling but I don't know but I knew I had to be in town that day and I was so glad that I did I felt so much more spiritual than I ever imagined I could have done I knew several of the people that was there and singing and they recognised me when they had a break in song they came over to me and chatted and gave me a cuddle it was so nice and they asked me if I could remember my Grandma's favourite song I told them I did and they asked me what it was I told them it was Amazing Grace and whilst they were on a break they sat round me and we sang it together and I was crying for Grandma and remembering her and this song got to me so much that day but it was beautifully done and I went home after that feeling something very special and spiritual and peace on the inside of me I could not understand this or why I felt the way I did but it was such a wonderful feeling and a feeling that I did not want to lose regardless of anything that will and was happening to me.

I was over three hours late home that night and my dad was working late and my step mum was in a foul mood by the time I got in and she asked me where I had been I told her that I had gone to town to listen to the Salvation Army singing Christmas Carols she called me a liar and she kept asking me again and again were I was and each time she got the same answer which just infuriated her even more and made her so angry she told me that she was now late for work because of me as I was having to look after Marie and Rowena again which I had done every night now for the last six months and I was complaining about it and saying it was not fair that it was always me when she had two older girls to do it for her she told me that they had gone out to have some fun and under my breathe I muttered lucky for them. Unfortunately for me she heard it and then her fist was flying and she hit me in the face and thumped me in the back I was so sore and angry with her I told her that she is not my mum and she had no right to do that and I hated her and I wished that she was dead well I should have not said anything as she was laying into me more and more and she still was by the time my dad got in about forty minutes later my lips and nose were bleeding and every-time I coughed I brought some more blood up and I was crying, my dad came running in when he heard the commotion and told her enough is enough you have gone too far this time and told her to back off and he asked what had trigged this off and I told him that I was fed up of having to look after Marie and Rowena as it was not fair that I was doing this all of the time and for once he agreed with me and he stopped the two older ones going out and told them that they both were going to stay in and look after them for a change I was sore but thrilled that finally I could go out if I wanted to but I did not but it meant that I could do what I wanted for a change and I decide to go to my room and read a book in peace well that is what I was hoping anyway. I heard the front door shut as both my dad and step mum left to go to work and I breathed a sigh of relief but then a few minutes later my bedroom door swung open and Charlene and Donna were having a go at me for ruining their fun and dragging me down stairs with my hair what I did not know at this time Peter was back in but keeping out of the way and eventually he came down to see what was going off and he stopped the two of them from hurting me anymore and then when he thought it had all calmed down he went for walk and I was on my way back up the stairs Donna through a knife up the stairs and it hit me in the back of the leg and came straight out. I had enough that night and I had not ran away for ages but I did that night it was a cold and wet night and the wind was blowing strongly which made it hard to get anywhere very quickly but I had managed to get as far as radio Blackburn's radio station and there was a car parked there and I squatted down besides it and realised it was dry there so I laid down there and I was there for a long time I had fell asleep were I was, there was a lot of heat coming off the car and I was so cold and wet that it was nice to have this heat but I knew now that I was not going back to that house ever again well in my own mind I did I had said this every-time I had ran away but I always had to go back eventually. The next thing I knew I was waking up but I was no longer outside but inside and near to a heater with blankets over me and I was not sure how I got inside as I knew I had fell asleep outside. As I awoke someone said to me it is ok you are safe we picked you up and brought you in an covered you up to get you warm I felt frightened and scared and vulnerable I apologised to them and said I better be on my way but I was in a lot of pain and I could hardly walk they asked me my name and I would not tell them my name or anything else they had asked me I did not tell them anything they said to me " if you don't tell us then we cannot help you" I did not want any help then I thought to myself maybe they will be able to get me to my mum and I just said I wanted my mum they asked me where she lived and I told them she lives in Leicester somewhere. They seemed surprised by what I had said but they knew I was a local kid because of my accent. I know I laid back down and back to sleep the next thing I knew there was a couple of police officers there to collect me I could only presume that the radio station had called them and the two that came out knew me as they were the ones that came back with me regular when I had ran away before. They commented that it has been awhile since I had done this and something must have made me run away I would not even look at them I was afraid of what they might see. They asked me to put my head up and in time I did and they said that they think I should be taken home before I am missed too much and when we were in the police car they had asked me what had happened and I told them that my step sisters hate me and that they threw a knife at me and they asked me if it hit me anywhere? I told them that it hit me on the back of my leg but it was ok they had a look at it and said it needed cleaning up which they did back at the police station and asked me if I had any other injuries and I told them that I had not I was too scared to tell them that I had taken a beating from my step mum to I was terrified to go home but they took me home and no-one had missed me but the police did not just drop me off they went in and had a word with my dad and step mum and said that this is very serious and that they would look into the home situation a bit more and ask social services to come round.

I went to my bed room and both my dad and step mum was in my room asking me if any of my step sisters had thrown a knife at me and when I told them that they had and they told me that if anyone else asked that I should tell them that I made a mistake because they did not want any of her precious daughters getting into trouble it did not matter what they had done to me as long they did not get into trouble. Well a few days later a social worker visited the house and tried to speak with me alone but that was not allowed none of them would let them talk to me without one of them being there with me so I did not say anything rather than denying it. After the social worker had gone I got laid into for not saying that I had made a mistake but I did not see why I should protect her precious daughters and I hated them so much.

The next day when I went to school I had got two black eyes but I still went to school neither my dad or my step mum had seen me that morning when I went to school and was un aware of how I looked and when I had looked in the mirror I was scared of how I was going to avoid people and especially staff at school somehow I was going to have to keep my head down as much as I could and I hope that I would have got away with anyone asking me questions or two many of them but I was hoping for too much that day. I had two lessons at the lower school and I had one at the upper school the first and third lessons was at lower school and I managed to keep my head down and the one at the upper school I tried to keep my head down but it was harder for some reason that lesson the teacher was getting me to answer her questions a lot that lesson and I kept my head down but I got into trouble for not looking up and looking at the person I was talking to and in the end I had to lift my head up and even the class had not seen the state I was in at the point and the whole class and the teacher gave a gasp when they saw me. She then set some work to do for the class and called me outside the classroom to talk to me and she asked me what had happened and I said nothing I just want to get on with the lesson and keep my head down which is all I wanted to do, she apologised to me for making me look up in front of everyone she went to make a phone call down to lower school but by the time she had come back I had left the classroom and the upper school and I made my way down to the lower school ready for my next lesson but I spent most of that lesson in the girls toilets then I heard some girls talking that the deputy head and other members of staff were looking for me and I came out of the toilets and I asked the girls not to say they have seen me and I made my way to my next lesson and kept my head down there we had set places to sit and I slipped in and sat in a different place and it was not noticed that I was in the lesson and the class was more or less the same ones from the previous class with the odd one being a different pupil but they did not say anything about me being there. At lunchtime I tried to avoid all the teachers and getting out of the class was going to be hard if we were not dismissed as a group and sometimes we were not but lucky for me we were dismissed as a whole class which meant I could get out with the other children I headed for the tuck shop and sat in there for most of lunch time and when a member of staff came within feet of the tuck shop I hid so I was not seen and the person that ran the tuck shop told me that I was going to have to face them sooner or later and when the coast was clear he let me out and I headed for the main hall and just as I went into the main hall so did several members of staff and I saw a group of girls I knew and started talking to them and staff were calling me and I was ignoring them hoping that they would think that they got the wrong person even though I knew that they were calling the right person in the end I was cornered and I had to speak with them I was taken into the deputy's room and several other members of staff were summoned to her room and they were all asking me questions how did it happen and I would not tell them and then another member of staff came into the room and asked me if he could touch my face and I told him no way is anyone else going to touch me then the deputy spoke to me and said nothing is going to happen to me with four other members of staff present so in the end

103

I agreed to let them in touch my face and he said I had taken one heck of a beating and I would not tell them by whom or why this had happened they told me that they would be contacting my welfare court officer and social services and told me that they would be there after school that evening and they took several photo's of me when I got home from school that evening I went straight to my room but I was soon called down and then taken to the doctors for a full examination with my dad as both the social worker and court welfare officer had insisted on it and had already arranged it they allowed my dad to take me but it was only me and the doctor in the examination room as she was told not to let my dad or step mum come into the room with me in case I said anything she asked me loads of questions and I still would not say too much but when she asked me if I knew the person that had done this I told her that I did she asked me if I was hurt anywhere else and I said I was she examined me fully and discovered all the bruising from this beating and previous beatings and the belt marks that were on my back she asked me if I got hit a lot I told her that I did she asked me if anything else had happened and I told her that I did not want to talk about it so she left it at that and told me that it would take several days before I felt comfortable and I begged her not to mention anything I had said to my dad and she said she was not allowed to discuss a patient with anyone without my permission and if I did not want my dad to know anything and I did not want him to know anything and I was frightened that he would find out again that I had something but not everything. On the journey home my dad was asking what she had said and what I had said to her and told him I did not understand the medical talk and I had said nothing to her I was scared to tell him anymore and he called me a good girl for not saying anything.

In the car on the way home he started talking about the Choir Sunday and the Choir Sunday meal which we always had and asked if there was anything I would like to do and I wanted to do a reading on my own this time as in the past an adult always shared the readings that the younger choir members had done just in case they were a bit nervous or felt that they could not do the reading when it came to the day I was amazed that he agreed that I could do this but an adult had to come up with me just in case I needed them I told him that I would not and when the day came the adult went to get up with me and I said I was ok I can do this on my own and I did and I was so proud of myself for doing this but more than

104

anything it meant a lot to me to be able to do this and I was given a very long reading to and I felt that was deliberate so I would fail but I did not and I was praised by the rest of the choir and the vicar afterwards and I felt so proud that I had done this and I was only twelve at the time and I was going to be confirmed the following week which I felt so proud of being able to do this. During the Choirs lunch there was always an opportunity to ask any question and all the years I had gone to the choirs meal I had never asked a question but this year there was something I wanted to asked my dad and I wanted the rest of the choir to hear what I was asking and the hope was he would not say no to me. So I got up and stood in the middle of the tables and asked my dad how much he loved me and he replied loads why then I said if you love me that much then you would let me go. He asked what do you mean I am too young to be let go of yet so I said to him" would you let me go to live with my mum if you love me as much as you say you do" after all you cannot keep hold of me forever and you do not own me I want you to let be become free to choose what I want to do. He looked angry but he agreed that this could happen but not yet. Some of the choir clapped me for saying what I did and there were others that looked disappointed in me and some actually said that they were disappointed in me and that this was not the place to ask that sort of questions I had done this deliberately as I wanted witnesses if he said yes that way he could not back out of it after he said yes to me in front of everyone. I got the third degreeby the time we got home that night and I got laid into for embarrassing him in front of everyone. He was not happy at all but I needed to ask him and if that meant asking him in front of other then so be it. Anyway it was easier to get his attention about things like this when others were around and he was not expecting it but I suffered for it later on. I was amazed when he said I could go and live with my mum if that is what I wanted to do it was the happiest I had felt in such a long time.

A few days later I was outside with my stepsisters and we were all having some fun for a change which was rare for us all to be getting on and having some fun it was nice whilst it lasted which was not that long we had been playing in one of the out buildings when I went into the outbuilding my stepsisters ran out and shut the door on me and then they locked me in and I heard them saying to my step mum well she is out of the way now for a bit it was a set up to get me in there and that is how I felt it was maybe it was not but I was not so sure that it was not. I took it as a bit of fun at first but as the day went on it was no longer fun and I knew there was often mice in there at night and I hated rats, mice and they terrified me and I had bad memories of them from when we had lived at our old house and I was still frightened of them and I was also frightened of being bitten again by one but I was going to have to get use to it for the time being but I did not like the idea. I had been in there all day and it was now getting dark and the light in this out building was not working so I was in darkness except from the street light that was shining through the small window at the back of the out building and it gave enough light to be able to see enough of the inside building which was good, I sat on the table that had been put in there so we could go in there when it was raining with drinks and sandwiches when we had friends around as we were not allowed friends in the house very often. It was quiet cosy in there we had a few blankets in there and some stools but it did not feel very cosy in there at this time of night, there was a lot of noise coming from the pub as there was one that our back garden over looked and the only thing that separated us and the pub was a wall and a small road but you could still hear them. I started to feel cold and hungry and I needed to go to the toilet but I knew I had to wait till the morning if I could, somehow I managed to get some sleep and settle down for the night but it was nice that I was undisturbed that night well in a way it was but I wanted out of there now and I wanted to be somewhere else anywhere but there. I was surprised that I got as much sleep as I did that night and it was fairly settled sleep. I awoke in the morning with the birds singing but it felt cold and I felt cold I heard someone come outside from the house and I jumped off the table and knocked on the door and shouted to them to let me out but they were ignoring me and went back inside the house and I heard the back door close again I sat down on the cold and damp floor I cried I was beginning to feel scared about how much longer they would keep me in there hopefully not much longer. After awhile I went and sat back on the table and covered myself up but then I got off again soon afterwards I needed to go to the toilet and I was frightened that I was going to have an accident and I knew I would have got belted for that one. I decided to go back on the table and try and keep warm and pray and think about other things and I did for some time and then it started to rain lightly at first then rain got heavier and heavier which did not help. There was a lot of activity in the neighbour's garden but then again there usually was and I saw them pottering about I the garden and they saw me and smiled and waved at me I waved back but we always did with them. The raining seemed to be raining for hours but our neighbours did not mind the rain they were always doing something in the garden whatever the weather was doing. It looked like they were planting some more of the beds that they had been working on for the last few days and were trying to get it finished. Someone nearby was cooking something nice to eat and it made my mouth water; I knew I was hungry but I did not realise how hungry I was until I could smell other people's cooking. There was very little activity coming from our house it seemed strangely quiet our house was never quiet and it seemed to be now. I started moving around a lot more and staying on the floor I was crying and in a lot of discomfort and I was praying that this would be over very soon for me. It was a dull day that day and it did not seem to get very bright at all and there were a few storms around I was ok whilst it was in the distance but as it got closer to me I was terrified and it was not that long before it was over head and I was trembling and I had nowhere to go or hide I just had to stay where I was the part about it was I did have an accident and I had wet myself and I was more worried about this than the weather I suppose it helped keep my thoughts away from the storm and that storm seemed to last for ages that day. It was getting dark again and I could not believe that I was still stuck in this outhouse and I was getting scared I was feeling uncomfortable cold and scared. I found it hard to keep warm that night and get much sleep. I did manage to get some sleep but not a lot and the only good thing for me about being in there was no one was bothering me or touching me. I went into a deep sleep in the early hours as it was starting to get light as I drifted off. I was awoken suddenly with some shouting at first I thought I was dreaming but then I was being shouted at and hit I was told to get up and that I smelt worse than a pigs sty and my step mum was the one who opened the door and finally let me out two days after I was locked in there and she was laying in to me, then my dad was out there having a go at me and told me that was only the beginning of my punishment and there was more to come and then he realised that I had wet myself and that was it he was laying into me and then my step sisters were calling me names to I just kept saying sorry to them and Peter came over the garden wall and had a go at all of them for the way they were treating me and he asked me how long I had been in there and when he discovered that I had been in there for two days he went berserk at all of them he lifted me into his arms and carried me upstairs and ran a bath for me and stood outside the bathroom whilst I was in there. There were a lot of words that was said between Peter and my dad and step mum and they backed away and left my brother to. I was sitting in the bath smiling that they could not defeat him and could not get away with anything whilst he was there but I knew that I would suffer for this at some point. When I got out of the bath and a had a change of clothes I felt much more comfortable but I was so hungry I opened the bathroom door and Peter was still standing there and I fainted and he carried me into my room and shut the door behind us. He had some drinks and some bits of chocolate in his pocket and when I came round he gave me both a drink and some of the chocolate and then he said that we were going out for something to eat and drink I was delighted that I was going to be spending some time with Peter we went to my favourite chippy and one of my favourite meals I really enjoyed it to. Peter told me that I was not going back that night but I was going to be spending a few days at his place and my dad did not know that this was going to happen and Peter was not going to tell him either he did not deserve to know after what he had done to me. I did stay with Peter and for longer than I thought I would have done I stayed there for almost a week he was only letting me go back because my dad had got the police in saying that Peter my brother was keeping me against my will but they soon realised that I was there because I wanted to be there but advised Peter to take me back home soon and this was not the way to get things sorted out and the sooner I was taken back home the better it would be for all concerned Peter told them that I was going to be spending at least another couple of days with him and then I would be taken back just in time for our mum to collect me and he even came down to my mum's with me that time and it was the first time in a long time that he had come down with me but he made it clear that he was only coming down to keep an eye on me and to make sure I was going to be ok. The time at my mum's was ok but not that brilliant there was a lot of tension there and I could not work out why. The time soon came for me to go back home and I was to be taken back to my dad's and I did not want to go but

I had no choice at the moment but to go back to my dad's.

By the time I got back to my dad's I had been out of that house for almost three weeks and they were good weeks for me it was a shame that I could not stay with either my mum or Peter but I could not do I had to go back sooner than later and when the day came for me to be going back I did not want to go back and I got very upset about doing so.

I went back in the end and I was promised that I would be able to go down again very soon and Peter promised me that he was coming back with me for awhile and saying something's to them and he did have some very stern words with all of them but everything was ok whilst Peter was there but when the time came when he had to go back to his place I knew that things were going to come up from over three weeks ago and I knew that there would still be some punishment from that I just did not want to go back into that out building again I was too scared to go in there again. I was scared to go back home to my dad's to it is the one place I did not want to go back to I did not feel safe there anymore I wanted to stay with my mum. The time came for me to go home came round so quick but it was nice to have some company on the train on the way back and Peter did spoil me a lot and he also said that mum will never look after you properly I told him she would but he was convinced that she would not why he was I do not know.

We soon arrived back at Blackburn station in no time on the train did not seem that long that week but that was probably because I had company on the way back and that night Peter took me all the way to my dad's and we walked part of the way home and that was nice to but it was a bit chilly walking back but it was nice to be with Peter and I can remember thinking why was he not around more often I felt safe whilst he was around and loved.

By the time we arrived at my dad's house it was around 11.30 and I walked in first he commented oh she has put you on an earlier train she has got some common sense after all and then my brother walked in and said "she did not but I did". My dad soon shut up.

Peter went to his room then shortly followed by me going up stairs and into my room as I approached my bedroom door Peter stopped me and gave me a big hug and whispered to me that he loved me and I would only be safe whilst he was around but he would not always be around to help me. I was worried by that I thought that Peter was always going to be around but he was there one day and gone the next and then he would just appear out of nowhere again.

It had been ages since I asked my dad if I could go and live with my mum alls he kept saying was soon and he would not commit on anything or tell me a date when I could go and live with her. My mum was getting inpatient to as she wanted to know herself and was always asking me to keep asking my dad but what she would not understand the more I asked him the more he would not give me an answer and I knew it Easter came and went and there was still no decision about me going to live with my mum Whitsun holidays were fast approaching and my mum wanted a decision and soon and I could not get one yet but I knew that I would do eventually but we just add to wait until he was ready to let me go whenever that may be but I felt that it was going to be never. Whitsun break I was spending with my mum and I was looking forward to it even though I knew that I would not be doing a lot I am still looking forward to seeing her. The house she was now in had a huge back garden more like an orchard with all the trees that was there and some of them had fruit growing on them it was a very hot that year and me and Mark had the paddling pool out for the full week and had loads of fun and whilst me and Mark were messing about in the water I glanced up and saw that my step-father Isaac watching me but I made out that I had not seen him because it bothered me that he was watching me and it made me feel uncomfortable. Mark got out of the paddling pool and started playing quietly on his own, so I laid down on one of the sun loungers and fell asleep I regretted doing that as I got badly burnt and I had some bad blisters on my back, shoulders and back of my legs and I was in pain I had some sun block on but not that much and I did not expect to fall asleep in the sun. When I awoke several hours later Mark had also fell asleep but he was in the shade and got a towel over him. I went into the house and I had not realised how much I had been burnt or how badly I was and once I got in and started to cool down a bit all my back, shoulders and legs felt they were on fire and I could hardly move and my mum made me lay down on the sofa and started placing ice packs on me wrapped in towels to try and cool me down and cool me down quickly and to bring the burn out of my skin and I was feeling ill and several hours later I was vomiting a lot and felt very dizzy and my step father got told off for not keeping an eye on us whilst we were out in the sun and Isaac just said that he thought that we were going to be ok and he did not expect any of us to fall to sleep in the sun so my mum asked what he had been doing and he told her he fell asleep for about two and a half hours and she was surprised that we had been out there in the sun for so long and she suddenly realised Mark was nowhere around and I told her he is ok he has got a towel over him and he is in the shade but he was also asleep but at least he was in the shade she sent Isaac out to check and he was still asleep and in the shade just like I said he was. That night mum did not go out anywhere she stayed with me and continued with the ice packs I started to shiver and feel very cold but at the same time my skin felt on fire this felt strange and I was not sure why it did. My mum sat up with me all night and she would not leave my side she was worried and concerned which made a change when she had not had a drink she were loving in her own way. Could I hardly move and when I awoke the next morning my mum was still putting ice packs on my back, legs and shoulders my head was hurting to mum told me that I had got sun stroke and I had to be careful for the next few days and stay indoors and stay warm but keeping my skin cool that did not make any sense to me but she knew what she was saying, my back was the worse I had loads of blisters on my back rest of me was not to bad but sore, mum had also been putting moisture into my skin to make it easier for me.

I did not go out for a few days I felt to ill and I was still not right when it was time to go back to my dad's so my mum phoned him using a neighbours phone to tell him we had gone away for a few days and she wanted to stay a couple more days and she wanted to keep me with her and to my surprise he agreed to that. I was glad that I was not going back for a few more days I did not want to go back at all but I knew that I would have to. At least a few more days with my mum was good to be with her and I was not as sore when I got home and the blisters were settling down a bit but I knew that they would be burst when I got home especially once they realised that I had caught the sun and was burnt well I was not so much burnt now but a bit sore as I was starting to tan.

When I had to go back to my dad's he was not pleased that it was a few extra days he said he would put a stop to me going if he had to and I said he can't do that my mum as rights to which got me a slap round the face he told me that was for being cheeky. There was no love from him or hugs unless it was for what he did to me that was the only time he came near to me rather than giving a child a hug and welcoming that child back home it did not feel like home to me it felt like a prison.

Later that night I was getting changed in my room and I had my back to the door and my dad came into my room I had not realised he had even opened the bedroom door and he was stood there watching me and when I went to put on my night clothes he told me not to bother as I would not be wearing them for very long. He took his belt off and hit me several times across my back and I felt most of the blisters on my back burst the pain was unbearable and I screamed out in pain and he told me to shut up but I screamed even more and I was crying I had been looking out of my window and someone had just pulled up on a motorbike and when they took their helmet off I saw that it was Peter so I screamed even more and Peter heard the screams at first he looked around him then he looked up to my window and then he came running into the house and flung the bedroom door opened and my dad was not expecting this and he was startled that Peter was there behind him but before my dad could do anything Peter took the belt off him and started hitting him with his own belt and he was cut across the face and on his chest and then he left my room. Peter came over to me and saw the state my back was in and he asked me what had happened and I told him that I got badly sunburnt whilst I was away with mum and I had only been back just over a hour when this happened he asked me why was he doing this to me? What had I done wrong? I told him that I did not know he went to get something to bathe my back and took the moisturiser out of my bag that mum had sent me back with and he spent a lot time bathing my back and rubbing in the moisturiser and he left me laying on my bed in just my underwear as that is all I had been wearing when my dad had came in and also Peter to. Peter respected my privacy and made sure he kept my dignity and that I did not feel exposed to him or anyone. Shortly later Peter went down the stairs and he was not at all pleased, he left me laying faced down on my bed with the moisturiser soaking into my back but it was not half stinging at the moment.

There were words said down stairs and my step mum shouted at my dad I did not understand what was going on there but she was soon in my room and asking me if I was ok and she saw the state my back was in and told me to stay where I was and the next thing I knew a doctor was coming into my room and he said I would heal in time and I was just going to have to give it time and he prescribed something for me to take and also some other cream to be rubbed into my back which would be better for me than moisturiser alone and she went and fetched the prescription and she gave me a tablet to take and she rubbed this cream into my back but it did not half feeling like it was burning my skin away but in a way it was as it was sealing my skin to prevent infection it was like having another layer of skin on top of my own skin. It felt a lot better than it had done for days but it was still very sore and my step mum did this four to five times a day for the next few days she had never been this nice to me before so why now I was not sure what was going on here. A few days later she said to me that she did not want me to go and live with my mum as she would miss me being around but she had never paid any attention to me before and or even been interested in what I was or not doing before all's she did was punish me.

The next month at church they were deciding who was going to be the Rose Queen for that year and this was one thing I wanted to do for so long. I hoped that it would be me that year which meant if I was I would mean another year before I went to be with my mum and I would have done that to if I got it. One Sunday after morning service they approached my dad and told him that I had been chosen to be the Rose Queen and he turned them down and he told them that I did not really deserve to be it but they said differently but my dad refused it. I was gutted as this is what I wanted to be so much and I had wanted to be this for years and I hoped and hoped that one year they would chose me and when they finally did it was turned down. I hated my dad for doing that but he made all sorts of excuses up like but you go and see your mum, how are we going to make the dress I said these were just obstacles we could have sorted out but he would not have it and I was surprised that he did not jump at the chance to keep me there for another year. I cried a lot that night and the next day I asked my dad as I was not going to be Rose Queen can I go and live with my mum again he said yes I could but I would have to wait for the time being that is all he ever said.

The school holidays came round and he still would not let me go and live with her he just kept making excuses up and whilst I was seeing my mum and step dad he said to me that something is not right with me and something is happening back at my dad's and I said there was and he asked me a lot of questions until he got it out of me what had been happening and that was hours before I was due to get back on the train to go back to my dad's. I did go back on the train and he was staying that I should not be but I had to go back for now anyway.

I was back at my dad's for a few weeks and he had been into my room early this Saturday morning and he was all over me and he was trying to get me to do things to him that I had not done before and I refused to do what he wanted he told me that he was going out for while in a bit and I better still be here when he got back. As soon as he had gone out I went down to the phone box and reversed the charges to my mum but my mum was not in it was just my step dad and Isaac asked me if I was ok I told him I was not and I needed my mum he told me to stay where I was and she would be back soon and they would ring me back, I was waiting outside the phone-box what seem ages and it was a scary time for me waiting there because I knew that my dad would be back soon and he would drive past me and tell me to go back home if not drag me back home which I knew he could have done if he wanted to do. I was getting worried that my mum did not want to ring me back but she did and told me to make my way down to the train station and train tickets would be waiting for me there, as I was walking down the street my dad went passed me and flashed his lights at me and told me to go back home I ignored him and continued down the street instead of walking I started to run as fast as I could, and when I got to the station I had to wait about ten minutes for the tickets but they were there for me and I got on the train and arrived at Hinckley station and my mum and step dad were there to meet me. There was not a lot that was said on the journey back to my mums and I was kept out of the way from everyone one once I got to the house, I was upset and scared, they went out for a drink that night and they also took the phone off the hook so I would not be disturbed by any one. I went to bed about ten that evening and my mum and step dad did not get in until after eleven and at about eleven thirty the phone rang and there was some heated words so I knew who that was and my dad turned round and said you can keep that evil witch with you as I

don't want her back and I don't want to see her again. That is how I came
to be living with my mum.

Chapter 6

I WAS NOT SURE WHAT TO EXPECT NOW I was finally with my mum I was nervous and frightened but I was glad to be there, my mum was drunk when she came into my room in the early hours and she started pulling my hair and asking me what really happened and I told her time and time again, my head was beginning to feel sore she was pulling clumps of my hair out. In the end my step-dad Isaac came into the room and told her that were enough and I had been through enough as it is, and she left my room but he did not and he told me that things are now not going to be as they were when I was just visiting. I did not understand that or why things were going to be different I felt frightened and did not feel safe now I felt that things were going to be no better for me there, than they had been when I was with my dad I hoped and prayed that they would be better and I was just frightened with me being there all of the time now I should have been happy but I did not feel very happy.

There was an argument that night between my mum and step dad and I heard them saying that you don't expect this on your wedding day it should have been a happy day and now they where, having to deal with all that I had brought down with me. I never had any idea that they were getting married and not on the day I turned up I actually thought that they had been married years ago. They started to argue more and more and I could hear things but their argument was not always clear what they were yelling at each other, I was frightened and I had not known anything like this before and I was not sure what to do I just stayed in my room and I started to cry. About a hour later I heard the front door slam shut and I looked out of my bedroom window and it was my mum walking out of the house and I did not know where she was going or when she would be back, I went to check on Mark and he was sound asleep I was not sure how he slept through all of that noise but he had done maybe this was not the first time they had argued like this, and at this point my brother did not know that I was down there to stay and I was not going back to my dad's. About half a hour after my mum walked out of the door my step dad came into my room to see if I was ok and said it is not what you expect on your first night at being in someone else's house and being with my mum something I have always wanted to be with my mum but Isaac told me it was not the first time they had argued like this it was just that they were careful not to argue in front of me before as they did not want to frighten me with everything else that I was going through at my dad's, I asked him how often this happened Isaac told me very often, I was surprised at that as I had never heard them argue before. Isaac then came and sat down next to me and he was comforting me and it felt nice to be comforted but I did not expect his next move and he turned very violent on me Isaac then grabbed my right arm and pushed it back and kept pushing it back and he kept the pressure on it I felt and heard a several cracks and it was hurting me so much. I was frightened and crying and I did not know what I had done for Isaac to turn onto me the way he was doing now. Had I been naughty I kept asking myself? Should I have done something when they had been arguing? I don't know what I should have done and what was right or wrong to do when two people were arguing I felt it was better to leave them to it. So maybe I had been a naughty girl and always was and I deserved this but I was only a child. It was not that long before he was then getting himself undressed with one arm especially taking his trousers down and this frightened me and I knew that I was now going to get the same treatment from him as I did with my dad but I did not expect it to be any worse than what my dad had done to me and what I had just escaped from and had not expected to get the same here he had not shown any interest in me before I came down so why now? I still did not know if it was going to be worse or the same to what I had just come from, but it was and I was so scared and was unable to move as he had kept the pressure up on my arm. He was now undressing me and taking my night clothes off me and before I knew it he was laying on top of me naked and I felt this horrible pain deep inside of me and he kept telling me that I was better than my mum and it pleased him. Isaac said that "I would do what he wanted and what he told me otherwise I would suffer." As he got off me and withdrew from me the pain I got was unbearable I had not felt anything like this before and I felt completely violated and I was scared and I was bleeding to and not bleeding in a way that I had known myself to bleed and it was heavy and dark and clotting unlike I had ever known and I knew I was not due to have a period as I had not long had one in the last week and it would have been unusual for that to happen for me. I was so frightened and I felt like I was dying I had not experience the pain I was now getting. I did not understand this and what had just happened had never happened to me before and I did not understand it either and it was different to what I had experienced with my dad. My arm was so sore and it was swelling up and I just had to put up with it. I waited up for my mum to come back so I could tell her but she did not come back whilst I was awake so I thought that I would mentioned it to mum the next morning but she said there was nothing she could see or that there was anything wrong with it and told me to stop complaining.

My arm was still hurting and it was difficult to move when I did move it I was in a lot of pain so I found a comfortable position and left it there and tried to keep it in the position that was most comfortable that was easier said than done and I was crying with pain to not that my mum was bothered she only cared about her drinking than anything or anyone else.

That morning the police were at my mum's house they had come to talk to me about what had happened whilst I was with my dad and to tell me how serious it was and it was up to me if I decided to do anything about it but they could take action on their own with or without my consent they were only there to talk to me so I thought but they were there to take a statement of what had happened whilst I was with my dad, I felt that I had no choice and I felt uncomfortable about this they asked me what had happened as far as they could do before they decided if it was possible to take things any further they took a few brief notes and then left but they had arranged to come again the following Sunday where a police lady would come on her own as they felt it would be better a lady taking the information and they thought that I would be more open with a police woman.

That week was a hard and long week and it was far from peaceful week. It was difficult living with my mum and worse than I ever expected it to be I knew moving to her was going to be hard however I never imagined that it was going to be this hard or so difficult and I thought that I would have a proper family for the first time in my life but I was so wrong this was not a proper family at all. My mum and Isaac were arguing every night sometimes it was not to bad and it only lasted for around a hour other times it lasted all night it felt so strange being in this environment and not something I was use to and was not sure what to do most of the time that week I stayed in my room out of the way. Sometimes I was left alone sometimes I was not. He was coming into my room more and more and he did not care how much he hurt me as long as he got what he wanted. He said it was my duty to give him what he needed and what my mum was not giving him as I was her daughter I had a duty to full fill this duty even more so when mum was not there. He had been in my room for sometime this particular afternoon and he told me that we were the only ones in the house but I had heard someone come in through the back door but my step dad had not and my mum came up the stairs and I thought that if she walked in that she would have killed him and been so shocked that she would have done something but she walked into my room and shut the door saying nothing but she just stood there and watched what he was doing to me and I was crying out with pain he was again holding onto my arm this time he had it twisted up my back and that was hurting me so much and more than it was already the pain was unbearable and ripping through my whole body, then I felt this horrible pain that I had not felt before I was laying on my front with my arm up my back and he lifted my hips up and before I knew he had entered my back passage and that hurt me so much and I was crying and asking him to get off and I started to wriggle and more than I had done before but I just got hurt even more my arm was being twisted even further up my back. He told me that the more I fought the more he enjoyed what he was doing to me and all this time my mum was standing in my room and watching what was going on I thought she would have gone mad at him but all she told me to do was fight him more than I was doing and after a few more minutes my mum walked out of the room and shut the door and went down the stairs I was shocked that my mum had done this I never thought that my mum would have stood there and let one of kids get hurt the way I was being hurt at this moment. He was in my room for ages and smiling and said no one is going to do anything about this and if I told anyone he would make me pay. I could not believe this was happening to me I wanted to be with my mum to get away from all this not jump into a fire from the frying pan because that is what I felt I had done.

I was scared to move after he left my room and I stayed were I was I felt so dirty and unclean and was in a lot of pain not just with my arm either but my back passage was hurting and I was bleeding from there to I did not know what I could do. I started to pray and asked God to guide me and help me and I prayed for such a long time that afternoon. I did not move for ages I was too scared to do and when I did the pain in my arm was unbearable that I screamed with pain and my mum came running up the stairs to see whatever was the matter I just said to her "my arm" she then looked at it properly and told me it looked broken and she would take me to the hospital where she was working it was not one of the main hospitals but they had a x-ray machine there and they told her that it was badly broken and in more than one place it was broken in a total of thirteen places and mum was told that she would have to get me to casualty but mum insisted that we can sort it out here and my mum just asked them to strap it up and try to set it as best as they could until she could take me down to casualty, I knew she would not have done as she did not want the questions that I knew that would have been thought or even asked and there was no-way she would have wanted that. As I thought she never did take me to casualty and my arm was going blue she started pulling on it to try and get the circulation back in my arm as much as she could and said that it would heal in time and said that I should not complain about it and I am lucky that I am living with her and that any one wanted me at all. Most people would not want something living with them who were damaged, damaged goods and no-one would want damaged goods. I did not understand what she meant.

The following Sunday the police did come back and as promised they did send a policewoman to take down the necessary information from me and she also asked me how things were working out for me here I told her it is just as bad here and that the same was happening here but much worse to what I had just gone through with my dad, however she seemed to dismiss what I was saying to her and nothing else was mentioned on this after that. I was on my own making my statement and it took me ages to do it as I was so frightened and was not sure what was going to happen I was not even sure how to describe to her what had occurred I did not understand it myself so how was I suppose to explain it to a stranger. She was getting impatient with me for not giving her the information quick enough and that she had a home to go to as she had already gone into overtime and she was not supposed to being doing overtime either so I told I her if she wanted to go home then she should, and she did not take very kindly to my remarks she then said to me that she is here to take this information down and that is what she will do. Finally come around 8.30 in the evening I had given her all the information that I could or prepared to give her after all of this she then told me to go and read it and sign it at the bottom of each page which I did and then she asked me if I wanted to add or change anything on it I told her that I did not. The police officer then told me that she would be in touch very soon and I would have to go and see a police surgeon within the next couple of days I could not understand why I had to go and see a police surgeon I did not understand all this and what was now about to happen and no-one explained it to me in a language that I could understand I found this all very confusing and frightening. This was arranged for a few days time and I was very frightened about this and there was no reassurance from anyone I felt alone and very scared. Before this there was more arguments and they were going on for longer than they were doing and they were beginning to sound worse than I had heard previously and I was scared and I dreaded them arguing I was always afraid of what would happen next this particular night for some reason I went downstairs what made me I do not know they were well into an argument and they were both going for each other mum with a knife and Isaac using his fist on her and kicking her every-time she hit the floor which she did often after all they were both drunk, I ducked just as a punch was swung otherwise I would have got it straight in my face. I was shouted at for being downstairs and I just said that I was going to the bathroom, in mum's house the bathroom and toilet was downstairs off the kitchen and through the living room. I was told to hurry up and go to the toilet and get back to my room and stay there. I ran back upstairs and shut my bedroom door and I was shaking and crying from what I had just witnessed between them. I thought to myself if this two people who have just got married then I never want to be married. I always hoped that he would leave me alone and they would stop arguing so much that was frightening enough. As I thought, and as she always did after they had argue my mum walked out of the house and this particular night he had been in my room for some time and he was hurting me and he was holding me by my throat and he entered me and again this hurt me he took something from me and I could not understand what it was about me that people did what they did to me, I felt so dirty and humiliated and so very scared, there was a knock on the door and I was made to go down stairs to answer it and as always I put the chain on the door before opening the door and standing at the door there was a couple of police officers. I went to shut the door so I could open it for them but they put their foot in the door but when I explained that I had to shut it to take the chain off so they could come and talk to me, once they were in they asked me if my mum was there I told them she was not as she had left about a hour ago so they asked me if I was in the house alone and I told them my step dad was there and they said that they needed to have a word with him he nodded to me that it was ok for him to speak with them I took them into the living room and I was in bare feet and there was glass everywhere and the police told me to be careful that I did not cut my feet and I went through into the kitchen and it was just as bad there I did get a small cut on the side of one of my feet but I just went into the bathroom and cleaned it up. The police had come round to tell us that my mum had been in an accident but she was ok they said because she had been drinking it saved her life because she bounced differently when you have had a drink and that she had been taken to Leicestershire Royal infirmary and someone needed to go and pick her up the police took my step dad to pick her up and brought them both back home to by the time they got back I had cleared all the broken glass away and the house looked almost liveable in it again and you could not really tell that anything had kicked off a few hours before even the police officers commented on it when they came back just by saying this is different to what it was a few hours ago. I went to bed around 04.30

that morning and at last I got some peaceful sleep not a lot but I got some and I had to be up early the next day as I had to go and have that examination but before I did my step dad asked me when my next period was and I told him that I had just started and he kissed my head and said that goodness for that because now all their results and test they did they would not be able to pick anything else up. I did not understand what he meant and I was scared enough about this examination as it was. I had to go over to Leicester to have this done at the main police station there and I was horrified to get there and they had got a male police surgeon to do this examination and I felt even more embarrassed than I already was feeling and the worse part of it the police officer who brought us there had to stay in the room with me and also my mum I had to get undressed in front of them they did not even turn their backs so I had some privacy but that did not happen. It was bad enough but having to have the examination that I did have to have and by a male to and my mother standing there watching in the end they had to ask my mum to leave the room because I just would not co-operate whilst she was there and I did allow them to do the examination but they could not do it properly as they said I was to scared and not very co-operative however they got enough information from me what they needed but they did he said that there was some evidence of abuse and that someone had intercourse with me no more than three times in the last few weeks no-one picked up on that I had been with my mum now for almost four and half weeks and I was due to go to a new school in the next few days. My step dad had gone a lot further than my dad did and he was a lot more violent towards me to get what he wanted to.

At this point social services was not aware that I was living with my mum until they came for a routine visit and they asked me how long I had been there for I told her just coming up to four weeks and she was stunned that my mum had not informed the social worker said that is another child we need to keep an eye on and will probably end up on the same register as my brother was I did not know what she was talking about at this time. A few days later I was starting my new school and I felt nervous and scared about this and was not sure what to expect from a new school I found it hard to settle in and found the school environment hard as it was totally different to what I was use to and it took me a long time to get use of the different methods used within that school and I was laughed at a lot to because the school I had just left if anyone entered the room we had to stand up out of respect for that person and I automatically did this at the new school and the rest of the kids made fun of me and laughed at me for doing this and I would only answer anything if I was asked because that is what I was use to. It took me a long time to get use to the new school but some of the habits I had from my old school stayed with me and I could not get them out of me after all they were a part of me. The first time I stood up when someone walked into the room the member staff was surprised that I had done this and so was the class teacher the other kids just laughed and I would not sit down until I was told to do so. After the staff member walked out of the classroom there was a discussion why I did that and what it meant I just said it was about respect and showing respect and it was something that I did at my old school and I had thought that all schools did this. The teacher told me that I did not have to do that here and I found it very confusing so I asked does that mean we do not show respect to people coming into the classroom here, she just smiled at me. I continued to do this and several children followed me and it was catching on slowly it got to the point that as someone walked into the classroom we all stood up and immediately we were told to sit down sometimes I was told to remain seated before anyone walked into the classroom it was the only way I could get this out of me and the rest of the kids got use to me and I slowly made friends and started to settle into the school. I had only been at my new school for about three weeks then it was half term break for a week it was after half term things started getting worse for me and going downhill for me at home things were bad enough before then but things got a whole lot worse after half term for me. They were arguing every night and getting more and more violent towards my mum and me to. I was thirteen in a few weeks' time and wonder what was going to happen as the weeks went on and how much worse things could get not that I thought that they would get any worse and I hoped and prayed that they would not but I was so wrong on that one things got a hell of a lot worse and everything was becoming unbearable for me my birthday that year was the worst that I had ever had I even had a visit by the police to see if I wanted to change my mind with my statement and I told them that I did not. He told me that was fine and they just wanted to check before they took things any further I was angry that they had not done anything about my statement that had been made nearly two months ago.

As usual that night my mum and Isaac went out for a drink and came home late went to bed and about three in the morning they started arguing and you could hear how violent things were becoming between them and how much more they seemed to be arguing and as always it was my fault and how much more it felt like it was my fault and that this was somehow my doing I was not sure how it was but I felt that it was. As usual my mum walked out for while and I was watching out of my bedroom window and for some reason she turned round and saw me and stuck her two fingers up at me so I opened my window and asked what I had done she told me it was all my fault everything was ok till I turned up here and it would be better if I left as soon as possible, my step dad was in my room by this time and she must have seen him as she shouted that it is right get me out of the house so you two can screw each other I was really hurt by this and Isaac told me that it was nothing to do with me but my mum had something going off in her brain that was not quite right. I did not understand that one no one explained anything to me after all I was just a child and knew nothing well that's how little they knew isn't it. Something else I felt that I had to blame myself for and maybe my dad were right I was evil. I had not heard from him or Peter since I had been down with my mum and I missed them all dearly and I was not adjusting to the life with my mum the way I thought I would have done and it was nothing like it had been when I came down to visit and it was not home for me I had no-where to call home anymore and I had not had that for a long time now and I feared that I would never have a home again. That night my mum came back after only a few minutes and he ran down stairs and they started arguing again and then mum came up to me and told me that she was not going to give me that long tonight and then she took her cigarette lighter out and started to set my bedroom carpet on fire and when it was just alight she went out of my room and shut the door and somehow fastened it shut so I could not get out of my room I was frightened and I tried to open my window but that was no use either had it had been fastened tight and I don't know how it was fastened shut or when it was fastened shut but it was and the room was beginning to fill up with smoke and I heard Isaac coming up the stairs and shouting at her and asked her what she had done and she said making sure you can't get to her again because she will be dead before long she said that I was a witch and needed to be burnt and that is what she was doing he told her that you must have been mad and he kicked my door in and put the small fire out in my room and he threw a chair through my window to let some air in and also to let the smoke out of my room and fresh air in. I turned round my mum was coming back in my room with a knife and she was going for me but Isaac stopped her and she cut his left forearm and a small cut on the throat and he just flipped and started shouting at her and saying that she belongs in a Looney bin and not on the streets and she deserved to stay there for the rest of her life. She turned round you would say that it means you will be able to have my daughter to yourself then wouldn't it? That night it got more violent and they were still arguing when it was time to get up for school mark and I got up and got ready for school and we did not even have breakfast that morning I got my brother to school as soon as I could and got myself into school and I was over ten minutes late and the reception asked me why I was late and I was not in the mood for twenty questions and I just replied that I was and it was nothing to do with them but unfortunate for me the deputy head was in the reception and she collard me on my way pass she told me that in the future that I was asked a question that I should answer it so I told them that my parents had been arguing all night my mother took a knife to me but my step dad stepped in the way and I had to take my younger brother to school and without breakfast she seemed stunned and told me to go onto my class and she told me to say that I had been with her because there was something that I had to sort out with her. I hope that the teacher believed me and I was not in any mood for any more questions and thankfully the teacher did believe me apparently she saw me talking with her that was ok for me. The deputy head contacted the social worker and she paid them a visit and by the time she got there you would not have known that they had been any bother there the night before and my mum and Isaac denied that there was any problems there the previous evening. Well I certain got it in the neck once I got in from school and was told whatever happens behind closed doors remains there and must never be discussed with anyone else ever again. I had to promise that I would not otherwise I would be in serious trouble. Nothing new there then I thought to myself I always seemed to be in trouble and I was becoming more and more convinced that I was evil and all this was my fault. I could not see it being anyone else's fault I only had myself to blame for everything. Again that night there was even more arguing and just as violent as the previous night but this time mum went out and did not come back he was soon in my room and he was holding my head and pulling my hair I was on my bed I was laying down before he came into my room well that was until he pulled me up with my hair he was standing up in front of me with his trousers and underwear down round his ankles and he was telling me to open my mouth but I did not want to, he would not release my hair and bent me down towards his trousers and I thought that he was going to leave me and not doing anything but I was so wrong I even thanked him for not hurting me but what he had reached in his trousers for was a penknife and he held that at my throat and told me that if I did not do as I was told he would use it on me he held it to my throat and told me again to open my mouth at first I still refused but he dug the penknife in my throat and eventually he got me to open my mouth and he put his penis into my mouth and I felt so frightened and I did not know what was going to happen this felt strange to me and I felt so dirty and scared, and what he was going to do next he told me that I was good and that I am better than my mum and this she would not do which is why he wanted me to do this. I felt like I was being used and I felt like he was always comparing what mum did and what I did it was not that he gave me any choice and he told me that there would be something in my mouth in a minute and I had to keep it in my mouth opened and swallow it and he stayed there until I did I felt sick and so afraid the taste made me feel sick I wanted to spit it out but he would not let me he continued to hold the penknife at my throat until I did what he asked me to do I was so frightened. I felt so dirty and disgusting and felt that I was evil. Maybe I was the witch that my mum said I was.

A few minutes later there was a knock on the door it was the police again and they had come to say that my mum had a mild heart attack and she had been taken to the George Elliott hospital and she was ill but stable. My step dad said that is good to hear and said he would go up to see her first thing in the morning. As his commitments here with her children and he did not feel it was fair to leave us alone. The police officer agreed with that one and they said by the looks of things it had been a tough night and they could see that they had been problems there because of the state of it and the amount of broken crockery and glass that was on the floor. However they did not say anything and left. I knew what they were thinking as it was the regular officers that came round and when they left the house I had my window opened and they said usual going ons there then but it is the kids I feel sorry for. I thought we don't need your pity.

I went to school as usual that day and so did my brother and he was collected by a family friend and I was collected by my step dad in his works van and I thought that he was going to take me to see my mum first he said I could only go and see my mum once I had pleased him I just wanted to see my mum and make sure she was ok I did not care what he wanted and I certainly did not want to please him I was not some sort of trophy for him or anyone but I was beginning to feel like I was.

He pulled in a lay by and I felt very scared and very conscious about being in his works van I began to feel panic raise up in me and very frightened he even shut the curtains in the wagon and pulled the seats down to turn them into a bed. I felt that I was going to continue to be punished and be hurt for always and that I must be evil and a horrible person I began to hate myself more and more as each day went by. I found the simplest of things very hard not just to do but to cope with too and hard to face and deal with I started wishing that I was dead and wished that God would take me away from all this pain and I even prayed he would do to but he did not. Even asked God why does he let these bad things happen to someone and why does he not do anything about it do you care God and this was the first time that I had ever questioned God I felt I had done wrong in questioning this and I knew all his teachings and it was not God's fault but I then asked the question more to myself than anything if God had created man like I believed he did why did he create such monsters and why could he not do anything to stop this monster. I knew it was not God's fault but it was each individual's fault we chose if we were going to do good or bad things not God and I kept telling myself this over and over again even though I was asking this question I did not know what to do or what I had done so wrong maybe what I was told that I was evil, naughty and a witch. I knew in my heart that this was man's doing not God's doing but it was hard to understand this whilst you are suffering. I was looking for someone else to blame besides me I could not blame anyone else accept me this was my fault and my dad was right I was evil and I deserved to be punished but I was becoming very withdrawn and very quiet, school began to notice this a lot more and started to question me but I would not talk to them and they just said to me that if I wanted to talk I could in confidence but I did not trust them I did not trust anyone not any more I was alone and so isolated and so very scared and I also became very uncooperative to everyone not just at home I just did not want to be here in this cruel world anymore. I was missing my Grandma and her love and care even more than I had done before and now I was nowhere close to her so I could be with her but in my heart I knew she was always with me. I kept wishing I was dead I would be better off if I was dead I often thought.

I was sat in the school library doing my homework and looking up at the ceiling it was a high ceiling and the ledge I was on one of the upper floors of the library and I stood leaning on the safety barrier and thinking if I had something to tie on here I could put it around my neck and just jump off here and that would be it for me but there was nothing laying around and we did not have to wear school ties but I was looking around though for something to do what I had just thought about doing but I could not but I told myself that I should keep an eye out for something and return here at a later day with something that is if I ever did find anything.

Things at home was becoming worse and worse and I began to stay in school for longer and longer I was in the library most nights until they kicked everyone out sometimes I hid in a corner out of the way and I often hoped that they would forget that I was there on a number of occasions they nearly did but they always spotted me just before they closed the doors and put the alarm on. I was actually hoping that they would have locked me in but there was no chance of that happening.

It was just ten days before we broke up for Christmas and I was dreading breaking up for the Christmas holidays and being at home all over the holidays.

A few days later I was in the library again and there was a new member of staff on and she thought that we had all gone and I was in my usual place and I was saying to myself that give her a few minutes to leave and set the alarm and then I could move I knew how sensitive the alarm system was but there was no camera on the level I was on as there was no other way in on this level. I had found some rope and hid it and I got it out and started to attach it to the safety barrier and once I had done that I started to put it round my neck and telling myself that my life is not worth living and no-one wants me or cares for me and I would not be missed if I did this, as I was just about to climb over the safety barrier when someone came back in I stayed where I was and I was hoping that they would not have seen me but for some reason they looked up and saw me there maybe I cast a shadow on the floor or something. But she looked up and saw me and screamed which got the attention of other members of staff, I quickly climbed back over and took the rope off me just a members of staff were fast approaching me they were running towards me and I could see the panic in their faces and worry to. As they got closer to me they began to slow there pace down not to alarm me any further by now I was already clear of the barrier and back to safety, one member of staff did approach me very slowly and carefully and when she was a few feet away she asked me if it was ok for her to come and sit next to me for a while and I agreed that she could do this by now I was crying and I was saying sorry to them for frightening them she sat next to me with her arm around me and giving me the comfort that I so badly needed, and then the questions started of which I would not answer they said that we would talk about this in the morning but I did not want to talk to anyone no-one could do anything to make things right for me or stop people hurting me I felt that I was beyond help and no-one could make this right for me no-one could take the pain away for me. How could anyone understand what it was like for me at home why would they care what it was like for me after all they had such perfect lives and never been hurt the way I was being. Well I did not think that it would have done and anyway I do not trust them and they did not know me and I did not know them and I did not want to get to know them and I was not sure that I could trust them as they kept going to the social worker every-time I did mention some things I did not feel that I could trust them at all I was scared to trust them because that only got me more hurt.

I went home that night feeling even more withdrawn and felt I failed in what I was going to do and felt I was not worthy enough to be here on this earth and I deserved everything that was happening for being so selfish, unfaithful and sinful.

131

When I got in that evening they were already arguing and throwing things around the house it was like they were both having temper tantrums I suppose that is what they probably were well that is what it looked like to me.

They had been drinking most of the day and I was in trouble yet again for being late home even though they knew that I was going to the library every day so I could make sure that I was keeping up with my studies and do the best I could I wanted everyone to be proud of me but the one person who would have be proud of me was my Grandma and she was no longer with me. I still miss her so much.

I walked into the back door and it looked like a war zone with the amount that had been flung around probably at each other. The first thing I got was you have got the meal to do sort whatever you can out, we are going to bed to lie down and that I was not to disturb them under any circumstances what so ever. I had no intention of disturbing them because whilst they were in their room and being quiet the house was peaceful. I manage to make something for our tea it was not a lot but at least I managed to do something and I knew that they would not appreciate it but it was the best I could do Mark and I enjoyed the meal they did not want anything and they were going out drinking again that evening I was puzzled how they managed to afford to drink and as much and as often as they did but could never afford to buy any food in the house I could not understand how parents could do that and continuously putting themselves before their children that did not make any sense to me at all I felt that they were very selfish but did not dare say that to them. About a hour later they were up and on the way down to the pub and they seemed calmer with each other now I was not sure how long that would have last but I was hoping that it would last for sometime but somehow I doubted that it would last for too long once they started drinking again.

I went to bed early that night I figured it would be better to have a couple of hours sleep before they got in than have no sleep at all I was laying in my bed and I was thinking about my Grandma and how much I missed her and I was finding it hard to remember her face and then from nowhere I saw her image and I felt her presence and she was soothing me and cuddling me and I could feel her close to me it was such a warm feeling that I was getting and I drifted off to sleep thinking of my Grandma and dreaming about her. I was having such a lovely dream and I heard a commotion outside and they had not got through the door but they were not on their own that night they had brought friends back with them and they were going to carry on drinking which did not please me but the friends were trying to be quiet but my mum said "stuff the bloody kids it is my bloody house and if I want to make some noise in it then she would do and no one was going to stop her either." Their friends kept saying "calm down it is not fair on your neighbours or us if you are going to continue and not calm down then we will not be coming back in with you". Someone actually telling my mum what to do there was a first not many people got away with that one with her she would usually have gone for them and would have been so verbally aggressive towards them that they would have wonder what had hit them but this time she just laughed at them and went a little quieter.

They all came in and everything seemed calm and quiet and then voices started being raised but not everyone's just my mum's and Isaac's he was asking one of their friends to leave my mum alone and she turned round and said it is only what you are doing with my daughter so why don't you go and find her and do what you do best and I will get what I can out of what was happening here and at least I would feel love for a change instead of being compared to that bitch I was so surprised that she had said anything like this and more so in front of people but her friends just turned round and said your drunk it is the drink talking you don't mean what you have just said. Then tempers started flying and the friends left quiet soon afterwards and they did not see them again after that night but that was not the end of what my mum had started she was determined to finish it. She stood at the bottom of the stairs and shouted up to me she said " you, bitch get down here now," I ignored her at first then she repeated it again and added if you don't get down here now I am going to come up there and drag you down the stairs I still refused to come down and I thought that she was in no state to drag me down stairs ,but how wrong I was she did drag me down the stairs and with my hair and she dragged me down backwards and she started having a go at me for what he was doing to me and told me that I am the one that as ruined their relationship everything was fine until I moved down here and spoilt everything for them I am just in the way and then she started belting me and swearing at me and she was not making any sense to me I did not understand half the things she said to me and when she finally let me go to bed she shouted up to me going go to bed you hoar whilst you can how much is he paying you I ran up the stairs crying and I sat behind my bedroom door crying. I could not understand why my mum was being so cruel and mean to me it was not my fault what was happening but then again maybe it was I was not so sure either way anymore. I was beginning to get more and more scared and I started to fear for my life but then again I did not want to be there anyway but I wanted to be the one that took my life away not someone else I started thinking about earlier on in the day and what I tried to do but did not follow it through maybe I should have just let go of that safety barrier. I listened to them arguing and it went on for hours every-time I thought that they had stopped and things had gone quiet for a while and just as I was drifting back to sleep they started up again and this went on like this for hours and it seemed to take her longer to walk out of the house now to she seemed determined to stay in the house in a way I was glad of that but in a way I was not because all that I wanted was some sleep but I knew I was not going to get that and I was getting less and less sleep now I was with my mum, I wanted to run away but I had no idea where to go I did not know the area well enough or the best ways to get anywhere I was not sure at all it was not like being with my dad were I knew all the short cuts and the best ways to go and where I could hide out I did not feel safe here this area frightened me but I did not know why.

The next day at school I was dreading going in and I was worried about what questions I was going to get but it was not the teachers that spoke with me but the social worker and I would not tell her anything I was too afraid to say anything about what I tried to do and would have done if my members of staff had not come back in. The social worker kept asking me about how I was settling in and how I was getting on now I was living with my mum and Isaac I just told that it was ok I suppose I was terrified of saying to much because of all threats that I had and about keeping things behind closed doors after a while she left me to go back to my lessons but as I left she said they can only help me if I tell them what is going off I was afraid of her and I did not know her or trust her. I heard the member of staff say she is so withdrawn and depressed but she will not talk to anyone and the social worker said that we are all going to have to work hard to gain my confidences and my trust and then I will open up to them.

It was only a few days till Christmas holidays and we were due to finish early on the last day but I did not want to finish but I knew I had to and that day came round far too fast for me.

I got in at around 1.45 from school and then I went to collect my brother from school which I did not do very often and it was great spending some time with him and he was really excited about Christmas he was only six and he thought Christmas was so special and that Santa still came to visit him but he smiled and said he had been a good boy that year but I knew how little we were both going to get and I was concerned that my brother was going to be disappointed. We took our time going home we even stopped at the park for a while it was cold and trying to rain but even so we still went to the park and had some fun and we were both laughing and I had not laughed like that in such a long time I had almost forgotten how to laugh these days, the wind began to pick up and there was a few spots of rain so we started to walk back home neither of us wanted to go home but knew we had to as we got closer to the house the rain started to come down and very heavy to so we started to run so that we would not get to wet and we got in without getting to wet, our clothes were damp but they would soon dry off. We were playing when my mum came down and she told us off for making so much noise and asked us what have us two got to be so happy about. Mark just said he was excited about Christmas mum was cruel she told him that Santa would not be coming to this house this year as neither of us deserved anything, Mark started to cry and I was the one that was comforting him not our mum and I just looked up at her and she told me not to look at her like that. It was not long before Isaac got in from work and they were going down the pub nothing new there that is always what they did her kids did not matter we had to fend for ourselves all of the time I was getting so use to that one but it was getting harder to do so as there was very little food in the house and they were not doing any shopping so I had no idea what I was going to do for a meal, they had been gone for a couple of minutes when our step dad came back he said he needed the bathroom but he actually came back and give me some money to go to the chippy but told us not to tell our mum as she would not be pleased he did go into the bathroom though because he knew mum would have be watching for him to go pass the window. A few minutes later he was gone again and they were walking down the street to the pub. I was getting mine and Mark's coat on to go and get something from the chippy for tea this was so rare for us to have anything like this so we were going to make the most of it but when we got to the chippy there was not a lot I wanted to eat so Mark and I shared some chips and we both had a battered sausage and took them home to eat and we did enjoy them and it did make a nice change for having not a lot to eat.

It was not long later that our mum came back on her own and was furious I asked her what was wrong and she said that he had just got us thrown out of the pub, a few moments later our step dad came in through the door and they were arguing again I took my brother upstairs and out of the way and left them to it. I was not bothered about what had happened alls I was bothered about was that my brother and I were out of the way and out of arms reach for a while. About an hour later they went out and went to a different pub and they were then out for the rest of the night till the early hours of the morning. You could always hear them coming back they made so much noise the whole neighbourhood heard them coming back. As usual they were arguing I had learnt to put cotton wool in my ears when I heard them coming back up the street and I did that night and it dulled some of the argument but not all of it. I dozed in and out of sleep that night you could not sleep properly in that house there was no peacefulness, no calm.

My mum was soon walking out of the house and into one of her friends whom lived half way down the street from us I watched her as she went into the house and then he was in my room at first he just cuddled me but it did not stop at that he told me that I knew what he wanted and if I did not give it to him I knew what would happen, I fought him to a point and in the end I just let him do what he wanted less chance of me getting hurt anymore than I had to I know that was the wrong to do just giving in to him but I did not know what else to do at least this way he was not as violent with me which was better for me I remember thinking that he was nothing but a big bully and a nasty one at that. About a hour or so later there was a knock on the door it was the police they had come to arrest him for assault on my mum I thought finally she was going to do something about him and get him out of our lives once and for all but he also made a complaint that my mum had assaulted him to and she was also arrested but she was let out very quickly and she came home to us but she went straight to bed, it was a reasonably peaceful night from then onwards no arguing, just peace but it felt strange the house being so quiet and I found it hard to get to sleep but I did eventually then at around ten in the morning there was a thump on the front door and shouting it was Isaac trying to get into the house mum had locked the door with every lock that was on the door and even put the chain on, she came in and told me to be quiet and told me not to answer it and she did the same with my brother and mum and my brother came into my room because if he wanted to climb up onto the roofs of the sheds or onto the shelter above the door he could have got in through the windows and in the end he went round the back and climbed up onto the sheds roof and in through their bedroom window and then he was searching the house looking for us my mum and my brother were in my wardrobe and I had slipped under my bed and it was such a narrow gap to I was surprised that I managed to get under my bed but I did and he left my room and walked out of the house and we stayed were we were for sometime just in case he came back but he did not and a short while later mum left the house and left me with my brother nothing new there I was always left with my brother but I did not mind it was probably the only time that we had some fun and found something to have a laugh about.

It was the night before Christmas Eve and it began to snow very lightly at first and then it got heavier and heavier but we loved the snow and we were soon out playing in it and so were the other kids on the streets and we all started making snowballs and throwing them at each other it was great to have so much fun with other kids then everyone stopped and looked at us and I turned round and saw my mum and step dad coming up the street together and for a change not arguing but the other kids soon left the street and we went inside to.

That night was quiet a calm night and they did not argue at all that night which was a relief for us it was still hard to sleep and when I did sleep I was having restless sleep.

Christmas Eve was fairly quiet to and they had not gone drinking either and had not bought any for the house which I found strange but then I thought maybe they are going to stop drinking. Christmas Eve was another peaceful night that was the first two nights since I had been there that they had not argued and things seemed a lot calmer which was so good for all of us. I just hoped that all this would last but somehow I doubted that it would have done. Christmas day soon came round and we were back to the usual routine of things I did not think things would have lasted for too long but I was hoping that they would have done the only difference that day was they took me and my brother down to the pub with them and we were in the games room having some fun for a change it was not a bad day but my step dad kept offering me a drink and not a soft drink he told me it would do me good and help me to relax a bit, but I did not want I just kept asking for a cola but it did not taste the way I expected it to taste and I said so to and I was told it was because it was not from a bottle that is probably why it tasted different to me but I suspect that it was something else and I began to feel ill and everything started spinning a short while later we were going back home I could not understand why I felt so ill my mum was in a dreadful state and was all over the place whilst she was walking back home but she was not shouting like she usually was she was laughing the rest of the day was a bit of a blur to me and I don't remember much about it, I had something to eat once we got in then I was laying down on my bed and I was naked and I don't know how I got to being like that and there was no way I was going to ask then everything went black the next thing I knew anything of they were arguing again and it was getting very violent but I wanted to stay out of the way and Mark came into my room crying and asking me to stop them I told him to leave them to it they are big enough to sort things out for themselves and he said to me that Isaac had took me up to my room because I was on the floor downstairs so the only thing I could think of was he had carried me upstairs and undress and done whatever he wanted to me and I had no recollection of anything that had happened and I was scared about this and scared about what was going on now down stairs.

That night they seemed to be arguing none stop throughout the night and they continued through boxing day, they went out briefly and were back arguing again and through boxing night and until around three maybe four the following morning before she walked out of the house and she was holding her head and wobbling all over the place she looked so drunk.

A short while later he was in my room and all over me and told me how good I was to him on Christmas day and I got very angry with him and I started hitting out at him and I spat in his face and I told him that he was disgusting that was a huge mistake for me he was so angry and told me that I was just like my mum for doing what she wanted and I need to be put in my place I did not understand what he meant. I was about to find out and he was not at all pleasant in what he did he drew the pen knife out and told me that I would do what I was told he then said to me that he would be back and then he came back in with some rope and the penknife was in his hand but he put it down to use the rope he told me that he was going to do what he wanted and have his way with me and there was nothing I could do about it he tied me up and in however he wanted me to lie every-time I tried to fight him he would put the penknife on my throat and telling me he would used it if he had to and I continued fighting him the rope was tight and digging into my skin and was hurting me he then put the penknife on my chest and told me one push into me it would go straight into my chest and I would be dead. He did whatever he wanted and into which, ever side he wanted me to be lying the pain for me was unbearable for me and I was so scared and I did not know what to do. He told that I was now being good and doing what he wanted and I was pleasing him but I was not sure how I was pleasing him.

He seemed to be in my room that night for ages and I was worried about my mum and he said don't worry about her she is not coming back I have made sure of that one I had not got a clue what he meant by that at all but it frightened me even more than I already was. I was beginning to feel uncomfortable, sore and in so much pain. When he finally finished and left my room he left me tied up and he said that he would be back in a little while, I was terrified and scared of what was going to happen next my wrist were throbbing and hurting so much so were my ankles to. I was in an uncomfortable position and felt all twisted I felt sick and I was terribly sore. I was frightened of what was happening to me. Mum had been gone for well over two hours now and there had been no knocks on the doors, which there usually was, but not today. About another hour or so went by I was still how he had left me, and feeling very numb, getting cold and in a lot of pain. I was hoping that he had come back to untie me but he had not it all he just started again and I was screaming with pain and in the end he put his hand over my mouth but I bit that so he used my pillow to shut me up and held that over my mouth to stop me screaming out in the end he had to use his belt tied round the back of my head and in my mouth and that was so tight to I was terrified I felt I could not breathe and it tasted horrible in my mouth. He kept telling me that I will do what I was told and allow him to do what he wanted and things will be easier for me in the future. I was not sure that they were going to be I felt that things were going to get a lot harder for me. I was beginning to feel that I had made a mistake coming to live with my mum and that I would probably have been better staying with my dad but I don't feel that either situation was the right one to be in I wanted out of there and fast but I was not sure how I was going to do that or what I was going to do to get away from here but I was starting to think about this a lot more to.

I was also beginning to miss going to Church but I knew that was forbidden whilst I was with my mum but there was nothing to stop me praying and I had been praying a lot more recently and more than I had realised to.

Maybe this was all part of my punishment for the evil person that I was and I deserved all of what was happening to me, however I did not think that I had been that naughty or I was really evil as everyone kept telling me that I was.

He finally left me alone and untied me almost three and half hours later after he had left my room the second time. I felt so numb but in a lot of pain, I finally sat up and felt sick with pain and the sight of all the blood that was there I did not understand were all this was coming from but I was so sore I felt like I was dying and when I looked in a mirror I looked like I was dying to. I wanted to be dead it was better than what I was going through at this time. The rest of that week was no different to the beginning of the week and New Years Eve came round and friends of my mum's asked if I could look after her kids on New Year's Eve and she said yes I can as I was only across the road and if Mark needed or wanted me for anything he could easily contact me if he woke up and needed anything or come across to us. The atmosphere at her friend's house was so different to what it was at my mum's house I could not understand how two different families could be so different as they were I thought that all families were the same as mine I never imagined that my family was so wrong and so different to other families. I was spending the night at this house and it seemed strange that it was peaceful even though there was four young children running around all over the house but they were so well behaved for me and went to bed as soon as they were told and I was in bed just after midnight and I looked across to my brothers bedroom window and wished him a happy new year not that he would have heard me but I said it anyway.

I was soon asleep and for the first time in ages I felt safe. In the early hours of the morning the people I had been babysitting for came into the room where I was sleeping and their mum was sitting on my bed and brushing her hand over my head and saying to me that everyone is going to be ok and that it was just a bad dream and I realised someone was touching me and I started screaming to get off me and leave me alone and she said she was not touching me her husband came running in to see what was wrong and she told him something was not right here she put her arms around me and just rocked me and soothed me until I was back in settled sleep, they left me to sleep in the following morning and around 8.45 there was a knock on the back door it was my brother coming to fetch me and the friends let him but told him that I was still asleep and they were leaving me to sleep, he thought that something was wrong with me because I was still asleep they just told him that your sister had a bad night but he could come in and wait for me to wake up if he wanted to do and he did and he was there waiting for me when I got up. When I went down stairs I was surprised that he was there and how late it was when I got up but the neighbour's house it was did not mind and asked me if I was ok and if I would like some breakfast and they asked my brother to and I just asked them is that allowed and they told me that it was allowed and I had a full cooked breakfast that morning and so did my brother. I noticed my brothers hair was greasy and I asked him what was in his hair a first I thought it was gel but it was not it was chip pan fat he had got in the way when they were arguing and he got hit across the head with it because I was not there he went down stairs and I felt guilty for not being there with him and not protecting him from harm. I felt it was my duty to protect him as no-one else was doing our mum should have made sure that we were both safe and out of harm's way but no chance of that one happening anytime soon.

I was dreading going back over to the house as I never knew what I was going to wake up to or find once I got back in there I never did know, but I was the one that cleaned it up afterwards and made sure my brother and I were ok as much as I could do.

I finally went back over to mum's place about lunchtime and it was in a right state and the people whose children I had been looking after their dad came over with me and said he did not want me to go back in on my own as I had no idea what I was going to find I was expecting to find one of them dead one of these days and that frightened me. I went in through the back door and the kitchen was in a mess and there was fat everywhere even on the ceilings and then there was no end of broken crockery and glass all over the floor and we were beginning to run out of crockery if this carried on there would be none left. I worked my way through cleaning the kitchen up and the parent of the children I was looking after helped me and made sure the living room was ok and there was no nasty surprise for me but there was not and he asked me if I would be ok sorting this mess out and I told him that I was getting use to it by now he says does it always get into this mess I told him this is nothing compared to how it can get sometimes he left me alone shortly afterwards and kept my brother at their place until I sorted everything out there and went back to fetch him it took me several hours to sort the mess out downstairs and when I finally went back over to the neighbours house I was made a sandwich and they were trying to talk to me about how often this happened and I told them almost every day it was part of everyday life for me and then they told me about my nightmare and how distressed I was and asked me if anything was happening to me that I wanted to talk about what was happening but I was scared. I was very wary about talking to them especially with them being friends with my mum. I said not at the minute but thanked them for their offer to listen and they told me if I ever needed to talk to anyone then I could talk to them and they would not tell them that I talked to them I said it was ok and again thanked them. I told them I was dealing with things they told me that they did not think that I was but it was up to me they could not force me to tell them and they were not about to do that. I smiled at them and thanked them for their kindness and said I think my brother and I should be going now and I thanked them for their hospitality towards us both they told me anytime.

Once I got back home I felt so relieved that someone else had seen the state of the house after they had an argument and that somebody cared enough to make sure we were ok.

A few days later we had a visit from social services saying that they had been informed that they had been arguing a lot lately and my brother had been hit in the process of their argument again they both denied this and we were not allowed to speak with them, I had an idea who had said this but I had an idea of whom had contacted them and I know it was out of concern for Mark and me. I knew they were trying to help but I did not dare say anything to them about what I thought because I knew that it would have been trouble for the neighbours to. After the social worker had gone and sometime later I asked mum if it was ok if I went over to the neighbours to be with their eldest daughter and mum said it was ok. A few moments later I was knocking on their door one of the younger two open the door and walked away it was only when their mum came to the door and invited me into their home that I went in, I asked her if I could have a private word with her and she told me that was not a problem and we went into her room and she closed the door I felt safe not threatened at all talking to her in her room, once I was sitting on her bed she asked me what I want to talk to her about and I replied to her "well you know New Years eve when I stayed here and everything you knew and what your husband saw at the house did you contact social services?" she hesitated for some time, and I told her I was just asking for me, she then replied to me " she told me that they did make a call to them but they did not leave their name as far as anyone else was concerned but she said they did this because they were worried about me and my brother and felt it was the only way she could do anything to help us both. I looked up at her smiled at her and thanked her for caring and as I did this I started to cry because no one had been so kind to me in such a long time. She told me that if she could help anytime then all I had to do was knock on the door and talk to her. Again I thanked her but this time I got up and give her a hug and she hugged me back and that felt so nice and safe. I could not understand why someone else could give me this affection when my mum did not. I asked her if she thought that I was evil and she laughed at me and told me that I was not evil but one of the kindest children she had ever had the pleasure in knowing again I was crying.

I was looking forward to getting back to school and getting away from everything for a while and especially that house and everything that went with it. We still had a few days to go yet before we went back to school and those few days could not go quick enough for me but they seemed to go by so slowly. Everything continued the way everything had been going for weeks now.

Finally the day came for us to go back to school and I was so relieved to be out of that house for a while but I was so very tired as I was getting very little sleep some nights we did not get any sleep at all.

When we got back into school everyone was talking about what a wonderful Christmas they had all had. I felt myself getting jealous of them as everything sounded so perfect for them and when I was asked did I have a good Christmas I just said it was the same as any other day for me. They looked puzzled with that and I did not say anymore to them I did not feel the need to say anymore to anyone either as far as I was concerned it was none of their business. I was so tired whilst I was at school I started to full to sleep in lessons and I was getting asked why I was so tired and I just said that I do not get much sleep at home and I apologised that I had fallen asleep in their lesson and I told them that I would try not to do it again and before I knew it I was a sleep again but this time they did not wake me up and left me till the end of the lesson and then they had a problem waking me up but I was also calling out in my sleep telling them to get away from me and crying, the teacher asked the class to go outside for a few minutes whilst she woke me up, she woke me so gently and I told her that I was sorry again and then I realised that the classroom was empty she called the rest of the class back in and took me out of the classroom and asked me who was I asking to get away from me and why was I crying I told her I did not know school was getting more and more concerned about me but until I could talk to them there was nothing that anyone could do to help me. I knew that but I was afraid to talk to them.

Things were going from bad to worse at home not that I thought that they could get much worse but they did in a lot of ways to. Kids were laughing at me at school but I did not know what they were laughing at and they were talking about something that they had read in the paper about them both something that I did not know about, but it went back to the night that they both charged each other of assault and I had not thought any more about it since I had actually forgotten all about that one, but what they were laughing at was that they both been done for assault and ordered to pay a fine and were bound over for disturbing the peace and were both ordered to pay each other £200 in compensation. I did not understand what that meant for my brother and me and I was shocked about this to and some kids were even picking on me because of it, and during one of our English lessons some kids were talking about it as we often did about things in the news at the start of some English lessons it was away for us to debate what was right and wrong and a way for us to express our opinions in a controlled environment. It was usually enjoyable to do this but not this particular day I felt so small and uncomfortable at first the teacher did not noticed that I was so quiet and usually I would join in these discussions but I did not want to today I found it too hard and it was my family they were talking about and I felt vulnerable. Then after about ten minutes or so the teacher asked me how come I am not contributing today I told her I did not know and one of the kids shouted out she is a liar she does know, so the teacher asked them what did they know and they told her that it was my parents that they were discussing and the situation that they had read in the paper and one of the kids even had a copy of what was in the paper which shocked me to actually read what was there and upset me to. I was sent out of the room for a while whilst she talked to the whole class and asked them how many knew that what they were discussing was about my family and someone they knew most of the class put their hands up and I was horrified to think how many people knew and how much they were now going to question me she asked the class to say they were sorry when she brought me back in and they all agreed to do so but before she took me back in she asked me how bad things really were at home I told her that they were bad and the bit that was in the paper is no way a reflection on what was going on at home that was just a small part of it and that incident was over six weeks ago. She then went onto ask me if I wanted to go back in to the classroom or not and I said I did and so I did go back into the classroom and I sat down at my seat and most of the class said they were sorry for teasing me and for picking that article to discuss and that was the end of the discussion and we had to go on to do something else for the rest of the lesson which was not long left by the time I had got back in to the class room. It would soon be break but I did not feel like going out at break and I asked permission to stay in the classroom and it was agreed that I could do just to stop some of the snipping that was going on and also to give me some peace from everyone I was still feeling very shaken about what had happened. I was sitting in the classroom alone for a few minutes whilst the teacher had popped out of the classroom to get herself a drink and she even offered me one but I declined. When she came back into the classroom I was crying. She asked me "if anyone else had been in and if anyone else had said anything to be" I told her that they had not and I apologised for crying and she walked me round to my next lesson and I was hoping that it was going to be a better lesson than the previous one but in some ways it was but in others it was not and the topic we were talking about in human science was sex education and pregnancy I just sat there stunned and at one point during the lesson I walked out crying and someone said she was upset in the last lesson and she stopped the slide show that we were having and came to have words with me and told me that I either go back into the lesson or she would go and fetch the deputy head down to talk to me so I went back into the lesson and I sat down but I put my head down on the table and started to cry it was the first time I had anything like this but it was the first time it came real to me what was happening to me. It was the first time that I had realised what was happening to me was not normal that it was so wrong all sort of topics were discussed including rape, abuse and sexual education it seemed strange having a lesson on this to me after side show had finished again I was called out of the lesson and was asked why I was not taking notes on what was being said and also asked if I felt I did not need to take notes because I knew all what was in the side show and therefore I did not need sex education I told her that it was not that, then she said something very sarcastic

146

that I was not making notes because I was to experience and knew about it all anyway I was shocked with that and I told her it was none of her business and ran off down the corridor it was not long afterwards that the deputy head was catching up with me I was crying and I said she had no right to say these things to me or be so cruel and the deputy agreed with me and took me back to the lesson were the teacher apologised to me.

I started to feel very frightened that they would now work out what also was going on at home and I was scared that they would think that I had said something at school and I was so scared about this and I hoped and prayed that they would not have worked to much out or if they had they were not say anything.

That was one day at school that I was glad to see an end to and one day I did not want to have a repeat of ever again well not if I could help it there would not be a repeat of that day but this was not something I had any control of. The only good thing that came out of that day was the sex education class because it also made me realise even more with what was happening to me was so wrong. However I had no idea what I was going to do about it I felt that it was my fault still and that it was me that was evil even though I knew differently now but it did not stop me feeling the way I did.

I was quiet when I got home and went straight to my and got changed from my school uniform and I was surprised that there was something on my bed and card it was from my mum she was thanking me for everything I had done since I had been there and told me how much she loved me under the card she had left me some chocolates. I could not understand why she could say it in a card but could not tell me to my face but this was better than nothing I suppose. But it was the most I had from her since I got there.

It was already half way through January and things were getting worse all of the time and nothing seemed to be changing either and we were not getting any sleep at all during the night and I was finding it hard to see the best time to sleep was during the day, whilst he was at work and this particularly day when morning alarm went off just as I was going back to sleep most days I did not need my alarm to get me up but I always set it just in case I did have a good night's sleep, when it went off that morning I turned it off and rolled over and went back to sleep it was the first time I had not been to school since I got there. Which also meant my brother was not going to school either but even he did not wake up I decided to leave him in bed and let him have some sleep. The next thing I knew it was gone one 'o' clock in the afternoon and that was the most sleep I had in ages and mum was still asleep when I got up I checked on my brother and he was playing quietly with his toys and when I went into his room he came down with me and we had some toast and a drink and shortly afterwards my mum was down stairs it was a fairly quiet afternoon and we were laughing together and we had not done that in such a long time but that did not last for too long as when he came through the door a couple of hours later her attitude to us changed and she started shouting at us and I felt very confused and upset I was not sure what to make of her change in attitude with us and we had a fairly good afternoon to and that spoilt it for us then again that was mum all over give you something in one hand and take it away with the other.

They started arguing almost as soon as Isaac came in and they were arguing about me and I don't understand why they were arguing about me. I was in my room with my brother out of the way it was better that we were out of the way and I was saying to my brother if the day comes were I am not here to look after you and they are arguing like this keep in your room out of the way and stay there and he promised me that he would but then he said but where are you going? I told him no-where but if I was not here that is all and told him I would always be there for him. What I did not tell my brother was I did not want to be there anymore and I wanted to die because that would have just been too cruel for a six year old to take. I loved my brother and cared for him so much and I did not want to hurt him at all not if I could help it.

The next two weeks were getting harder for me and there was not a day that it was peaceful in that house and there was not a day my step dad was not in my room and it was anytime of the day and mum was there sometimes watching and saying to him I want to see everything that you do to her and how you treat her, I cried and screamed at her mum no please don't make him do this. She insisted and he did show her everything and she seemed to enjoy the pain and suffering her daughter was suffering and going through he was crueller and more violent with me than he usually was but I came to expect the violence more and more and knew that one day he would become more violent with me but I was not expecting him to be like that now and not in front of my mum I kept thinking why is she enjoying this and not stopping him, why does she want to see this? Why didn't she care? That is what I kept asking myself over and over again but I could not come up with any answers. I felt this awful internal pain he was off me but still touching me I not seen the penknife in his hands I no idea he had that with him and I was scared when I saw it but I had now realised that was the reason for the internal pain I was getting it was only when I saw the penknife covered in blood and I felt something sharp pull out of me and he said to me I would never have children now he was going to make sure of it. Once they both left my room the arguments started again. I could not move with all the pain I was in and I was bleeding so much to and I did not know what to do I did not know who I could take me to a see a doctor but I knew if I had seen a doctor they would have asked a lot of questions and these were questions I did not think that I was ready to answer or talk about yet. I slowly sat up on my bed and started to get dress I did all I could to stop the bleeding but there was not a lot I could have done I just hoped that this would stop on its own but the pain was unbearable and I was doubling up with it. I put on my shoes and walked as best as I could out of the house and I made my way down to the park and I sat on a swing and leaned over to try and stop the pain but as soon as I straightened up it was too much to stand. I felt spots of rain on my face and I stood up then everything went black and the next thing I knew people were there and around me I did not know where they had come from or who they were and there was an ambulance there to but they did not know about the bleeding at this stage, I think I must have fainted or collapsed or something but I do not recall anything from me standing up to all these people being around me. They were asking all sorts of questions but I could not answer them straight away and I know they wanted to take me to hospital and I don't know how they found out but my step dad turned up to and said it was ok she has been ill and it was the first time I had ventured out since I had recovered and he said he would carry me back home and make sure I rested. Well he did carry me so far well till we got out of sight of everyone and then he made me walk and told me that I will not survive this I was terrified I wanted to die but not by someone else's hand. If I was going to die I wanted to make sure that it was going to be by my hand not someone else's but something deep inside me kept telling me to be strong I will repair and things will become easier but it is going to take time. I was in pain for days my insides felt like they were on fire all of the time and I was so sore, what hurt most mum did not seem to care what she had seen or how much I was hurting. She just seemed to care about her-self I still could not understand why she would not do anything or why she did not stop him, I even started asking myself why she was staying here with him why could she not take me and my brother away from here and keep us safe.

The arguments and fights continued and one particular night towards the end of January I had enough and I went down stairs and I started shouting at them to grow up and stop this fighting I was sick and tired of hearing the same arguments day in and day out and there was no need for all this violence I was at first told to shut up as it was none of my business but I would not shut up I wanted to make her listen and to get her to think about things and about her children but she was not having any of it. She began calling me names and he defended me, which did not help the situation and mum told me to go to my room and get out of her face I did not expect the next thing that she said and I was stunned by it. She told me that they were going to London later on that day and by the time she got back and it would be late that night when she got back but I better be dead when she got back otherwise she would do it herself.

I ran to my bedroom crying and felt so hurt by what my mum had said I did not think that she would have been so cruel to one of her own children but then she was not behaving like a parent who should have cared and loved their children unconditionally that was what my Grandma always told me children come first and foremost before your own needs and anything else and she give them your protection and love no matter what was happening in your life, so I could not understand why my mum was not and she was being the way she was with her children.

The arguments got louder and louder and more things were broken including several windows were things went through them whatever I did I felt that I was wrong and I felt so betrayed by mum and that sort of betrayal I would never forget I had been at my mum's for only four and half months it was all I ever wanted for years and now I wished that I had not come to be with her it was a very long four months and a lot had happened since I had been there and not just in the home but to me, I was very down and depressed and I did not have anything to live for anymore. At about 3.45 my mum came into my room and told me that they were leaving and she told me to remember what she said that I better be dead when she got back.

I got up for school that morning at around six, I got my brother up sorted him out for school and made sure he had some breakfast and I went in the cupboard under the stairs and took a handful of my mum's tablets and put them in my purse to take to school with me but first I had my brother to get to school. I dropped him off and headed for school myself I had no intention of returning to the house ever again that was going to be the last time I left that house if I had anything to do with it. I was not looking to good, as it was I felt ill and my mum's words kept going through my head over and over again I could not concentrate at school and by lunchtime I could not cope with it anymore. I went and fetched myself a cup of water and I went into one of the cloakrooms and started to take the tablets and one of my friends was looking for me and came in looking for me as she knew if there was something on my mind I would be in there because it was out of the way of everyone and it was quiet and peaceful in there she had often found me in there asleep and that what she thought I was doing that day but when she saw my purse opened at first she thought that they were sweets and when I said they were not she ran out and ask me not to do anything but I had already took several of these tablets and by the time she came back with members of staff the was only one or two left and I was asked if I had taken anything and I said might have done but I wanted them to leave me alone. They told me that they could not do that and they started to walk me to stop me going to sleep eventually they took me to one of the offices and called my social worker and she was there about a hour later and she took me to the doctors and he said I was lucky and the effects I was having were my heart rate had slowed right down and my blood pressure was very low he told me if it was not for teachers at school walking me I may not have been here now and I said good I don't want to be here and he asked

151

me if I really meant to do that and I told him I meant it to. We collected Mark from school and went back to the house and it was in a hell of a mess after yet another night of fighting and violence and she asked me does this always happen I told her all the time. I picked up a couple of bits and took them with me and that night me and my brother was going into emergency care for my sake more than anything but it was only meant to be for that night. My mum got back at ten 'o' clock that night and there was a note from social services asking her to contact them as soon as she got in and she phoned them just after ten thirty that night demanding that we are brought back home immediately and she was told that it was not a good idea at that time of night but your children are safe and being cared for. She was furious but I was not sure who she was furious with most social services or herself. My dad was contacted and asked if he wanted me back and what he wanted to happen he refused to take me back and said that is not what I wanted and it was better for me that I was looked after properly for a change he was given all the contact numbers if he or any of the family wanted to get in touch with me.

The next day both me and my brother went to school and social worker asked me and my brother if we wanted to go back to the house and my brother said he wanted to be back home with his mum but I refused to go back to them and it was my refusal that started care proceedings to keep me in care. I had to be taken and collected from school as they were hanging around school and trying to grab me back and in time it was felt that it would be better if I got the school bus as it may be easier for me to get in and out of school in a crowd but that was not the case I often had to go back in to school to get staff to take me on the bus because they were sat outside the school gates they made no end of attempts to speak with me they even followed the school bus to the short term foster parents and they were giving a lot of grief there and on a number of occasions the police were called to move them on and they could not understand why I would not go back with them, they could not see what they had done wrong and how much I was hurting all they were bothered about was themselves about a month later social services got an interim care order and a full hearing was set for a month later. They had also invited both sets of parents to attend the full care hearing and not one of them attended I was even asked if I wanted to be with any of my parents and I said under the present circumstances I did not want to be with either but I also said that if anything changed then I may reconsider. An order for a full care was put in place and I was now in the care of social services. That night I had a phone call from my brother and he told me that is nice to know that I was now safe from any harm we chatted for a long time that night and I was so happy to hear from my brother again and to have someone in my family that cared about me and loved me. He gave me his address and telephone number and promised me that he would stay in touch with me.

That is how I came to being in care.

Chapter 7

BEING IN TEMPORARY FOSTER CARE WAS THE MOST peaceful time I had in such a long time but it took me a long time to settle and I was constantly worried that I was not safe there and there was going to be a repeat of what I had already been through I was having nightmares all of the time and was afraid to leave my room at night as I had to go through another room and I was frightened that Isaac was lerking in a corner somewhere to get me when I went through the other room even though I was reassured that he could not get into the house without anyone knowing I would not believe this, it was difficult for me to accept yet another change in my life and there had been a lot of changes so far in a very short time, and I found it very hard to accept them. There were nice enough people and they were kind but it was different and they were strangers to me and I was feeling frightened. I was remaining at the same school for the time being and in a way I did not want to leave that school as I was starting to make some good friends it took me a long time to get the friends that I have got but only time would tell or not if I had to move school or not. I was going to school on the bus everyday and coming home the same way it was getting harder and harder for me to go to school without me getting some hassle from my step dad and him trying to grab me he wanted to take me in his works van to get me back with them he kept telling me things would be different this time but I just refused to go back with them and then he got nasty and told me that I would regret this. I could not see how I would regret it now I was not in their home anymore and it was a relief to be out of there to.

I few weeks later social services got a full care order on me and it was granted as none of my parents had showed up at the hearing and the judge commented how little they must have cared and loved me for them not to show up and fight for me I agreed totally with those comments I felt they did not love me or cared for me. I was now in full care of social services and I was told that I would not be with the short term foster parents for very long as they had found me some long term foster parents and they were keen to meet me and have a daughter around the house they had two sons and very much wanted a daughter and I was looking forward to meeting them but I was nervous and worried What if they did not like me or me them there was a lot of what if's for me and it was yet another unsettling time for me. These last few months had been good and peaceful for me I was having a lot of nightmares whilst I was there and I had not realised how many or how much things had bothered me and I did not think that I ever would realise how much things have got to me or effected me maybe I never would but I could not know that at this time.

The day soon came for me to meet my foster parents who were going to look after me for the long term and provided that they like me and I liked them and we were both happy then I would be moving in with them very quickly after that visit things were moving very fast for me and I was very scared of this and I was not sure what I was going to make of them. Everything felt like I did not have any control over my life anymore.

I arrived at their house in a small village they seemed friendly enough but I was not sure it seemed miles away from anyone and I knew that I would have to change school again and that was something that I did not want to do but I was not going to be having a choice in that one if I was to stay there. Their cottage was nice and spacious and the son that I met seemed nice but I was not sure about staying there so the social worker said maybe it would be a good idea if I came to stay with them the following weekend and see how I felt, I agreed to this if it was only going to be for the weekend to see how I felt. I was then taken back to my short term foster parents to think about it and decide what I wanted to do and on the way back to the foster parents the social worker kept telling me that they were nice people and they were looking forward to me staying there and getting to know me and they would have plenty of time to spend with me if that is what I wanted them to do it was up to me, she told me church if that is what I wanted no-one would force me to do anything I did not want to but I was not convinced of that. The social worker was doing her best to get me to feel ok with going to them I suppose that was their job to do that.

The day came for me to go and spend the weekend with them but I was actually going to be moving in with them straight away as my step dad was becoming very aggressive and sitting outside the house a lot and phoning constantly and it was felt that it would be better if I was moved quickly for everyone's protection I was taken to my new foster parents at night and when I left three different cars left at the same time so to confused them which car I was in and with the hope that they would follow the wrong car and not find out where I was living and their plan worked they did follow the wrong car which meant I could get to my new home without them nothing because this time I insisted that they do not know where I am and that they were not told any information the only one person that I wanted to know where I was that was Peter for the time being. He was the only one that was told were I was going and my contact telephone number if he wanted to stay in contact with me.

I was nervous about going to live with these new people and I was still worried about being with some else and getting to know them, I kept thinking that they were going to hate me and would not want me there or want me to be part of their family.

They welcomed me into their home and made me feel very welcome and part of their family I was shown to were my room was and my foster mum was fussing and said I have only got to ask if there is anything that I need or want and they could try and sort something out for me.

I felt overwhelmed with them all and needed some space to myself and I could not cope with her fussing over me so much as this was something that I had never had, and my foster dad said to her give her some space and let her get settled into her room and feel comfortable and get use to her surroundings. I felt embarrassed but I had to ask were the bathroom was I was shown were it was and said that they would be down stairs if there was anything I wanted. A short while later my social worker came up to see the room and to chat with me she told me that I would be safe here and that I would be happy here I told her I did not like it here and I did not want to stay here she told me to give it time and it was early days here at the moment and then she said her goodbyes and left the cottage.

I sat on one of the beds and started to cry I felt so alone and isolated and so very scared. I was not sure that I was going to be ok here and safe I was feeling very vulnerable. I must have been in my room for ages when my foster mum came upstairs to see if I was ok and to tell me that tea was ready if I wanted to make my way down the stairs I thanked her but said I was not hungry she asked me to come and try to eat even if it was only a couple of mouthfuls at least I would have had something to eat. I was more hungry than I thought that I was I managed to eat it all and got up to the pots but I was told that I did not have to and that they would do them in awhile, and this after all was my first night with them. They asked me if I wanted to go and have a walk round the village so I could have a look and see what was about but I declined their offer as I wanted to get use to my surroundings first my foster mum said that was ok maybe we could go tomorrow. A short time later my brother phoned me and I was delighted to hear from him so soon and my foster mum picked up the phone and asked who it was and then she asked me if I wanted to speak with him and I told her yes I would and I heard her say to my foster dad that was the first time I had smiled all day since I got there, my foster dad told her to give me time and this was all new to her and she had been through a lot as it was. Don't push or rush here you know what the social worker said that she is very fragile and vulnerable and that she would need a lot of time and great care to bring her out of everything.

I was talking with my brother for over a hour and he said that I could go up and stop with him soon but I had to start to settle there first and the social worker would let me go and spend time with him I was delighted about this and I was going to be looking forward to that whenever that was going to be.

Shortly after coming off the phone I asked them if it was ok if I went to bed and they told me that I don't have to ask to go to bed it was not like that here.

I was glad to get into bed and be on my own for a while, it felt strange in that room and all the different noises that I heard some were peaceful and others frightened me. I knew that in time I would get use to the different noises and where I was now. I was scared and unsure of what was ahead of me.

I was woken by the birds that morning with the dawn chorus but it is was nice in a way and the church bells and it was the first time I thought about church in a long time but I wanted to go again and I would but not just yet everything was to new for me as yet. I was afraid of what I would have to face and if I would be accepted or not.

I went down stairs around nine thirty in the end that morning and my foster mum was up and asked me if I would like a cooked breakfast with it being my first morning with them and to set me up for the day and I thanked her and said I was not very hungry but she made me one anyway. I thanked her when I had finished and went to have a shower.

I was later introduced to a lot of the villagers but I felt over whelmed and I was also introduce to the choir master and was invited to join if that was what I wanted and as most of the village kids were part of the church it would be a good start for me to get to know some of the kids and then thing s would not feel so strained and strange to me I told them I would think about it but I did join again it was good for me and I did meet a lot of the kids but some of them I took an instant dislike to them as they did me. Why I did I do not know but I did. I was going to be starting the new school after the Easter break it was planned that way to give me the Easter Holidays to settle down a bit in my new home. I found it hard settling into village life but I did settle as much as I could do and I did make some very close friends there who stood by me and was always there to help me a couple of them even tried to protect me from some of the bullies. The problem was everyone knew who I was and that I was being fostered but I did not know who they were.

The school was ok it was bigger than I was expecting it to be the staff made me feel welcome and so did most of the kids in my classes but it was hard for me I was finding it hard to make friends and I preferred my own company and being on my own at least that way I was not going to get hurt by anyone. Some kids were really cruel when they found out that I had foster parents and they were making fun of me that my parents did not want me but I just turned round and said my parents are dead and they soon shut up but in my eyes they were and that is how I was looking at the situation that my parents were dead anyway it was easier saying that than trying to explain why I was with foster parents and there was a lot that I did not want anyone to know. I suppose it was my way of coping and it helped me in a lot of ways especially to get some time for myself and not to be asked a lot of questions that I did not want to answer. Maybe it was wrong of me but I had already shut my parents out as much as possible maybe one day I could see my parents again but at the moment there was no way I could I hated them and I felt so betrayed by my mum that I felt that I would never forgive her for that I still could not understand why she did what she did and why she did not do anything about it and I made myself a promise that day that I would not let my kids if I could still have them suffer anything I had suffered and I would be the mum to them that I never had from my mum I was going to be more how my Grandma was as far I was concerned my Grandma was the best mum I could ever have had and it was her love and care that I missed so much.

I had been with my foster family for over a year now and fairly ok for me but that was with my foster mother and one of their sons I got on great with them but me and my foster dad not so good he kept asking a lot of questions about what had happened to be before and how it made me feel and what I felt had happened, something's I told him and something's I did not the only problem was anything I had said he checked with my social worker and she confirmed what I had said I know there were long conversations at times between them if I should go in to counselling but it was always decided that it was not a good idea. I feel that was my mistake telling him some of the things that had happened because it give him the green light to do what he wanted and told me that I would not be believed or listened to and no one would do anything about it. There were problems and disagreements between us and I was getting on well with most of the family but not everyone.

160

But it had been a hard year for me as four months previously I got a call from a hospital telling me Peter had been in a motorbike accident and it was serious I was terrified of losing him but I could not go up to see him. Thankfully for me he came through it and rang me at his first opportunity and I cried when I heard from him and I realised how much I was missing him and how much he meant to me he promised me as soon as he was up to it that I could go up and stay with him again and I was looking forward to that he promised to ring me again soon. He did ring me again but not for a couple of weeks and I was very worried and argumentative and scared it caused a lot of problems for me but it was only what I deserved I suppose and I was worried about my brother I thought people should have been understanding but maybe I did not deserve them to be understanding.

Just over a year with me being at my foster parents I was going camping as part of my Duke of Edinburgh's award scheme and I was looking forward to it was only for a few days to and I loved camping and I was one of the few that knew how to put a tent up the site we were on already had them up but as part of doing the Duke of Edinburgh's award scheme we had to put a tent up on our own and survive one night on our own I loved it and the peace it gave me.

I can't explain why this made a difference and why things changed once I got back from camp but things changed again for me. I came back from camp with something in my foot and I could hardly walk on it and by the time I got back it was very sore I was not surprised that I got something in it as I was walking around in bare feet most of the time well as much as I could do which was more often than not.

I came back from camp feeling relaxed and a sense of feeling that I had finally made some good friends and strengthened the friendships that I had already got.

I was in my room and I had just had a soak in the bath and I was sat in my bed wrapped in my towel and trying to get whatever was in my foot out when my foster dad walked into the room and without knocking to and I started to feel very scared this was not the first time he had been in my room and this was not the first time something had happened but before it had only been a pass and I just ignored it. I blamed myself for this for not getting dressed straight after a bath and maybe then he would not have done anything to me he was having sex with me when he heard my foster mum coming up the stairs and he jumped off me very quickly and sat on the bed opposite me and started looking at my foot and making out that is what he was doing all of the time I was still wearing my towel and I had to re-adjust it to keep myself as decent as I could do. He did however managed to get a number to thorns and grass out of my foot and it was also infected which meant I would have to go to the doctors and get some antibiotics to clear it up but I said it would be ok and I did not go to the doctors and I was right it did heal on its own and fairly quickly to once everything was out of my foot. My foster mum stayed in the room whilst he was doing this and he left as soon as he had got everything out of my foot and my foster mum stayed and talked to me and said she was aware of what had happened before and I better not have any ideas of anything repeating here I told her that I did not but that was too late for that things had already happened.

I was enjoying being back in church and I was able to talk a little bit to the vicar but I found it hard talking to anyone and people were already starting to talk because he was talking to me a lot and a lot of villagers did not like and they felt it was not right and when I went for a walk he would sometime meet me on the walk so we could chat and I would be walking my dog and he is but it was one of the few times we could chat I did not see what was wrong with that and neither did the vicar and as he often said to me that he will do what he can to help anyone and that does not matter where he as to see them to help them and told me not to worry about what people were saying I did try to ignore what people were saying but that was not so easy to do but it did not matter who I had a conversations with there was always someone jumping to the wrong conclusion. I did a lot of babysitting for one of the families in the village and one day on the way back from a walk they stopped me and asked if I was free that evening and I said that I was and asked me if I would like to baby sit again that night from about eight till about eleven I said that should be fine. I went back to my foster parents house and made sure that it was ok with them and they said that it was so I looked after their kids it was not long before people were talking about me again and it was so hurtful to me and very destroying for me and I began to lose faith in people and became very wary of everyone and was scared to talk to anyone in case someone saw it as something else.

My foster dad was coming in my room frequently and having sex with me sometimes he hurt me and other times he was gentle. He told me that I would have to be careful because he could get me pregnant and if that happened he asked me to say that it was someone else's and I told him I could not do that because that would be lying and not fair to someone who is so innocent.

I was scared to tell anyone what was going on and my social worker picked up on something but she was not saying anything to me about it well not at first she did not but after a few a month's she did and asked me if I was safe here and I told her no more safe than I had been anywhere else it was now eighteen months since I first moved in with them and in a lot of ways this was the first family I had ever had that actually loved me and I knew deep down that they did.

I was slowly being accepted in the village but they were still talking about me and probably will do for some time to come or until the next new person came into the village but even then they probably would do it were the way they all were.

My foster dad was coming into my room more and more and saying all he does is think about me and how much happier he has been since I came to live with them and that I was a very attractive young woman I did not think I was attractive at all but I thanked him anyway for his compliment but I was not sure that he meant it as a compliment but away to get what he wanted. That it worked because he did not want me to do anything to him or make what he was doing to me right he was having sex with me on a very regular basis and I was becoming increasingly scared that something was going to go wrong.

I was wanting to see my mum again and it was a couple of days before new year it had been arranged in a local café for her to meet me but she did not turn up and give no warning that she was not going to turn up the morning of the visit she had phoned to speak with the social worker to make sure it was still going to happen and confirmed the place where we were going to meet and we were there in plenty of time and waited almost a hour for her to turn up and she did not she had let me down again and I was so disappointed that she did not come to see me. I went back to my foster parents feeling very upset and sad.

I had told the vicar that I was going to see my mum and I was looking forward to it, he was the one that suggested to me now maybe a good time to try and speak with my mum and I felt angry at him for suggesting this and ending in failure for me I felt I had failed, I did not feel that my mum had failed but me failing her. I could not understand why and what I had done that would make a mother hate their daughter so much.

A few days later a received a letter from her and it had been censored by the social worker because there was things in it that was not very pleasant and it was felt that it would have upset me there were only four or five words left but it was not crossed out that bad because when I held it up to the light I could almost read all of my mum's letter and yes it did upset me but I would rather have known what she felt than me wondering about it for years to come. She was saying that I had made the decisions that I have made and it was my decision only that put me where I am now and I had made my bed and I now had to sleep in it and not to contact her again until I was away from them and where I was staying that hurt me so much and it did upset me and I was crying so much. I felt that she had rejected me again and did not care about me. Maybe I had to accept that but I could not I still loved her but I was very angry with her and she had managed to hurt me again even without seeing me but that letter said all she would have probably said to my face if she had the courage to meet with me but as I well know she had no courage to me she was a coward.

I tried to forget that I had a mum and tried to get on with my life as much as I could do but it was not easy for me to forget this and I still wanted my mum to love me and be there for me as a mum should have been. I still wanted my mum but somehow I knew I had to find away to accept that she did not love me or want me.

I was having a lot of bullying at school but overall I had settled into the school and was getting a number of friends that were close to me or as close as I would let them and another year from now I would be taking my exams and leaving school and I knew that time between now and then was going to be so precious to me and I wanted to do well in them and I was already having to work as hard as I could because I felt I had something to prove to everyone and to myself.

Life was bearable at the moment but I could not stand certain parts of my life but I was pretending to myself that they were not happening I know this was running away from things and not facing up to anything but it was the only way I could cope and survive. As time got on I was finding things very difficult and things were becoming more difficult to cope with for me and I felt so trapped and scared and I was trying to work hard and revise as much as I could as I had got my exams coming up and I wanted to do well.

Late autumn I was in a lot of pain in my stomach and I was constantly being taken to the doctors and I had a grumbling appendix and the GP kept giving me tablets to take to ease the inflammation and this continued throughout Christmas but it was not getting any easier in the end I was taken to hospital but only stayed in for a few days and there was disagreements between my foster parents and I and they walked out and did not come back to see me until it was time to go home.

A few weeks later I was back in again and I had to have my appendix out I was lucky really that they did take them out when they did as they operated on me they burst it could have been a lot worse for me if it was left any longer. I felt so alone and so scared and I was facing this on my own as my foster parents refused to come to the hospital to see because I was not very nice to them the last time but I was frightened and it was the first time I had stayed in hospital on my own and I was frightened about what was going to happen to me the last time I had been on a ward was when I saw my Grandma and she died in hospital and I thought that was going to happen to me. When I came back from theatre there was no one there for me and I was very frightened the nursing staff were good and did all they could for me and when everyone else had visitors someone came and sat with me and chatted with me just so I was not on my own. After a few days I was moved to another ward and I got a visit from my social worker and she asked me had my foster parents been up to see me and I told that they had not and I felt that I was being abandoned and isolated she spoke with them and they told her because of how I was with them before they decided it was best not to come and see me my social worker told them that this is the first time I had been in hospital for any length and I was only a child and a very frightened one they still refused to come and see me and told my social worker that I had to phone to be collected when I was being discharged. My social worker was not happy and told them that they were being very childish over this and not being very caring or supportive to me

A few days later I was allowed to go home were ever home was I don't know anymore and I felt more scared than I had done for a long time. I got the nursing staff to phone them to tell them I was being discharged and they should come and collect me sometime in the early afternoon. They did come and fetch me but I said very little to them on the journey back home and I went straight to my room and stayed there until tea was ready I went down for tea but as soon as tea was over I went back to my room I needed time on my own and time to think about things. About a hour after tea my foster dad came in to my room and started shouting at me and telling me that I had upset my foster mum and I had to go down stairs and say sorry to her otherwise they would throw me out we were arguing and in the end he left my room and I went down stairs and went to walk out of the front door but my foster mum came running through to the front door and before I could get out she was blocking my way I let go of the door and the window smashed and I got a slap round the face for it I told them I hated them both. Their son came in not long after and the first thing he said was what dad done now he always goes too far. I heard my foster mum saying that I had broke the glass but my foster dad had done nothing but had a go at me since I got back and their son said what did you expect you left alone in the hospital and as soon as she got back you started having a go at her and she has had a big operation for someone who is so young and going through that alone must have terrified her. He popped his head round my door and I was crying he came and sat next to me and give me a brotherly hug an told me to not worry about things they will all calm down come the morning and he told me that they are worried about me and I replied they have a funny way of showing it he said that's my parents they don't always say what they mean. He apologised how his parents treated me and went back to his room and shut the door as he left a few minutes later my foster mum was in my room saying she was sorry to me and I said I was sorry to her and she cuddled me for ages and I just cried I feel asleep crying. The next

166

morning my foster mum was at work but my foster dad was not and he was in my room within minutes of my foster mum driving off to work and he told me that I had a lot to make up to them and I had to start now with him and I was going to have to do exactly what he wanted me to do otherwise I would be in more trouble and they would send me away and I would end up in a children's home because no-one else would want me.

He was in my room for most of the morning and having regular sex with me and wanting me in different positions and he told me that I had still got a lot of work to do to make things up to them and this was only the beginning of me making up to them. I hated them for leaving me alone when I was in hospital and leaving me feeling very isolated and alone and frightened I was also keeping a dairy for myself about how I was feeling and what was happening and who I had talked to about things.

I was still in some discomfort from the operation and I still had my stitches in and they were not due out for a few days yet I was also due to see my social worker in the next few days and I had requested that she came out to visit me as there were things I wanted to discuss with her and it was more about what was going to happen to me once I finished school than what was going off there I was not sure how to talk to her about that but I knew that at some point I was going to have to but I did not know how to talk to her about this and I was scared to as well.

I was talking to the vicar at my church and not said too much to him at this stage but I was talking to him a lot about a lot of things some very general things to at this point. I thought I could trust him. I found it hard in the village people started talking about me and the vicar and saying it was not right that he was spending so much time with me and talking with me when he could be talking to others I started to become more and more withdrawn and was struggling to talk to anyone and I was afraid to make conversation with other people because of what people may say about two people talking they were also talking about me and my foster parents to and more so my foster dad and me mostly what they were saying were that things did not seem right and he was very protected and overly friendly to me and they were convinced that something was going on that should not have been they were not wrong there but I did not say anything to them or anyone about this I just let them get on with talking about me because I knew eventually that they would find someone else to talk about and then they would leave me alone but I had got use to it by now they had talked about me since I had arrived in the village and they would probably talk about me long after I leave the village to that would not have surprised me if they did but it made things very hard for me in the village everyone wanted to know everything about someone and what they did not know they made up and tried to find out as much as they could about me and they had done from the word go. I was keeping a diary about how I was feeling and what was happening to me now, and what had happened to me before, I was angry about that she had read my dairy it was about me and had nothing to do with anyone else what I had wrote I had never expected to share what was in it with anyone else it was just my way of trying to come to turns with what had happened and it was only meant for my eyes only. This is where I was betrayed again my foster mum read my diary and made me tear it up especially anything she did not approve of that was in there but I felt that she had no right to have read it in the first place she had no right to go through my private things some things were very personal for me and about my life before I had even arrived there and she was like the rest of the people in the village small minded and jumping to the wrong conclusions if she had took a minute to ask me what it was all about she would have realised that I was writing about the time I was with my dad and my mum and what my step dad had done and how I came to become there and I was making references to the church and how that made me feel and I was asking myself a lot why was I going to church now to be betrayed again by the church if that was the case then what was the point to anything and what was the point to trusting anyone again if this is how I felt but I could not find the answers to my questions so I kept going and kept trusting people but I was the one that got badly hurt not them.

I began to hate everyone but more so myself and I stopped fighting anyone I just gave into them all of the time I suppose it was easier for me than to fight them all of the time, I was shutting myself away more and more and becoming very isolated and withdrawn even school was becoming concerned about this and how much I had changed since I had been there and I was be questioned a lot about things but I just brushed it off and told them that I was ok and just trying to keep my head down with my exams coming up and I was still not back in school from having my appendix out several weeks ago I was just going in for exams and going home again I was working hard at home though and I was always in my room with a book under my nose trying to revise and do as much as I could I wanted to do the best I could in my exams they were so important for me and I knew I had to do well so I knew I had to put the time in to do that which meant I was spending more and more time on my own and less time in other peoples company with the exception of my foster father coming into my room more and more for more sex when it suited him and I did not fight him anymore I did not see the point because I knew there was no point anyway he was going to get what he wanted if I objected or not so I just let him do what he wanted and if I got hurt in the mean time so be it I did not care anymore I just wanted to get away from here and die. How I was going to do that at this stage I do not know. I had been having problems from the wound from my operation and it was constantly seeking and opening up and I had already had it re stitched three times up to now and I was having to be careful that it did not happen again but I knew that it would do with the way things were going and I knew that I would be kept in if I had to have the stitches re done again as I had already been told this not so long ago. When he left my room I was in quite a bit of discomfort and the wound had opened again and I was bleeding very badly so I just laid on my bed on the half dresses state that I was now in and closed my eyes and prayed to God to take me away now and stop all my suffering and pain and take me from this cruel world but that did not happen I don't remember much else from that day or how I got to the hospital I was out of it for ages and feeling very confused but I was staying in hospital for a couple of days at least and they could not understand how come this kept happening to me and thought that I was doing too much and too much heavy lifting but I was not I got the same questions over and over again and they got the same answers back and I overheard a conversation between a couple of nursing staff and they were saying that they believed that someone was hurting me and doing this to me rather than the wound just keep opening up and I knew this was not right for me because I have always healed so quickly but not this time again my foster parents did not come to see me but took me back home a few days later and I was under strict instructions not to do any exercise or lifting for at least two weeks otherwise I would never heal properly and there was no way that I wanted to go back into hospital again I hated the places to me that is where you went if you were going to die in a way that is what I wanted to happen to me. I knew I had to be right for when I finished my exams in the spring I was going on a Red Cross holiday as a helper for disabled children and I was looking forward to it and knew I had to be right for then I was determined I was going to be going on this I had done all my training and I had met the child I was going to be in charge of for the week and I was going to be responsible for her and making sure she was at breakfast and she was ready to be down with the rest of the group but I was scared now that I was going to miss out on this with everything that was happening at home and with my foster father.

I was beginning to confide in the vicar a lot more because I knew I had to talk to someone and I did not like my new social worker in fact I detested her. So the vicar was my best option I had, I was too scared to talk to anyone else I believed what I said to him was safe and would not go any further.

Maybe I just asked the wrong question this particular day but it was one I needed to ask we only had a GP that came into the village twice a week and was not always a female doctor which is what I wanted to see I could not go to the main surgery without alerting my foster mum something was wrong or getting a thousand questions from her. I knew that the doctor that I wanted to see was also a friend of the vicars so I hoped that he could find out when she would be there next and fortunately for me it was the following Monday and then the question came why do I want to see this particular GP I simply replied because she is female and I need to discuss female issues and it was easier for me to speak with a female about these things then it was a male well that is what I told the vicar and I knew he did not believe me because the look on his face and unfortunately for me I did not get to see her the following week as I could not get out of the house on my own without a thousand questions why I was going out and where was I going, but I knew that before much longer that I had to see her otherwise I knew I could be in even more trouble than I possibly already was and for me I knew something was wrong I had missed my first period and about to miss a second and I knew that was not like me and I was beginning to suspect that I could be pregnant and I was scared that I was and then there was only one person that it could have been and that was my foster father's I was being sick every day and I was hiding it from everyone else in the house as I did not want anyone to know and I was so scared my foster father had suspected the same thing and told me that I better not say anything to anyone if I was and I had better say that it was a boyfriends but everyone knew that I had not got a boyfriend so that was impossible to be someone else's and I felt very confused I did go to the GP's a few days later and I walked out afraid to say anything to her but I was the last one in the waiting room and she came after me and told me that it was ok anything I told her was confidential and she was not allowed to discuss it with anyone else I told her that I think that I was pregnant and she asked me loads of questions and most of her questions I answered Yes to apart from the one about a boyfriend I told her I had not got one but she looked confused, I told her that I did not want to talk about it and she then asked me if it was ok if she was alright to examine me, I must have looked frightened and she told me that it was nothing to worry about and she would be gentle, after she had examined me she informed me that I was pregnant and about ten-twelve weeks and she asked me what I wanted to do about it I told her that I did not want it and I needed it doing without anyone else knowing about it. She made a few phone calls and told me to go to this ward on this day at this time and everything would be dealt with there and then I did everything she said and followed her instructions to the letter I felt guilty because of what I was doing but I knew that it was the only way for me. The day soon came for me to go and have a termination I was terrified and I was not really understanding what was about to happen to me or how I would feel afterwards but I knew I had to do this and I did this without any support accept from the GP that sent me there in the first place and as far as I knew no-one else knew this was happening. I was there longer than I thought that I would have been and I was in more pain than I was expecting to be in but I was told that this would soon pass. It did not feel like this pain would pass I thought that I was going to die and I wished that I would do to. I got back in about the time I would have got in from school maybe a few minutes later and when I walked through the door I was told how dreadful I looked and that I still had to be careful not to do too much and I was even asked if I had a hard day at school and I told them that it was considering that I had only just gone back from having my appendix out. I headed straight to my room laid down on my bed and cried I felt guilty about what I had just done and I was in so much pain to which did not help, I don't know why my foster mum came up to me but she sounded concerned with the way I looked when I came through the door and wanted to make sure that I was ok she also asked me when I last had a period and I told her that I was having one now why and she just said that she had not noticed that I had one in the last few months and was concerned because of what people were saying. I did not like what I was saying to her but what else could I do, I did not feel that she would have done anything if she had known I felt that she would have done exactly the same as my mum had done and turned a blind eye to everything and pretend that it was not happening and would blame me because somehow it was my fault and I deserved this but I don't know I felt this but I did. I did not feel that she would have done anything any different maybe she would have done but I was not so sure that she would have done and I did not trust her any more I already felt that she had betrayed me by going through my personal things and I could not forgive her for going through my dairy I still did not make it right what she had done she should have asked me before she jumped to the same conclusion as everyone else why couldn't she just have trusted me. I started to ask myself what is it about me why people want to hurt me so much and what had I done to deserve this, I could not think of anything I had done to deserve all of this but I must be doing something to deserve what I had been through and continue to go through maybe it was something about me why everyone wants to hurt me so much. Whatever it was I did not know what it was. Maybe it would always be like this for me but I hoped and prayed that my life would not always be like this for me.

It did not take my foster father long to come on to me again and I was terrified of becoming pregnant again as I did not want to go through what I had just gone through again and he was not bothered he kept telling me I was the daughter they always wanted I wonder why he always wanted a daughter maybe I know why so he could have done to his own child what he was doing to me I was beginning to become scared of him and feared what would happen next I was trying to study for my exams and cope with what was happening to me which was not easy for me to do it was easier for me to pretend to myself that it was not really happening to me but to someone else that way I could just about cope with what was happening some would have said to me I was burying my head in the sand but it was the only way I could cope with what was happening and to concentrate on my exams they were too important to me and I knew I had to do well I had my heart set on going into the police force. I was going to do that no matter what if I could get in then that is what I was going to do, that was why my exams and doing well was so important to me I wanted to do well I was determined to do well and get my dream if it happened or not was another matter.

I had eight weeks left of exams and before I went on the Red Cross holiday and I was looking forward to it more than anything I was looking forward to feeling safe and doing something worthwhile for someone else. I was busy all over the weekends with the run up to this holiday and extra training we had to go through just to make sure we understand every eventuality that could happen and we were as prepared as we could be to dealing with this holiday it was meant to be enjoyable for all of us we were going to be staying at the agriculture college in Warwickshire and there was loads of activities planned and loads of fun and games for everyone but there was also time that all the young helpers could have some fun to and that was what I was looking forward to having some fun and being myself for awhile whatever myself was I did not know anymore.

I struggled through my exams and I was constantly being sick and I was worried but I had to try and stay focussed on my exams and not let anything else get in my way but that was easier said than done for me. I finally finished my exams and I could now look forward to going away I was talking to the vicar more and more and starting to open up to him a lot more and he said to me how pale and withdrawn I looked and people were talking again about me I was getting use to that one now but even the vicar stated to ask me questions about what he had heard people saying and asked me was there anything going on with my foster father at first I denied that there was but he kept asking me he told me I could trust him and he would not tell a soul if I told him and I believed him and in the end I told that some of what was being said was the truth but I don't know where they got it from in the first place it certainly was not me he told me that is what this village is like the jump to the wrong conclusions sometimes and sometimes they come to conclusions and then people start talking and decide if it is right or not they were usually right though and that was the strange thing about that village. I was talking to the vicar a lot more and I was feeling so comfortable talking to him and over the next few weeks we spoke almost every day and at different times of day and he soon picked up on the sickness that I was having and he asked me if it is possible that I could be pregnant again and I told him I don't know and he asked me if I got in to see the lady doctor a few months ago I told him that I did. He promised me he would not tell a soul about what we were discussing I trusted him so much I asked him to contact his friend and see when she was going to be on at the surgery again in the village as it happened it was a few days before I went on the disabled holiday so I went to see her and she did all the test again and asked me to phone the surgery in a few days time I agreed to do that. I saw the vicar as I came out of the surgery and he asked me if everything was ok I told him I did not know and he said to me that he had no choice but to speak with my social worker and told the doctor more than he should have done I began to cry and then I ran away from him I hated him for that and he promised me that he would not speak to anyone or tell anyone about anything I had confided in him he betrayed me and he betrayed everything there was to betray as far as I was concerned including the church that was the not the first time someone in the church had betrayed me and would never forgive him or the church for this.

The day I was set to go on the disabled holiday my social worker rang me and asked me if there was anything I wanted to talk to her about and I told her that there was not she reminded me that they could not help me if I did not tell them what had been going off, I actually told her to mind her own business and there was nothing she could help me with and I hung up the phone I felt so foolish doing that but I did not want her interference and someone else to break my confidences and trust I did not trust anyone anymore. I was feeling very low and depressed and did not want to live anymore I would rather die than come back to this house. I meant that and felt that so strongly too.

I had to be up early the next mornng as we were being picked up by coach around 8am and I was going to be one of the first to be picked up as I was the furthest helper out everyone else was at the Rugby side of Warwickshire to me. There were several people there to wave me off including the vicar and he told me to have a good break and as we pulled away he told me he was sorry I just shook my head at him. I was beginning to wonder what the point there was to life and what was the point of life for me and where I was going to end up if I survived life as it was I doubted that I would survive life as it was and I kept asking myself what was the point of life and why was I here. That was one of many things I did not understand maybe I never would do. Most of the Red Cross holiday went by very smoothly until I had to phone the doctors up to see if they had got my test results back and it took me several attempts to get through to them and in the end I had to leave the number of the agriculture college for the doctor to ring me back and she did about a hour later and she gave me the results over the phone and I was devastated and I was scared and I just wanted to die and I knew I could not go back to that ever again the only problem was that one of the leaders had to come and fetch me when the doctors rang and left me to the call but she was obviously concerned that my GP was phoning me whilst I was there when I came off the phone I ran up the stairs crying and went into my dormitory and slammed the door shut and started crying I was laying on my bed crying when one of the leaders came into me and I told them to leave me alone she asked everyone in the dormitory to leave us alone so she could speak with me in private she asked me what was wrong and how come my GP was contacting me there I told her I had tried all week to get hold of her for some test results and she was phoning to give them to me she asked me was it anything serious I told her it depends what you call serious. I told her if being pregnant was serious then it was serious, I also told her that I wanted to die and then I was put on close watch, as they were concerned for my safety. Not that being on close watch did them any good. It was the last night of the holiday and all the helpers were allowed to have a party but before we could do that we had to make sure all of the guest were in bed and asleep I was lucky the little girl I was in charge of was a sleep very quickly but then she always was, the party was in full flow about a hour later when I went into one of the bathrooms and locked the door open the bathroom window and climbed out onto the ledge and it was a long way down from where I was and it was only a very narrow ledge and it was a cold night and there was a strong wind blowing I was considering jumping off the ledge when someone knocked the door and asked me if I was ok but I did not answer them so they asked me again I still refused to answer them and I wanted some time away from everyone however when they asked me a third time and I did not answer they were getting other leaders and clearing the area and asking everyone to move to another part of the upstairs they said that way it was better for everyone and it would give me some privacy if I needed it when I came out of the bathroom. I had no intention of coming out I had every intention of dropping off that ledge it was a long way down and I was surrounding by trees and then there was concrete under me and to my left there was the outdoor swimming pool and I knew that I could not make that as it was far too far from where I was at this time, I knew I did not want to be there anymore and I certainly did not want to go through what I had been through a few months ago again. I heard a lot of commotion outside the bathroom door and a few seconds later they had opened the bathroom door and I was still on the ledge and I was crying and there was a sudden gasp from the leaders maybe they realised where I was at this point but some grabbed me by my ankles just as I was about to jump off the ledge and I did not care if I lived or died, a couple of the leaders pulled me back in and asked me if I was ok I told them to leave me alone and then asked me if I meant to do anything or did I just slip I told them to work it out for themselves. They had to do a report and on it stated that I possibly slipped off the ledge and if it was not for the leader's quick thinking I would have fallen I wished that I had done and I wished that they had not grabbed me and pulled me back in. That night I was not allowed to be with the child I was looking after as they said that I was not in the right frame of mind to look after someone else let alone myself and of course it started a lot of questions for me and eventually I told them more or less what had gone off and what my GP was contacting me for and I told them I did not want to go back to them anymore apparently they had already contacted social services because they had their own suspicions and that night they contacted them again to take advice from them about me going home the next day and they were told that under no circumstances must I go back home and someone from social services would come and collect me from the centre but it would not be till later in the afternoon and I had to wait with the leaders and I was not left alone for very long from everyone else going home till the social worker arrived to collect me I was lucky if I was on my own for more than a few minutes as they were concerned about what I would do next. It seem ages before anyone came to pick me everyone else had gone in the morning we all said our goodbyes to everyone that was there and we all said that we hope to see you again soon and told me to take care and they would always remember the fun that I had with them, and it was now well into the afternoon and still no-one had turned up to pick me up but they were told that it would be mid to late afternoon due to staff shortages but they were reassured that someone would be there before four pm that afternoon and the leaders advised them that they had to be away from the premises by four pm as the students were due back in around then and it was better that all previous occupiers had to be away before they got back to take up their residence and carry on with their agriculture course. The weather had changed and it was now raining and I was still standing outside in the doorway just starring out at nothing just being with my thoughts and being in my own space that I needed so much and I was feeling very scared and uncertain of what was going to happen to me and where I was now going to go. I felt very frightened but I wanted to die I did not want to be in this world anymore but there was something stopping me from this and I did not know what or why.

It was just before four pm when the social worker finally turned up to collect and take me home but I was not going back to my foster parents I was taken to a kids home there was no privacy no peace just mayhem, I saw were I was going to be sleeping and I was horrified and felt uncomfortable and vulnerable the rooms were nicely decorated and kitted out for the purpose but the rooms were all mixed with different ages and sex I was one of two that was having to share with the boys they seemed ok but I hated that house it was not home for me I spent the whole weekend crying and I was very withdrawn and wanted to be on my own as much as possible.

That weekend seemed a long weekend for me and it was Saturday night and tea was being served when I got there but I did not eat anything and did not want anything the workers seemed ok but very distant after all I did not know them and not sure I wanted to get to know them I hated it there and did not want to stay there for too long but I knew I may not have any choice in that one on how long I stayed there for. During the evening on the Saturday I got permission to go for a walk on my own and off the grounds I needed time away from everyone and I needed time to think about things and how I was going to cope with where I was now or if I could live like this and scared of what was going to happen next? This was the unknown for me and I was so scared I was finding it hard to accept the situation and where I was now staying everything felt so strange for me and I felt very isolated I found it hard whilst walking as I did not know the area that well and I was in unknown territory and that was frightening for me to not knowing where I was or where I was going.

When I got back in from my walk I was offered something to eat and a hot chocolate I turned down something to eat but I accepted the hot chocolate I drank my drink and went to bed before everyone else came to bed the workers checked in on me regular during the evening and before the rest came to bed and told them that they had to be quiet as I was asleep but they were not and I did not expect them to be quiet, the house was busy and noisy throughout the night there was always someone moving around. We were all awaken early the next morning for breakfast and everyone said the new girl won't come down and eat with the rest of us as I was not civilized enough to do that the workers told them to stop being so cruel and give me time to start to feel settled I had just been through an awful lot and I needed time and patience they all laughed at me but I did not care but I did go down for breakfast and eat with all of them I was in the kitchen when they said what they did and I was upset by it but I thought that I had every right to eat just like they did and we were all there for similar reasons and we were all meant to be kind to each other not that happened very often but most of the time there was a lot of kindness around after breakfast there was a fun and games day planned and we could participate in what we wanted to be involve with or not whichever the case may be I did join in with quite a bit that day and it was a slightly better day for me and I was not crying as much but I was being sick a lot and the others picked up on it and I was due to go to the doctors at my surgery on that Monday but now that was not going to happen but I knew something would have to be sorted out at some point. The workers knew that I had to go to the doctors that Monday and was arranging for me to see another doctor as soon as possible.

We had quite a lot of outdoor games some were rougher than others but all very enjoyable. I was enjoying the games until I was tripped up and jumped on I screamed with pain and everyone got off and the workers came running out to see what had gone off and I was still on the floor in pain and all the other kids were sent inside and the pain got worse and I felt strange but could not explain it and one of the workers asked me several questions and then there was panic and a lot of activity very quickly and I was carried inside into one of the single rooms and was checked over this was the room that was used in case of accidents and a doctor was called and I was examined and one of the workers had to remain present for the examination because it was not felt that it was right for me to be examined on my own. I was asked when my last period was and when I told them that it was over two months ago they did not ask me anymore. The doctor gave me an injection but I do not know what it was or what it was for but he told me that it would help me and help things become easier for me it was not until about a hour later that I got even more pain and I was bleeding and not like I had before this felt different but I could not explain how it felt different and I doubled up in pain and one of the female workers were sitting with me and telling me that it is ok I am not alone and it will all be over soon enough the doctor was still there and I felt very drowsy and very scared and I was not sure what was happening or what they were doing to me but I suspect it had something to do with me being pregnant and I was now bleeding so much I felt faint and weary. Then everything went black for awhile for me and I was told that I had fainted and that I would be ok now and nothing would be mentioned about this again I felt confused and scared and I was told to rest for the rest of the day I was brought my tea and drinks to me and I was escorted every where I wanted to go including the bathroom they said that they were worried that I may faint or try something again I was not really understanding what they were saying.

The next morning my social worker came to visit me and told me that I would be moving from there that day and she was going to take me to another place which was better than were I was now and I would have my own room and be able to do things more like I am use to doing and look after myself a lot more than I could do whilst I was where I was now but again this felt very frightening to me and I was not sure where I was going and for how long I would be going for. My social worker tried to reassure me that everything would be ok and it was a very nice place that I was now going to and the people are nice and there is some good staff there who will be there to help and guide me if that is what I so wanted. I was not sure what I wanted and I was very withdrawn and feeling very isolated I was taken to the girls hostel as the social worker called it another kids home and one where I will be staying until I leave care or a bit longer if that is what I so wanted but that was up to me. When we arrived at the kid's home it was very busy and a lot of activity going off with different people most of the other youngsters were out at school/college or work so there was not that many people around when I got there which in away was nice because I did not feel like I was being starred at. After meeting the staff that was on duty I was shown to my room and allowed to settle into my room on my own it was a small room on the second floor and the view from my window was not very good, as I over looked the main road. It had everything that I would need in there for the time being at least I had somewhere warm to sleep and I was in a room on my own and I could lock my door if I wanted to which was something I suppose. I went down stairs a short time later and hear my social worker talking to the workers and she asked them if they thought that it would be appropriate for me to go into counselling but they felt that it would not be and it had to come from me first but they said they would discuss this further at my next review in a couple of months time, I stood and thought why do I need counselling I do not need to talk to some shrink there is nothing I needed to talk about and not to a complete stranger either. Anyway they had made their decision without consulting me that I was not ready to talk to anyone and it was felt better that it came from me rather than them implanting it I felt that they should have consulted me to see what I wanted but I knew I would not have agreed to go into counselling.

My first review was three months after arriving at this kids home but it was not as bad there as I thought that it would have been but I was not settled there or happy my foster mum came to the review and told me that I could go back with her if I wanted to but I could not whilst my foster father was still there but I was told that it would just be me and her and her son well that is what she told the review but I was not convinced that it would have just been us if I was sure it would have been just us I would have gone back with her I loved her so much and the review board felt that it was better that I stayed were I was but she was welcome to come and see me whenever she wanted and it would be discussed again at a later date.

Well my instinct was right she was still with him as next time she visited she brought him with her it was strained but ok as it could be. A few weeks later she brought all my things including my dog to the hostel they would not let me keep the dog but I had to get all my things into my room and very quickly to. It seemed to take me ages to get everything into my room and I was not sure where I was going to put everything but somehow I managed to find somewhere to put most things and it was all away and tidy. Whilst I was unpacking I found a letter from them saying how much my foster parents loved me and they were sorry for how things had turned out and they regretted the things that had happened and that they had not trusted me, and they hoped in time I would forgive them and go back to them and they missed me so much. When I read this I burst into tears I missed them to but I knew that I could not go back it was too late now and I knew it would not have been safe for me to go back there.

I spent most of that day in my room and in tears and I was left very much alone throughout the day and evening occasionally someone came up to see if I was ok and if I wanted anything if there was anything I needed I only had to ask. I told them I was fine and thanked them for coming up to see if I was ok. I was on my own till gone seven that evening and the hostel started to get noisy with everyone coming back in and getting ready to do what they wanted to do one of the other girls asked if I was in and was told that I was in my room and were I had been all day and it would be best if I was left alone and I heard her coming up the stairs and as she came onto the corridor she started shouting my name and told me that she was coming in to my room if I liked it or not. I had already unlocked my door as I know what she was like she would not take no for an answer and she would have come in regardless if she was invited in or not she was quite sweet in a lot of ways but sometimes very overpowering at first she frightened me but as I got to know her I got use to how she was and her little quirks and we were becoming friends. She came into my room and saw me crying and she sat down next to me and just hugged me and then told me that she would not hear anything of it I was coming downstairs and having something to eat I told her that I was not hungry she told me no arguments if I have to feed you myself she said I would be eating, actually when we went downstairs and started cooking something to eat I realised how hungry I was and I enjoyed what I had eaten and the company to it was not long before I was laughing and joking with her the other girls kept their distance from us she was not the most popular girl in the hostel but that was because of the way she was with people but she was calming down slowly and seeing things differently, the staff often commented on what a good influence I was on her.

Most of the time at the hostel was not that bad but there were times when it was horrible and I hated it but at least I felt like I had a home for the time being and at least I was safe there.

I started college in the Autumn and was doing a business course but I could not settle with it and I started to struggle with it, it was much more difficult that I thought it would have been I thought it was going to be an easier course to do but I was so wrong, I also found the kids difficult they were all in their own packs and it was hard to get in with anyone I spent a lot of my time on my own and I was being bullied a lot to the work load was ok but certain aspects I found boring and it was not really what I wanted to do and I was regretting doing this course now but I wanted to see it through. Just after Christmas that year I was considering leaving the course and looking for full time work I was already working part-time in the evenings and mainly at weekends and I loved it but there was no other hours for me. In the January I saw some work in one of the factories that made furniture covers and I loved sewing so I applied for it and got the post and I was delighted and worked hard I was there for just over three months and I was enjoying but I could not keep up with those that had been doing it for years and I felt I was no good at it so I started looking for something else in the end I got a temporary post till the Christmas in a biscuit factory and I took that and left were I was and started working in Nabisco fears full-time it was hard work but good work.

I had met a nice young man a few weeks before and I was seeing him regularly and I got on well with his parents and I was going to be going away with his family the following summer and I wanted to pay my own way with that and I did. We got engaged during the summer and I was over the moon about it but my social worker and the workers at the hostel were not very pleased about it they said I was too young to make these sort of decisions for myself and I had made the wrong decision but for the time being they were going to let me make my own decisions and see where things went. Well things were a lot further on than anyone knew but he was so gentle to me and did not do anything I felt uncomfortable with he was so kind and loving I felt so safe when I was with him I felt so protected to which was so nice. I was talking to him about my mum and how much I missed her and that I wanted to go and see her we cycled everywhere and was planning to cycle over on the bank holiday Monday and he discussed this with his parents and the best way to go and his parents offered to take us over to show us the way and once we got there they give us the opportunity to stop and see her and we took this opportunity and saw her his parents went off to Hinckley for the next few hours to give us time with my mum. My fiancé came in with me and held my hand the whole time I was there. I was shaking when I knocked on the door and it seemed to take forever for her to answer I figured that she would have been in the pub but she was not she was in and she seemed so pleased to see me but then I saw that she was still with him which made me feel even more uncomfortable we did not stay in the house for long she suggested that we went down to their local for awhile and we did and by the time we got back to her place my fiancé's parents were there and we had to go she promised to come to see me alone and she was going to arrange for us to spend the weekend there. I was not sure about this one but I still loved my mum and wanted to try and get to know her but I was not sure if that was possible or not.

I was very quiet on the way home and I felt very distance and unsure of what all this now meant to me and felt that I had made a huge mistake contacting her but it was too late for that one now I had already done it.

When we got back to my fiancé's place we went for a walk along the canal and he asked me what was wrong at this point he did not know what had happened to me not all that long ago he actually said that my mum seems nice and I laughed at that one he could not understand what I was laughing at and I told him she is far from nice when you get to know her she's is an absolute bitch but I still loved her but he knew there was more to what I was saying and then he asked me why I had not spoken to her husband and that was it I just started crying and sobbing and he sat me down along the canal bank and put his arms around and was so gentle and kind with me and then he asked me to tell him what was wrong and why was I not happy that your mum had invited you to stay with her I thought that is what you wanted he told me but it was but not now and not whilst he was there. It took me a long time to feel that I could tell him but he did not know the extent of what had happened and I was scared to tell anyone about it and I had not told anyone in any detail so far and I was so scared to do now I was afraid to lose what I had already got and I did not want to do that my fiancé meant so much to me and I loved him dearly, but I knew at some point I would have to tell him everything but I did not know how to tell him and the thought of sharing it with someone filled me with dread and total fear. I kept asking myself what if he thought it was my fault and that I deserved but what if he walked away from me and never want to see me again. I just could not bear this. He did somehow manage to get it out of me what had happened and he told me I should have told him before now but I told him it was something that you cannot easily tell anyone and I had to be sure it was not going to be used against me in any way he promised me that it would not and he never did. He was so supportive and understanding I was so surprise that he was and he took it very well to. We became very close after that and in many ways it changed our relationship but for the better I felt so special with him and he spoilt me and cared for me and loved me so much as I did him. I was feeling love that I had not felt in such a long time it felt wonderful.

My eighteenth was coming round and I was looking for other accommodation because as soon as I was able to leave I wanted to do at least then I could start building my own life without someone my back all of the time.

But before I came eighteen I was pregnant and my social worker was saying that when it was born that I would have taken from immediately and it would be put up for adoption as I was not fit to look after myself let alone a child I felt so devastated and so low originally I was planning to have it terminated but on the day I decided not to and cancelled the admission to hospital but said nothing to anyone at the time my fiancé knew and his family but was sworn to secrecy.

Somehow my mum had managed to arrange for me to go and spend the weekend with her but there was a condition that I took my fiancé with me so they knew I would be safe as I possibly could be and she agreed to that. I was a horrible weekend and there were still arguing after they had a drink which did not surprised me, in the end we only stayed one night and got his parents to come and collect us earlier alls we said to my mum was that I was not feeling to good and it would be best if we went home and she seemed to accept that without much confrontation from her there was always going to be some because that is the way she was if it was against what she was expecting then she would have to have her say on it. As it happened I fainted whilst she was having ago and my fiancé Thomas said to her I told you she is not very well and it is best if she went home and got her doctor out in the end she agreed to letting us go home early but I was not going back to the hostel I was going back to my fiancé's home and that was his parents insistence that we did to and we said nothing to the hostel as far as they were concerned I was at my mum's till sometime on the Sunday, his parents said to me that I needed some peaceful time and rest before I go back there and that is what I got.

A few weeks later I found a small flat and it was not too expensive either and I loved it, it felt so perfect for us and it would be a nice start for a baby to and I accepted the flat and was looking forward to moving in the only thing was I now had to get social services approval on it because I was not yet eighteen and to my surprise they approved of it and I could move in to it as soon as it was ready but it was not going to be ready for another few weeks and by then I would have been eighteen. I was still working at the time to and no one knew that I was expecting I was keeping it very quiet but that was deliberate to.

On my eighteenth birthday Thomas met me from work with eighteen red roses I cried when I saw them he really cared and loved me and he was always showing me how much he cared and he always told me how much he loved me to.

I was glad to reach my eighteenth birthday and being out of care but before social services could close the file they wanted me to have a full medical to make sure that I was ok and I had no health problems before I was going to be going into the world on my own I was pleased that this medical was going to be done at my doctors, however I had to ask my doctor not to disclose that I was pregnant to social services and he told me that he was suppose to disclose all information he discovered but I asked what about confidentiality and what I wanted however he said this was different and I continued to disagree with him that this was not different and he should respect confidentiality of his patient, and I felt that this was my private business and my life and therefore had nothing to do with social services any more now I was eighteen. regardless of social services wanting me to do this medical which I and in the end my Doctor could not see the point in this at all so eventually he did agree not to say anything to them about the pregnancy there was no way I wanted social services in my life any longer than I wanted them in my life I felt that I had been under their control for long enough I did say to my doctor that if he did say anything to them that I would make a formal complaint about breach of confidentiality if I had to, as after all I was no longer in care officially now for the last three weeks since I turned eighteen in the end my doctor agreed with me that I was old enough now and an adult and my wishes should be taken into account and respected.

Chapter 8

A FEW WEEKS LATER MY FLAT WAS READY to move into it and it was not
that many weeks till Christmas it felt so special for me and I was excited
to have my own place. To have the security, of my own place and I felt so
safe there however it did feel strange at times especially at the beginning
with it being so quiet after all the hustle and bustle of the children's home
and to what I had become accustomed to over the last few years it was so
peaceful and safe in my new home and I felt so safe for the first time in
my life at least that is what I thought. Thomas also moved in with me he
felt that I would need looking after as I got further on in my pregnancy
and he wanted to care for me and look after me and be there for me I
felt so much love and care I was crying. I felt very privilege to have all of
this and it made me feel so very special, something I have not in such a
long time. We were even planning our wedding day but it would not be
for a couple of years yet. I then made the decision to let my mum know
where I was living and asked her to come round on her own as there was
something that I wanted to tell her I was scared that I had done that and
scared that she would bring Isaac with her however to my surprise she
did come round on her own and was delighted to know that she was going
to be a Grandma and thought that Thomas and I looked good together
and was excited about becoming a grandparent for the first time, she
stayed for several hours and it was great seeing her and having the adult
conversations like we were having and it was the most we had talked in
such a long time come to think about it that was the most conversations

we had ever had. However that was my biggest mistake asking her to come alone because she did not really come alone Isaac had dropped her off outside and went and parked up further up the road from the conversations that we were having during the afternoon, I wanted her to go home but was not sure how I could get rid of her and that Thomas came out with darling you are looking pale and tired remember what the midwife told you about plenty of rest I told him to stop fussing and that I was ok and I was actually enjoying talking to my mum however my mum took the hint and left me promising me that she would come and visit as soon as she could. I knew that he would soon know that I was expecting and exactly where I was living. Even though I had asked her not to tell him because I felt deep down that she would not keep it to herself I still asked her not to tell him but this was my mother we were talking about she cannot keep anything to herself she always did the opposite to what you asked her and she was never any good about keeping secrets, she never could and I felt that it was nothing to do with him and I did not really want him in my life, my partner's life or my child's life I was six and a half months pregnant and I was looking forward to having the child but it was not a straight forward pregnancy at all I had threaten to miscarry on three occasions and I had been admitted into hospital on a number of occasions due to different complications and reasons they told me to expect to lose this child and I was determined that I was not going to give in and accept what the hospital was telling me I was going to do all I could to prove them wrong and I would continue with the pregnancy and by I was now six and half months pregnant and the hospital was surprised that I was still pregnant. I did not expect many more complications I had a lot of problem controlling my blood sugars and my blood pressure which were a couple of reason why I was in and out of hospital but I hated being in hospital and this particular day I had just got home from hospital after yet another stay in all because of problems with my blood sugars and blood pressure and I was being pampered and I was being spoilt rotten with all my favourite things but it felt so good to have someone to care for me the way Thomas did for me and I loved him and cared for him so much to.

We had not long eaten and we were snuggling up on the sofa watching a movie that we had been wanting to watch for ages when there was a knock on the door I told him to ignore it but he said he can't do that because it could be important I told him that it probably was not as everyone we knew always rang before they came round and including his parents as they wanted me to rest as much as possible and be well and of course to have a successful pregnancy.

I told him that I would get up and answer it, I was told in no uncertain terms that I would do and was told to stay where I was after all I had just got in from hospital and I was supposed to be on complete rest for the next few days and I knew it was for my own good but already I was getting impatient about this and wanted to move around and do things but this was not allowed at all not if I wanted the pregnancy to go to full term which of course I did otherwise I would not be doing what I was told to do and that was rest. However I wished that he had not answered the door though and had ignored it like I had ask him to but he insisted that he had to open it as it could be important. I had a feeling that it was not but trouble was at our door and it was.

When Thomas opened the door Isaac was standing there and he was demanded to know where I was and he was told that I had to rest and not be upset he shouted up the stairs to me that it better not be true what my mum had told him about me being pregnant and I quick thought went through my mind saying what if I am it got nothing to do with you. He pushed Thomas out of the way and came straight into the front room. When he saw me he just went mad and Thomas just wanted to protect me and keep me safe but he got a beating for trying to protect me and our unborn child I was so scared I thought and felt that my step father was going to kill him. Thomas took a bad beating and he was laying on the floor hardly moving I was so scared that he was dead he looked like he could have been, then my step father turned on me without any warning and he dragged me off the settee and through me on the floor and as I tried to crawl away, crying as I did he then pulled me back up and before I was on my feet properly he was throwing me across the room and I was scared and crying and begging him to stop it and that there was no need for him to do this, this just made him even more angry than he was already he grabbed me by my hair and got me into an almost standing position and I was so close to the top of the stairs and the next thing I knew he was throwing me down the stairs and once I was at the bottom of the stairs he began kicking me at first just nudging me with his foot then he suddenly turned on me with full hard kicks into my stomach at first I was thinking that he would not do this but then another blow in the stomach from his foot followed by another and as time went on I didn't think he was going to stop, somehow and I don't know how how he managed this but Thomas came down the stairs to see where I was and as I was not upstairs in the flat he was worried were I was and when he heard noises at the bottom of the stairs he came running towards the noise as fast as he could I was crying but I felt so numb, Thomas was soon at the bottom of the stairs and was shouting at Isaac to leave me alone and to stop kicking and punching me, I was surprised to when he did stop, however this was only to give another beating to Thomas and he was being told that he should have known better than to come down and to try and help a slut like me and that is all I was, I could hear Thomas telling him that was not true I was loyal, kind and the most loving person anyone would love to meet, and then he was told he should have known better than he did if he did I would not have been pregnant now, I do not remember much after this I do not know what happened to Thomas at this point or where he had gone or how badly hurt he was, as I had passed out. By the time I came to I was in the hospital and in a lot of pain I kept asking what was wrong what was I doing here I also kept asking for Thomas but no-one would tell me where he was either I was very frightened, I was crying in pain and feeling that I was so alone. It seemed to take ages for anyone to tell me what was going on but I knew something was wrong as I could not feel my baby moving and I was bleeding very heavy and in a lot of pain. They were giving me so many injections for this and that and not really sure what they were giving to me and why they were, having to give me so much. They then did the scan and they would not let me see the scan which I was disappointed about which just confirmed to be what I was already thinking and feeling that something was very wrong and I was so scared of losing my baby, and Thomas, and I was still not being told what was happening they were talking in whispers it was not until the consultant came in to see me that I found out what was happening and Thomas finally came in with me he looked a mess they would not let him in until they had assessed me and knew what they were dealing with. He came and sat next to me and held me he was crying and kept telling me he was sorry for not doing more to help me, I knew he could not do any more than he had done and he had took a lot in trying to help me. He was sitting in a chair next to me holding me close to him well as close as he could do, before anything was said to us. Then the blow came I had lost my baby he had managed to kill my baby I was crying and angry about what he had achieved how dare he think that he had a right to tell me when and when I could not have a relationship or a child for that matter, he was jealous because of what I had and he wanted to make sure I did not have anything that I had however there was still bad news to come and I was terrified at what was being said to me at this moment and I did not really understand everything that they were saying to me and I did not want to hear what they were saying I still could not believe that I had lost a child because of him. However I was not able go to theatre to make this easier for me at this time and was then told that I would have to deliver my dead baby here and now I had not even accepted that I had lost my baby and now they were asking me to do something I was not ready to do and was so very scared to do. I felt just one tear stroll down my face then more and more followed one by one then many more tears it was not long before I was crying uncontrollably. I had cried a lot before I was calm enough to ask the question was there no other way for me to do this? The medical team told me not if I wanted anymore children there was not. I can't there had to be some other way but I was told again that there no other was to do this and it was the best way for me if I wanted the chance of other children and the fact that I was six and half months pregnant at this time and if I wanted to have any other children which they believed was unlikely at this time with the amount of injuries that I had received from this vicious attack on me. However they tried to reassure me that they would make it as painless as they can for both of us but I just felt so angry and then unexpectedly my stepfather came into the side room I was crying when he came in all he could ask was as she lost the baby and when he discovered that I had he was smiling and told me that my chances of having any more would be very slim now and he was pleased with himself for what he had done to me, I was shocked that he had the nerve to show up here and come into the room where I was and I started screaming get him out of here his only reply was he was staying where he was and no-one was going to make him leave. I just started screaming and crying and begging him to leave and I had not known that Thomas had pressed the buzzer to get staff into us and they came running in once they heard the commotion coming from my room and I again screamed at him to get out and leave me alone and he just stood there and told me no and that no-one would get him out of the room. I just kept demanding that he was removed and left but he refused to leave and the doctors didn't seem to understand why I wanted him out then Thomas said to them that he is the reason I'm in here and going through what I am now about to go through. They soon had him moved from the room and the ward and security was then on the ward to make sure he did not come back onto the ward or near me. What did surprise me was they did not contact the police maybe Thomas said that I had been through enough and it was not right to do that now I don't know if that was the reason but I suspect that it was. I know he just wanted to forget about what he did maybe that was out of concern for how I was and what I was about to go through and I knew he was hurting to not just from the beating but he was also losing his child to we were going through this and was going to be getting nothing at the end of it. I had not realised that Thomas had called his parents or the hospital did on his behalf and they were outside waiting to see us and they were crying. We lost something very special to us that day and not just our unborn child we lost something special between us maybe he was just angry and hurting but he would not tell me.

That evening seemed to go on forever for me and I was in so much pain and I could not understand why I had to go through this why couldn't they just put me to sleep and take it away from me but it was something to do with how pregnant I was well that is what I was told anyway I felt what I was doing was very cruel but they must have their reasons for doing things this way. However at this time I could not see what these reasons were. I did not want to deliver my child not this way and knowing that it was dead. The medical staff was kind and gentle to us but it did not take my pain away or the hurt I was feeling I was in constant tears and no one could console me or Thomas could not, and he was hurting as much as I was if not more so. His parents kept asking if they could come in and see me but I did not want to see anyone at this time, but they kept asking to see me but I didn't want to see anyone apart from Thomas it was a very long night and my partners parents were there all night and so was Thomas's parents just before our child was born I finally agreed to let my partners parents in to see me and they remained in the room with us for many hours to come. it was the early hours when our daughter was born even though she was dead and I knew she was going to be I still wanted to know what I had given birth to it was a little girl and they still tried to revive her just in case there was any hope but there was none, I was crying and I was given my child to hold she felt so soft but so cold she looked almost angel like so peaceful at this point his parents came back into the room I had not noticed that they had left the room and I thought that they was still there until he asked me if it was ok for his parents to come into the room and I agreed that this was ok for them to do. They wanted to see what should have been their grandchild they took her away from me and I just cried and cried I sobbed that day and night and no one could comfort me. Thomas stayed with me for most of this time and we were asked if we wanted to do our own funeral for her I could not answer that one and neither can Thomas but his parents did and they said they would like to deal with that one for us, they asked us what we wanted to call her and for some reason I said angel because of the way she looked and it was agreed that is what she would be called. After that it was all out of my hands and I had not been left alone since she was born I felt empty and numb.

A few hours later my mum and Isaac walked into the room and I told him to get out I was so angry I jumped out of bed and went for him but I was not suppose to get up at all and as I reached him and went to hit out at him I collapsed on the floor and Thomas was there like a shot and so were his parents and several nursing staff and again he was asked to leave my mum stayed for a few moments before she was dragged away by Isaac. My blood pressure was so low I was meant to be on complete bed rest until that picked up but it was constantly dropping and getting dangerously low they were considering taking me into theatre to try and control the blood loss I was having and were beginning to suspect that I had got some internal injuries but they were going to monitor me for awhile and see how I did but a few hours later I was in and out of consciousness and they did eventually take me into theatre I had several ruptures including my uterus that had a small rupture in it and several other ones to and once I came out to theatre and had come round they told me I was lucky to be alive and the chances of me having further children was very unlikely with the amount of internal injuries I had obtained from him and I knew that I would never forgive him for this, the thought that I may not be able to have children in the future hit me very hard and I knew I would never forgive her for betraying me and now for what he had done to me. I just cried but said to myself that one day I will prove them wrong and I would have children regardless of the consequences it brought to me I would have children I was determined and I was not going to take their word for it having a child was so important to me and it was one things I wanted more than anything else in the world.

I began to think about the last few months or so and for some reason I demanding everyone that was in the room to leave me alone for awhile, I need to sleep and rest and so do all of you it has been a long day for all of us and you should go home and rest and come back later any way I need some things from the flat for my stay in here, and finally it was agreed that I had some time on my own and the staff promised them that they would keep an eye on me whilst they were gone and would contact them if anything changes.

A few minutes after they had all gone I requested that I was taken down to the hospital Chapel and be near my daughter and it was agreed that I would be allowed to do this but I was taken down in a wheel chair and was to have someone with me at all times and I agreed to this.

I sat there in the chapel so silent and so very still and the nurse who was with me stood at the back out of the way and allowed me my time in there and allowed me quiet time to. I was praying and asking God to take care of my little Angel and to let her be with my Grandma but I was also asking why had this happened and why had he allowed this to happen I was just as angry with God for letting this happen as I was with my step father for his actions in this. I was crying and I shouted in the Chapel I shouted God please take me to I kept repeating this I just felt I could not be here without my baby.

Then the nurse came to me and put her arms around and told me that everything is going to be ok and said she felt it was time I went back to the ward when the chaplain came in and asked me if there was anything he could for me I asked him to pray with me and the nurse left and went back to the ward we prayed for almost a hour and then I asked to be taken back to the ward he took me back to the ward and sat and talked to me about my loss for a little while longer then he left as he left he told me that day or night if I needed him to come back up to see me that I should just ask the medical team and someone would contact him and he would come back up and sit with me for awhile. I was soon asleep but unsettled sleep I was in hospital for nearly ten days because of various complications. I was due to go back to the flat but could not go back there so I went home with Thomas and stayed with his family they were so good to me but they had not told me that it was the day of the funeral for my Angel but they had not called her Angel but to me she was my Angel and always would be, I felt numb and confused at her funeral I could not understand why they wanted to do this and sometimes now I still cannot but they did what they felt right to do, I felt numb but I had cried so much and exhausted myself and when we got back to their place I just sat on the floor in a corner and cried even more and I did not want anyone else near me I just wanted to be on my own and in my own space.

Not many people attended the funeral because it was meant to be a low-key funeral that was the only request that I had. My wishes were taken in account. I still could not accept that I had lost my child because of someone in my past and because of their actions to I was still very angry at him and angry at my mum for telling him where I was. But if I need my mum in my life then I would have to accept that he was going to be part of it to and that was one thing I could not accept.

A few weeks later we emptied the flat and I had found somewhere else for us both to live but he said he was sorry he could not live me again at the moment but he would still come and stay with me occasionally, he said he needed time to adjust to everything that had happened and he was finding it hard looking at me now and not seeing me pregnant he said it was ripping him apart. It ripped me apart, the time we had together became less and less and one afternoon I went round to see him and he told me he could not do this anymore I could not understand what he meant at first but he just kept saying he could not do this anymore, I loved him so much and I could not believe what he was now saying to me I just kept asking him what do you mean I don't understand what you are saying he told me he still loved me but could not be with me any more I was devastated. I could not believe this was happening to me not after everything we had just been through I could not believe he would do this to me and then he hurt me even more that he was just staying with me for the sake of our child I knew that was not the truth but he was now hurting me in a way that he knew he could and would have the biggest impact on me after all a member of my so called family had hurt him.

I left his home and just said goodbye to everyone as I always did and went to my place on my own and I was in tears as I walked home, it was raining slightly now to and tears were streaming down my face. I could not understand why this was now happening but it was, it seemed to take me ages to get home that evening and I did not walk particularly fast I was not in any hurry to get back to my place I did not care if I ever went back to my place I could not understand why he had done this now we were so good for each other I loved him so much why had everything changed so quickly, it just made me cry more and then I got angry again it was all Isaac's fault if he could just leave me alone then maybe we would have been ok and my child would not have been dead now and I would have been a mum now almost to if Isaac had not done what he had done. The pain was so unbearable and I just cried when I thought about what I had now lost and what would have been. I realised how much I had lost in such a short space of time why was the place we live in such a cruel world maybe I was being tested in some way if I was I just wished I knew why and why did I have to pay such a high price for it?

As I approached my front door I saw a car parked outside and not one that I recognised either and I was still crying. And as I got to my front door I heard someone calling my name behind me I tried to ignore it at first but I couldn't it was Isaac he told me that it had took awhile to track me down and he wanted to talk with me I told him I don't want to talk with him and I turned to walk away from him and he grabbed my arm and I told him to get off me and I was so angry at him for what he had already done to me but at the same time I was scared what he was going to do to me now.. I turned round and kicked him and pulled my arm away but unfortunately for me I could not get away quick enough and he got hold of me very tightly and his arm was around my neck he was threatening me if I ever did anything like that again I would pay dearly for it I thought to myself that I had already paid dearly because of him. He was still holding my neck when one of my neighbours looked out of the window and asked if I was ok and somehow I let her know that I was not and before I knew the police were there and asking what was going on. I asked if it was ok for me to go into my home and they agreed that I could go inside and one of the officers followed me in but they would not allow him to follow me. I was asked a lot of questions and if I knew him I told him it was my stepfather but he was not invited or welcome here and he prevented me from entering my home. They soon had him moved away and charged him with disturbing the peace I was too frightened to say anything else to them but they told me that they can't help me unless I tell them what was going on, I was too scared to do and I did not feel that they would have not believed me anyway. I just told them I am use to it by now. The truth was I was terrified of telling them what had happened because I knew the consequences if I did and they were just not worth it for me. They soon took him away for the night regardless because of what they had witnessed themselves and the police had kept him over night and they escorted him back for his car the next day and escorted him away from me it was not long that I was packing up again and moving somewhere else I could not stay there now he knew where I was, I was too frightened and I knew the consequences of what would happen with him spending the night in the police cells a thought crossed my mind what was he going to tell my mum where he had been all night that is going to get interesting I thought but then again if she did say anything he would just beat her to he had done it so many times before to her. There was nothing stopping him coming back to mine anytime soon and I knew he would have done to.

I was very depressed at this time and regretting some of the decisions I had made including giving up my career and I was thinking is it worth me re contacting the police and seeing if they would now allow me to continue with my application form after all I had been accepted and was not far off me going for my training but I decided against that one for the time being I didn't feel I was ready to handle this one now and I was not in the same frame of mind when I first applied for this or in the right frame of mind to handle this or anything that may throw at me along the course of the career. I didn't think that I could do that now it was too soon for me but then maybe it could help me at least take my mind off things for awhile but I also knew what was expected in the training and

I knew in my heart that I could not have given one hundred percent so or that it felt right to me anymore I knew I would not have done myself any good or anyone else and I was not prepared to be carried by anyone I had to stand on my own two feet and depend on no-one and I knew if I had continued with what I always wanted to do somebody would have carried me along the way and I did not feel that was fair and I had already reside myself to the fact that was not going to happen now and it would have reminded me of what I had lost and I was not ready for that one at this time right here and now I was not and who knows maybe I would never be ready for the police force again I don't think that I ever will be either so I decided against it for the time being. I knew deep down though that I would not go back to that now or the future.

I moved out of my flat three weeks before my nineteenth birthday and moved out of the way and hopefully were I would be safe I was still speaking with my mum on the phone but I would not tell her where I was or where I lived in fear that she would tell Isaac again however this just made her angry about that, and all she kept telling me was that she was my mum and had a right to know where I was and to know that I was safe. I just kept telling her I can't tell you were I am living now and certainly not whilst you are still with him however I did promise her that I would be in touch very soon.

A week later she said to me that my birthday was coming up and were was she supposed to send my card if she did not have address to send it to so at first I told her not send me one how can I do this to her was all I kept getting from her, I should be able to give her love and trust her without worrying about what she was going to do but I kept thinking you have broken my love and trust so many times that I did not want to take the risk of her breaking it again, then came the question do you love me she asked me and I told her that I did well if you did you would trust me and give me your address. I then started to feel guilty for not trusting her but she had not given me any reason to do that and I do not know why I did but I did end up gaving her my address she just kept the pressuring and blackmailing up on me until she got what she wanted, and when I finally caved in as I always did were she was concerned I was again frightened for my safety. But I still needed my mum and still wanted my mum. I knew as soon as I had given it to her it was a mistake and it was this time a huge mistake.

Within in days Isaac was round at my place and he knocked on the door and told me that mum was on her way to see me and she had a heart attack and I had to come quick, I believed him to and went with him but he said I could not sit in the front that I had to sit in the back of his wagon because he would get in loads of trouble for having people in the wagon that was not supposed to be there so he lifted me up in the back of the wagon and pulled the door down so no one could see me in there and he got back in the driver's seat and started to drive and I seemed to be ages in the back and I knew I should have been at the hospital by now and started to panic but kept telling myself that I would be ok and he was really taking me to see my mum but deep down I knew he was not taking me to see my mum something kept telling me that he would not take me to my mum. I knew that was just a ploy to get me to come with him and he knew it would work to he knew how much I loved my mum and how much she meant to me and that I would go with him knowing that my mum was in hospital.

I seemed to be in back of the wagon for such a long time and I was feeling very scared and worried and it was not the most comfortable of places to be travelling by and I was not dressed to be travelling in the back of a wagon, I was not expecting to go out and it was warm in my place I was dressed for the summer not the winter and this wagon was so cold. Carpets and poles, not the most comfortable of items to be sitting on surrounded me and the plastic round the carpets was cold to sit on. I was wondering where we were I knew we had gone several more miles and gone out into the country somewhere but I did not have a clue where I was and I was so scared I started to cry at first it was only a odd tear then another and the tears were streaming down my face I was so scared I started to pray and hoped that I was going to be safe but I had a feeling that I was not going to be safe. Even so I kept praying, and asking God to help me but my faith was not what it was and felt my prayers would not be answered and God and no one would answer them I was on my own now. I heard the engine begin to slow and then there was nothing but silence for a while not even from the front of the cab, nothing but silence. I held my breath for what seemed ages but it was probably only for a few seconds in real time but it felt ages. Still nothing but silence, I had not heard the cab door open and did not hear any movement outside so thought he was still in his cab but a moment later the wagon door flew opened and made me jump but he dropped it behind him as he came in and told me not to be so jumpy and as long as I did what I was told no harm would come to me. I was now regretting having such a short skirt on and wished I had dressed for the weather he told me I must have known he was coming and it made things so much easier for him and he said to me that I looked good in what I was wearing and he told me I must have known he was coming round today because it looks like I had dressed for him. I asked him about my mum and he told me he said that just to get me to go with him. I went to slap him but he grabbed hold of my arm and stopped me hitting him and he knocked me down to the floor unfortunately for me I fell in such away he told me that I was getting ready for him I told him no way was he going to do anything like that to me ever again and he asked "me who the hell is going to stop me" as I was no better or stronger than my mum well I was so angry with him I started to swing my arms around to hit him and I did land a couple of hits on him but I paid dearly for doing this. He slapped me around my face and I screamed and he told me to shut up before I got some more so I kept screaming hoping that someone would walk pass and hear me then he got up and opened the wagon doors and showed me were we were he had pulled up in the middle of a field and in the middle of nowhere and then he closed the doors again he told me that it was just in case anyone did walk pass but it was very unlikely were we were. He took some rope from behind one of the roles of carpet and started to tie it to my wrist and ankles I was fighting him all the way once he had got it round one ankle I was kicking him with the other and then he pulled out a knife and I stopped fighting him instinctively and I was crying and asking him why he was doing this to me why did he have to be so cruel to me. He taken down my underwear and dropped my skirt he was stripping me bit by bit I was shaking and I was so scared of fighting him anymore he was holding the knife at my throat and by now we were lying on the wagon's floor the rope was so tight around my wrist and ankles and he undressed from his waist downwards and it was not long before he was penetrating me and he was hurting me the pain was unbearable and I was crying he told me that I was soft and weak just like my mum. I was so scared to move and I allowed him to do what he wanted I was so frightened that he was going to kill me and I believed that he would have done to, I know I should have fought him more but I knew that there was no point as the more I fought the more I got slapped and beaten up and the more he raped me. If I did not do what he said and what he wanted. All the time he was digging the knife in my throat and I was scared that I would not survive this one I really felt I would not but as long as I did what he told me I felt sure that he would not do anything to hurt me any more than he had done already. I was praying to not sure it was doing any good for me but I hoped that it was at this point my faith was not what it used to be that was going from me rapidly at least that is how I felt. I was thinking about anything apart from what was happening here and now and in this wagon, it was so uncomfortable for me and he made it even more uncomfortable for me there was very little light coming apart from the light that were coming in through the gaps around the wagon there was more than I realised to. We seemed to be ages in there I was too scared to move and I knew if I did that knife would have gone in my throat and there was no-way I was going to let him do that and kill me if anyone was going to kill me then it would be me and certainly not him, and not this way either. It was feeling cold in here now and the light was beginning to fade. I was beginning to feel that I would have been in there all night and I could not move as I had this dam rope tired around m my ankles and wrist. I could scream as he had stuffed a rag in my mouth. The rag tasted horrible and quite oily it was horrible and my mouth felt very dry and I was struggling to breathe I was beginning to panic about not be able to breathe properly but I was trying to tell myself to stay calm but it was too late for that I was panicking already and so scared I knew that one of these days he was going to kill me one way or another but I was not going to let him I kept telling myself if anyone was going to do that then that would be me not him and not whilst he was in control and doing what he wanted to do to me and here in this wagon. He eventually got off me but I was hurting so much and I was so very scared, I was in unbearable pain and I was fighting back tears. Even though he had got off me he left me tied up and gagged. He stood above me laughing at me and told me how pathetic I looked and how pathetic I am. He eventually took the gag out of my mouth and I felt so ill, I was sick in the end and he give me a slap for it and kicked me in the stomach and stood there laughing at me. He started shouting at him and I was crying but it only got me another slap and a kick. I still could not move to well he still had not untied me; I started begging him to untie me he was just laughing at me. He went to get out of the wagon and left me tied up he got out for a few minutes but it seemed a lot longer than a few minutes.

He eventually came back in and untied me; my wrist and ankles were so sore. He threw some money at me and told me that is what I'm worth and then started calling me names including a hoar, a prostitute and said that is what I was to him. I hated him so much and I swore that no one would ever do anything like this to me again how I was going to make no-one would do this to me again I did not know I was determined that I MADE sure no-one hurt me like this again. I made myself as decent as I could and he threw me out of the wagon and I did pick up the money he threw at me and there was over ONE HUNDRED POUNDS, and told me to walk back from here, I started to walk and I was crying a few tears at first then I was crying un-controllable I was already depressed from losing my child and this had just made me feel a whole lot worst. I had money he threw at me in my hand what I was going to do with it I did not know. I hated myself and hated how I felt. I was not even sure where I was but I didn't care.

It was not till I actually got to the main road I knew roughly were I was I got a good walk to do but that was fine with me I was hoping it would clear my head a bit but it didn't. I was walking along the road when a car went past me who I recognised and they did me and they stopped and give me a lift back home they asked me what had happened and I told them I did not want to talk about it and they left it at that and said to me if I did they would be there for me, thanked them but said I didn't want to talk about it and I never wanted to talk about it I was too scared to talk about it. I was due to go on shift tomorrow lunchtime and at this moment in time I did not feel I wanted to see any or face the world again.

I went into my home and just stirred around and felt very shaken and dirty, I felt so violated and scared I went to run a bath and I was too scared to answer the door and I could not see who was there I was terrified he had come back to do more to me so I ignored the door and went and carried on with my bath whoever was at the door was very persistent but I could not answer the door I was terrified it was him again. I was sitting in the bath and I was trebling and crying and I started to scrub myself clean but I still did not feel clean. I used a nailbrush to scrub myself clean but it did not matter what I did I did not feel clean. I eventually got out of the bath and got myself into my dressing gown, and went down stairs to get myself a drink but there was still someone at the door and I had a peep through the curtain to see who it was and it was a friend and one that would not go until I answered her and I did and she said I looked rough what the heck has happened to me I told her nothing I just don't feel very well, she accepted it for the time being but I knew she did not believe me she knew me to well and knew something was wrong, however she told me she could not force me to tell her but if I ever wanted to talk to her about what was wrong then I could I thanked her for her kindness and got up to make us a drink. As I got up I doubled in pain and bleeding but I knew I was I had been since I got away from my stepfather I knew he had hurt me in a bad way but to scared to do anything about it because I did not want the questions and she respected my wishes even though she was not happy with them. She was the one that went and made a drink not me. I was sitting on the sofa when she came back in and I had my feet up and she saw the marks on my ankles and said to me "ok now what is going on something serious has happened hasn't it," I started to cry and just nodded my head she told me that I need to go to the police but I could not but I could not explain why I could not but I just couldn't I was to scared of the consequences that I would receive if I did go to the police. She just held me after that and she stayed at mine all night that night but left for work as I was getting ready to leave I wanted to do some shopping before I went to work. I did make an appointment to see my GP and went to see him and I told him that I was in pain and I was hurting he said it sounds like I had an infection so he prescribed some strong pain killers and some antibiotics for me and advised me not to go to work for a few days as I needed rest, I did phone in work and said that I was not feeling to good today and would not be able to make my shift they told me what my next shift was and told me to let them know in the morning if I could make it or not.

I then went to the local pharmacy and got my prescription and then went into another one and bought a box of one hundred paracetamol and then went into boots and bought some more I had picked up a total of four hundred paracetamol and my antibiotics and the pain killers that my GP had given me. I went back to my place and just looked at what I had bought and thought what reason have I got to be in this life and I could not think of any reason to stay in this world for all I could see was pain and despair and I did not want a part of this cruel world anymore. Tears were streaming down my face I started thinking of my Grandma and being with her. The more I thought about this the more I wanted to be with my Grandma and my Angel I felt that there was nothing left here for me now. I had taken a lot of the paracetamol before I went to bed but no more than the daily dose.

I went to bed that night crying and very, very depressed. I woke up in the middle of the night and just looked at the tablets I had and started to take them one by one it was not long before I had taken all my antibiotics and painkillers from the GP, then I started on the paracetamol, then one box was soon gone I started to feel ill so went to lie down but I had to get up and going to the bathroom and I was ill so I started again with the paracetamol and soon was on the second box and I was feeling drowsy now to and feeling very numb to. It was around six in the morning now and I was in work later that day if I made it that was another question. I had already gone through my second box of paracetamol and came out of the house with the rest of the paracetmols and made my way to work and was starting my third when I arrived at work I bought myself a drink and went to sit down I threw the empty box into the bin and got the final box out of my bag and I was part way through that when one of my friends were talking to me and I was asked if I was ok I asked if he could watch my bag whilst I went to fetch myself another drink and he agreed to watch my bag whilst I went to get myself a drink, I got served with my drink and the young girl that served me asked me "if I was ok" "I told her I was. Why? Do you ask" and "she replied that I look like death." I just smiled and walked away and went to sit back down, my friend who was waiting near my table asked me if I was ok to he said, "I don't look to good." "I told him I would be fine." He was one of the security staff at MacDonald's and he was constantly coming back to me to see if I was ok, I must have looked dreadful for him to keep coming back to see if I was ok maybe he was just being a good friend, everything was starting to look blurred to me and I was very drowsy and feeling very sick. I was still taking paracetamol at this time and drinking my drink. I had the paracetamol in my hand and I'm not quite sure what happened but there were suddenly a number of people around me. A lot of them left me very quickly someone said I had just fainted and there was nothing to see. I was still not with it but I was talking but only just. I know my friend saw what was in my hand and discreetly took them out of my hand and went to the manager's office at the back of the restaurant and I know what was left was counted and there was only forty six left in the box I was then taken through to the staff room and all staff that was in there was asked to leave. I was being asked questions but was not sure what I was being asked I was answering but not sure what I was answering it was a strange feeling I know they were trying to keep me awake. I did not want to be kept awake I wanted to go to sleep forever.

The ambulance was there now to, and they also were talking to me and asking me questions but could not really answer them, I heard them saying this is more than just fifty two paracetamol and they took me to hospital with the lights and sirens flashing. I was in and out of sleep and I was given this and that and poked here and there and was given so many different things but I did not know what I had been given, but what they give me made me violently sick and this went on for what seemed hours it was hours. I was then allowed to go to sleep and I did but I was crying I did not want to be here and felt they should not have done what they had done they took my choice away from me but I now had to accept that I was still here for now well that is what I thought anyway. I was in the hospital for a several more hours yet and most of that time I just slept and when I awoke it was the next day and I was allowed to go home but before I left the asked me if I would like to talk to a physiatrist and I told them I don't need to see any shrink I just want to die. I left the hospital feeling very weak and very depressed I also knew that I had more paracetamol at home. I knew though that there was not that many left though. My head was pounding and I felt very dizzy how I managed to walk home I would never know. I had to keep stopping on my way home and sitting down to stop myself fainting it seemed to take me ages to get home but I did not want to be going home I wanted to be somewhere else.

Once I got home I kept thinking what the hospital said to me that I was lucky that there would not be any permanent damage to me but a few more tablets then that would have been a different outcome for me. I went to take a couple of paracetamol for my headache but I could not tolerate them that had something to do with the drugs and stuff they had given me to counteract what I done. I went and laid down on my bed and I just cried.

I was off work for the next week on sick leave and to give me time to recover and get back on my feet.

It was soon time for me to go to work again and I was glad to be back at work but I was being watched very closely for awhile but they were very supported of me and made sure that I was ok and that if I need to talk to someone then they could sort something out for me. It was nice to have people there that cared enough about me even if it was just work colleagues.

Whilst I was working I got a phone call from my dad asking me if I had got the invitation to Donna's wedding and I told him that I had not and was not sure if I could make it anyway but it was for a few days time and I told him that I could not get the time off work to go as it was to short notice but I asked my boss anyway and he said I could take the three days off as long as I made up for it later when I got back because now he had to find someone to cover my shifts for the next couple of days I hated working were I was but it was a job and it got me out of the house for awhile. I hated working there so much. The day of Donna's wedding I could not get up to see her get married but I could get up for the evening reception, that day after my shift ended and I was going to be travelling up straight away if I could get a train that got me there at a reasonable time and there was one in about forty minutes time that I could get on. It would get there with not a lot of time to spare but at least I was there for the reception and she was so pleased to see me all of them were and were glad that I could make it for them, the reception went well and I was introduced to all her friends and saw some people that I had not seen in such a long time the reception was soon over and we were heading back to my dad's place. At this point sleeping arrangements had not been sorted out I was offered the single bed that was in my dad's room but I said no to that so I was then offered the sofa which what I took it did not feel right having the single bed in my dad's room. The sofa was comfortable enough I had slept on much worse and much less to I had been known to sleep on the floor many times and on occasions to sleep rough and in doorways. So this sofa was not that bad and it was somewhere to put my head down for the night and at least it was warm. It took me ages to get to sleep and I when I did I did not have restful sleep it was very unsettled sleep and I had some nightmares to which I had not had for a while now and I was constantly waking during the night. I did eventually settle for a couple of hours but that did not last for long. I must have gone into a deep sleep as I had not heard anyone come down or come into the living room where I was my dad had come in and was sitting on the floor next to me I felt something on me but thought I was dreaming at first but I felt something deep down telling me this was no dream and something was happening to me and I awoke up suddenly and my dad was only in his dressing gown and that was un done to and he was not wearing anything underneath it and I felt scared and things from when I was younger was flashing through my mind I could not believe that I was in this position or situation again but I was and I was not sure what to do, I felt to numb to scream or shout out and felt in shock to. I thought that I had chosen the right option about sleeping on the sofa but obviously I was wrong on that on I suppose that was my mistake sleeping alone and downstairs. My dad's hands were all over me and he was pushing more than he had done when I was a child I had slept in very little the night before but my underwear was very quickly removed and I was laying on the sofa naked in front of my dad and I felt very embarrassed and extremely scared something felt different this time to when I was a child but I could not say what felt different something just did. The next thing I knew my dad was laying on top of me and I could see and feel how aroused he was and before I knew it he was penetrating me and he told me that he had waited a long time to do this and he could now as I was over eighteen and I could legally have sex now which is why he waited so long to do what he was now doing to me I felt so violated and so dirty it was bad enough what he had done to me when I was younger but to do this now I couldn't believe that he wanted to do this to me I hated him even more. I felt numb and I could not move it felt like it was happening to someone else and not me.

I had the choice of two trains to take back home and I was originally thinking of the later one but now I wanted to get the early one and get out of there as fast as I could that morning even if it meant that I was sitting round in a train station for awhile I just knew I had to get out of there as fast as I could and get away as far as I could and that is what I did, after he got off me he asked me what time my train was and he would take me to the station and he did take me to the station and on the way he told me that what he had done he had waited so long to do and it felt so good to him I wanted to hit him and scream at him but I could not say anything to him. I just sat there in silence and feeling numb. How could a father do this to a daughter your own flesh and blood? How could anyone do this to anyone?

I was so relieved to get to the station and get on the train and be away from him he came up on the platform with me to see me off I started to get angry I could feel it building up inside of me but I did not let it go my train was there moments later and I got on but my dad had to give me a hug and a kiss before I boarded on the train I felt myself cringing at that and I quickly got onto the train and found a seat I was looking over my shoulder in case he got onto the train but he did not thank goodness and to my relief he did not. I felt panicked and scared and I felt a single tear then more came until they were streaming down my face and I no longer could stop them coming. I was not sure why I was crying I was not sure if it was because of what had happened or because of anger maybe it was a mixture of everything that had happened. It was a relief when the train was moving away and I felt safe again well as safe as I could be at his time I was not really sure that I would ever be safe again.

It seemed to take me ages to get back home but it gave me plenty of time to think and wonder what I would do next. Even when I got back home I did not know what I was going to do I felt numb and very withdrawn and very scared.

I could not believe that he would do something like this to me again I couldn't believe he always wanted to do what he had just done and why because I was over eighteen had that made any difference. Surely it was still wrong what he had done to me or was it I kept asking myself I was not so sure of anything anymore. There was so much doubt in my mind maybe it was my fault, maybe I had deserved everything that had happened to me or was it my punishment I asked myself. I felt it must have been he was still my dad after all surely that made it wrong, it felt wrong to me so it must have been wrong. Why it felt wrong I do not know but it did, I also felt that it was my fault and this was my punishment. I felt numb for many days and I was very quiet at work and I was constantly being asked if I was ok and how did the wedding go, I just told those that asked me that the wedding was lovely but I have got a lot on my mind and I just want to get on with my job. I was left alone and Left to do my job, My dad phoned several times whilst I was at work and when I was told that there was a phone call for me I always asked who it was and told them to tell him that I can't take personal phone calls at work and I would contact them when I finish which the management did then I was called into the office to ask what the problem was and why I could not take the phone call I just told them that it was personal and I thought that you would be pleased that I had not took the phone call but it just got me more grief and it was grief that I did not need. I was not working there that long after that but in a way I was relieved not to be working for them again, but things went from bad to worse for me I spent a lot of time going from place to place and spent some time on the streets with nowhere to go then I got a place that I really liked but once again I told my mum were I was as always she told my stepfather and before long he was round at mine wanting what he always wanted from me and I felt I could not get away from him no matter what he did but he left before he could get what he wanted and he was not pleased and told me I would pay dearly next time he came round. I was frightened of him and I knew next time he came round he would be more aggressive and violent towards me. I hope that would be a long time in coming.

Chapter 9

I was soon moving out of Leicester and moving away from that area and hopefully a new life and new beginnings and I knew that I did not ever want to go back ever again well not to live but one day I hoped that I would be able to go back and visit the few friends that I had left there now. I needed to be away from here and everything that had happened to me over the last few months and years. I wanted to move on with my life and start all over again well that was my intention that I would be starting all over again and hopefully have much more peaceful life to what I had, had so far in my life well one can hope that this will happen can't they?

I knew a couple of people that lived in Derby, it was not that long after I made my decision to go that I made contact with them and asked them if they would mind putting me up for awhile and they said that they would gladly do this for a short time. I was shortly moving to Derby. I was nineteen and three months when I moved to Derby and it was not long before I found work, working in a hotel as a breakfast waitress and it was not that long before I was working a lot of extra hours and no longer just the breakfast shift. I was enjoying the work but not the long hours but it paid my bills and some money in my pocket. Which was fine for me and it was a nice job but tiring however, I did enjoy it even though it was hard work it was the cycle ride to work and back that I had enjoyed the most as this was a time that was my time and I was free.

Whilst I was with my friends, my step father came to visit me I was so shocked to see him there and I was so scared and I was annoyed with my mum for telling him where I was she promised me that she would never tell him I should have known better for her to keep it to herself where I was. He told me I had to go with him and I refused to go with him and then told me that my mum was in hospital with another heart attack so I asked him which hospital and he told me she was in casualty at the Derbyshire Royal Infirmary and she was going to die and this could be my last chance to see her. I was adamant that I would not go with him I did not trust him and after what he did to me the last time there was no way I was going to go with him, I would have rather have got the bus into town or I would walk rather than go with you, but I would go and see her, He was furious that I refused to go with him and before I could say anything else he picked me up in his arms and carried me to his truck and I was screaming put me down I don't want to go with you and everyone was looking at me and asking if I was ok and he just shouted back at them screaming to them to mind their own business this was nothing to do with anyone else. He again threw me into the back of the wagon and shut me in I began to panic and feared what was going to happen next I started having flash backs to the last time I was in this wagon why does he have to keep doing this to me? What is it about me that makes him hurt me the way he does? I was panicking and sweating and trembling with fear, I was having flash backs of last time that I was in here and I was terrified that the same thing was about to happen again. I began looking round the wagon and when I found some rope I was even more scared than I was before, I began to cry and I had to keep telling myself that the same thing won't happen again to me and not now I was much older well I was but not by much and I thought that I was stronger now and I could fight him off better now if he tried anything, but I was so wrong on that one. I was actually worse off by trying to fight him and I got hurt even more I was so angry with him for using my mum the way he did and he knew how much I loved her and cared for her even now I still did after everything she did to me. Isaac was not very pleasant to me but then he never had been but I was trying to fight him more than I had done before but that just ended up me getting a beating, him still doing what he wanted to do to me and it also included me being tired up again but I would not lie still and I kept moving and I wanted to make it as difficult for him as I possibly could do I did not want him to do anything to me but I was going to make sure it was hard for him but the more I wriggled and fought him the more he hit me there came a point in my mind that I felt it was a waste of time fighting him whatever I did I could not win and he was going to hurt me one way or another and he did, I always felt that it was something about me why people did this to me and maybe it was. Did I deserve this and all that had happened to me in my child hood and adolescents? This just kept going through my head and again and again I asked myself the same question over and over again. I still felt violated and dirty for what was happening to me but in the end he got what he wanted, he did what he wanted to me, however once was not enough for him that day and he wanted more from me and much more than I ever imagined he would ever want from me, and I could not fight him anymore, I was scared and sore from him hitting me and him repeatedly raping me. I hated being forced into doing something I did not want to do, and what he did to me was much more than forcing me it was complete violation. I hated him more and more and I wanted him to die not my mum I was getting so angry with him doing this to me and I promised myself that one day he will pay for what he has done and continues to do to me. I was not sure how I could this, but I knew that it would always be my word against his if I went to the police or would it? I was too scared to go to the police again, but I knew somehow I had to find away to stop him raping me and hurting me like this, but I did not have a clue what or how I was going to do to stop him.

That day made me realise somehow I have got to stop him from ever hurting me ever again. He raped me every way he could during that horrible day and it was not very comfortable or pleasant for me and neither was the beating I took. By this time my nose had started to bleed and I had a cut above my right eye which was bleeding, my face was beginning to feel very sore and I could feel it swelling up. Whilst he was hitting me he was also raping me. He did not care how much he hurt me or what he did to me as long as he was satisfied himself, and with what he had done to me. He had done anal penetration before but it hurt me so much more this time than it had done before and I could not understand why it had? Well not at the time I did not. It also felt like something had torn inside me and when he came out of me and I was getting myself sorted out I was bleeding then he untied me and told me to get up and turn my back to him and learn forward I was scared he had not ask me to do this before and he took a penknife out of me and that Is what caused me to be in so much pain and to be bleeding the way I was doing. I did not know what to do but I was too scared to say anything to anyone about what I had gone through that day and I did not think anyone would have believed me if I had told anyone. How could I start to tell anyone what had happened that day and what I had been through as yet this sort of thing was not heard of and still very much swept under the carpet. I hoped that this would soon changed and you would be believed and you would be treated as a victim and treated gently when you did report acts of rape and abuse but at this moment in time you were not believed and when you did say anything it continued to be brushed under the carpet.

He told me I disgust him and that I was not worth anything and no one would want me and any way there was now to much damage to me for anyone else to want me I would disgust anyone who looked at me for the rest of my life I believed that this was true to but no one could hate me more than I hate myself right at this minute I wanted to die and no longer be in this world I felt this world would be better without me.

This time he dropped me back close to home and I looked a mess when I got in and I went straight to the bathroom and ran a hot bath hotter the better I thought and It was a hot bath and I went into the kitchen and got a new Scoller out and I started to scrub myself clean with it I scrubbed myself that much I was bleeding even more than I was doing already and then I went to bed and stayed there for a couple of days my friends kept coming up to see if I wanted anything but I did not and thanked them for their kindness I decided it was time to move out and find a place on my own and my friends said I did not have to and I could stay with them for as long as I felt I needed to be on my own for the time being I needed space and time to work this out in my own head and I was not sure that I could ever do that but being on my own was the best thing for me and for everyone around me and I was not sure where I would go but I felt that this was the best thing for me to try and be able do this at least I had my friends to come back to if I needed to. I did get a bedsit it was not a very nice one but it would serve the purpose for me and it give me the space I was looking for and I did not tell anyone were I had moved to because at that moment I did not want anyone to know where I was I did not even tell the friends that I had been staying with where I was going to be living at the start as I felt I needed to keep them at a distance to keep them safe and was not sure that was the right thing to do but I feared that Isaac would beat them to find out where I was. However in the end I did tell them where I was living as they would not leave me alone and kept asking me until I told them were I was going to be living, and they had been good to me for the last few months and I was grateful to them and they very supportive of me and they also knew that something was not right and something had happened to me but I just did not feel safe and I could not tell anyone what had happened to me I was to scared. I had also met a nice young man who at least I thought he was but I soon found out he was not so nice and we did not last more than four months but I was not going to take anyone else hitting me. I had enough of people doing that to me already and I did not need it from a partner to. I had no one who I felt I could confide in and felt very alone and I was scared to tell anyone about what had happened I was not sure that I would ever feel I would be able to tell anyone not even the friends I had stayed with. I was too scared to do I felt no one would have believed me anyway even though they saw the mess I came home in that day I still did not think they would have believed but they knew it had something to do with the visitor that I had received unexpectedly but even so I could not tell anyone I did not see the point of telling anyone it was just going to be another one of those things that I would be keeping to myself.

I had been working at this hotel for a couple of months now and I had only seen a couple of the Chefs but with working lunchtime I got to see all the chefs and there was a chef that I really liked and we got on very well and we started dating and I was already expecting and just going into the second semester of my pregnancy and I hoped that everything would run smoothly and I was scared that my mum would find out and tell Isaac and once again I would lose another child by his hands. I had already lost one at his hands and I was not prepared to lose another one or go through what I did when I lost Angel, one afternoon at work I started getting stomach pains and I ran to the ladies and discovered that I was also bleeding and I sat in the ladies crying and thinking oh no not again. I left the ladies after washing my hands and went into the kitchen and found the chef I had been seeing and he saw that I had been crying and asked if he could take a break for a few minutes and he was told he could have five minutes and no more and when he asked what was wrong I was not sure if to tell him or not but he had seen it in my face and he could see that I had been crying and at first I did not want to tell him but he asked if everything was ok with regards to the baby then I started crying again he knew then that something was wrong and that I was worried. He told me to go home and call my doctor which I had did but it did not go down very well with work but he told them that she can't be in work whilst she is being ill and it is not good for the customers to see her looking ill so they agreed that I should go home, I spoke with my doctor on the phone and he arranged for me to go to the hospital within a couple of hours. On arrival at the hospital I began to feel panic and scared and felt that I was losing another child, I was sent to a ward and shown to a bed and was put on strict bed rest in the hope to stop what was happening to me. I had been sat on the bed for several hours when I give out a scream as the pain became unbearable so quickly and without any warning. Within moments the nursing staff were at my bedside and told me that this not looking good for me and they would fetch a doctor to check me over, at first the doctor would not tell me what was wrong but something told me that I had miscarried that child. Adrian and I was moving in together and things were happening a lot faster than I ever thought that they would have done and I was putting a lot of trust in him and I was scared and feeling trapped but I loved him and before I knew it and I was expecting again and again I miscarried and I was told that I may never have children but I could not accept that and a child was something that I wanted so much that I could love and hold and have something that no-one was going to take away from me and not without a fight anyway. About a month after the miscarriage I was expecting again and I was afraid to tell anyone that I was so scared of losing another child I did not want to go through that again it would have destroyed me if I could not have any children and I did not want to tell anyone yet that I was expecting again and I feared that I would lose another one but I had to keep telling myself that this one is going to be ok and that it will go well but I was so scared

I also knew I had to keep it from my mum for some time yet if I could. A short while later Adrian proposed to me and I said yes and we planned our engagement party. I knew it was going to be hard as we were having an engagement party that weekend and all of Adrian's family knew I was expecting and they were all congratulating us and it was getting harder to keep it away from my mum but as usual she was too drunk to realize what was going on and so was Isaac it was a very strained night for me and hard to deal with I found it increasingly hard having two people in the same room whom had abused me and one of them was still doing so. It was a strange situation to be in and I spent most of the night trying to keep out of the way. Isaac kept trying to get me drunk but I was being careful not to drink too much I had a couple of glasses of wine and that was all I wanted to have I was trying to think about unborn child and I did not drink a lot anyway it just did not appeal to me that much and I had seen enough of drink to last me a life time whilst I was growing up and I really did not want to go down the same road that my mum had gone down. I was frightened that I would do if I did start to drink I knew the occasional drink was ok but I knew how easily it would be for one drink to have lead to another one, and before I would know it to and I knew if I did not have control now I would never have control and then I would have been drinking all of the time and that is something I did not want for me or for my children, I had seen enough of the effects of drinking to last me a lifetime and I had gone through enough of that to know how it feels and I certainly didn't want, my children to see their mum drunk all of the time or feel unloved and not wanted. I was determined I was not going to go down the same route as my mum.

However all through the evening Isaac kept trying to get me drunk every-time he bought me a drink even if I just wanted a coke or lemonade there was always something else in it and I could taste it to so I tended not to drink anything he bought me, and he even said to me how I am, are you feeling alright? He thought that I should be feeling light headed and drunk yet and when I told him that I was not, he seemed surprised that I was not and said that he would have to buy me more drinks because he wanted me to go to the hotel room with him whilst my mum was still getting drunk and she would not notice that we were missing and when I refused to go with him he got very aggressive with me which also drew attention from everyone else in the room which is when Adrian came over to me and told me he wanted me to meet some more of his relatives and I did, and it got me away from him which I was glad of. Next it was my mum coming over to me and asking me to sit with her for a while so I excused myself to go with her for a while but I didn't want to be with her for very long and as yet my mum didn't know I was expecting and I wanted to keep it from her for as long as possible it felt cruel but I felt I had to for my own sake and the sake of my unborn child. I was sat on a stool opposite to my mum and she was now very drunk and having problems staying upright let alone sitting on a stool the were a number of times when I thought that she was going to fall off and I found myself smiling at her. However she did not take to me smiling at her and I was thinking to myself how pathetic she looked. She was getting angry with me and began calling me names and pushing me and now she was laughing at me and telling me that I will always be a hoar and nothing will ever change that she then pushed me backwards off the stool and was laughing as she walked away and demanding another drink she turned round and shouted I am surprised anyone wants you as you are damaged property and nothing but a stupid hoar. By now I was on the floor crying and I wanted to hit back at her but I felt that there was no point in doing so she was not worth it, Adrian was now at my side and so was several members of his family helping me up and making sure that I was ok. I told them I was. My dad then went over to have words with her and told her that she would never change and she is only having a go at me because she was jealous of me that I had got someone who loved me and made me happy. She just saw read and you could see how embarrassed she was but something made her calm down and then she was asking us back into the main bar for late drinks once the party is finished we told her we would think about it.

The party finished somewhere around 1am and most people left at the end and my mum and Isaac invited us again to join them in the residents bar for awhile longer and have a few more drinks with them there was around twenty five of us that stayed on for a few drinks and even I had a drink and only one and they were all chattering for awhile and I sat there looking round at everyone that was together now and thinking to myself that it has been a long time since both my parents were in the same room as each other and they were being civil to each other instead of trying to rip each other's throats out which made a nice change for me however there were the words that they had earlier, I was not long before I had enough and I wanted to go home which, we did shortly afterwards and my dad was coming back to my place for the night and was suppose to be staying for a few more days to. My dad knew I was expecting but he was told not to tell my mum because I wanted to tell her and in my own time and as far as I was aware he had not but I did not feel comfortable with him being at my place but Adrian told me that I would be safe whilst he was with me and that I should not worry and he would be going home soon well that was not sooner enough for me, I wanted him gone home and I actually regretted asking them to the party and regretted having my dad to stay I felt very uncomfortable with him being there and it was one of those occasions where I felt obliged to have my parents there and it also give me an idea what it would be like on my wedding day. A few days later my dad decided to leave and go back home and it was a relief for me when he was gone but I felt sad to in a way in a strange sort of way I was getting use to him being around and I was going to miss having a parent around but I did not trust him at all. Adrian had gone back to work and it was nice to have some company throughout the day for a change. I did not feel safe whilst my dad was there and I was not sure what he was going to do next even when he gave me a hug I cringed I did not want him anywhere near me. I was relieved when he had gone home and I felt safe in the house on my own again but the thought that he would be back down again soon filled me with fear.

A few days later Isaac turned up and he was not being very pleasant to me and was not pleased that I would not go to his hotel room with him, on my engagement party and he told me that I was about to pay dearly for this and it was going to be right now. I was scared again especially knowing I was expecting a child and as yet he did not know, and I had no intention of him finding out well not if I had anything to do with it. There was no way I was going to tell my mum either as I knew that she would have told him as she always did and I knew she could not keep anything to herself. Somehow he always had a way of finding out but I do not know how he found out things but he did. He was a nasty as ever with me and as violent as ever and I kept holding my stomach in a protected way and he asked me if I was pregnant but I just denied it and I said that I had, had a upset stomach for the last couple of days but he called me a liar and he was right but I was trying to protect my baby and I was scared that I was going to lose another child at his hands. I don't know where I got the strength from that day but somehow I did and after he violated me I screamed at him to get out and he said I should not be so fiery and he would go in his own time and when he had finished with me I yelled at him that he had five seconds to get out or I would call the police he told me that I did not have the guts to do that if I had done I would have done it by now, However I ran out of the room and grabbed my phone and I started to dial 999 I had put in two nines before he got to me and he still told me that I would not have the guts to put in this last digit but I did and I had done unfortunately before I could say anything he grabbed the phone off me and said that one of the children had grabbed the phone and was playing with it and apologised and told them that this had happened and he would make sure that it would not happen again. He soon left the flat though and that was the last time he actually did anything to me but it was not the last time he tried to do anything to me but after that day I felt stronger and more able to stand up to him but I was terrified that he would have got even more nasty than he already had done. I don't know where this strength came from maybe it was to do with protecting my baby I don't know.

When Adrian got in from work I was in a lot of pain and I was bleeding I felt I was going to lose another baby and I was taken to hospital and put on strict bed rest and to see how things were going and I was checked and my child was monitored very closer and I was to stay in hospital for several days but I did not lose my baby this time. The heartbeat was strong so I felt that my child had a chance and I hoped that it would stay that way to. However I did threaten to miscarry on several occasions after that and each time I thought that I would lose another child,

But thank-fully I did not but it was not a pregnancy without problems and complications. Two months into my pregnancy I got engaged to my partner and we had set the date of our wedding, which was to be the 2nd June 1990. I eventually delivered late and I give birth to a son and that was the proudest day of my life holding my child in my arms. Adrian was present when our son arrived into this world and he looked so proud, due to the number of complications after delivery I was to remain in hospital for a few days yet, but I was reassured that these things sometimes happen and not to worry, I began to get very tearful and feel very alone and isolated but I kept telling myself this was stupid I should be so happy I finally got the child I had always wanted that horrible day kept going through my thoughts. When I went home I felt I did not belong there and Adrian was working long hours and I was left alone for very long periods with Daniel, I loved Daniel so much but felt I could not provide for him or love him the way I should have done. As the weeks and months went by I felt this more and more and at the same time I was planning my wedding day. I felt so isolated and so scared and did not know which way to turn. My dad was also living with us now to he came to stay for a while at first then told me he was not going back up to Blackburn as now he nothing to go back for and everything he had was right here with me and my son and my future husband, I never believed that was the only reason but he had been in court recently before coming down to us and I think it had something to do with that why he was now living with us, Maria had not long pressed charges against him for indecent assault on her by my dad and as soon as that was over he was at mine and the next thing I know he was living with us long term it was very hard and stressful for me to have him there with us and I found this so hard and emotionally and physically to he was constantly undermining my confidence and made me feel that I was not coping and I was not good enough to be a parent he started working with Adrian so in the end they were both working all hours and I was left on my own so much and I was frightened that I would fail my son and family. I was also getting a lot of grief from my mum to do with the wedding and she was not going to be there if Peter was invited to our wedding and my dad was saying the same but I wanted all my family to be there but in the end I had to make an uncomfortable choice and not invite my brother Peter to my wedding however I did send Peter an invitation to Peter for my wedding behind my parents back but he declined as he did not want to be there with either of our parents and I found this very hard and afterwards Peter told me he did not want anything further to do with me. I obviously wanted my parents after everything they had done to me.

The run up to my wedding did not go smoothly my mum was constantly hassling me and saying she wanted me to do this and that on my day and she wanted to have more say in what I wanted but in the end she allowed me to do the wedding I always wanted to have I did not want to do it the way she wanted me to have it as it did not feel like it was my wedding if I had done it her way it felt more like her wedding and I wanted my wedding day to be the way I wanted it to be and not have my day through someone else's eyes and how they would have got married. It did not go by smoothly the weeks up to our wedding day there were a lot of problems that I had to deal with as well as looking after a small child by the time the wedding day came round I was having serious second thoughts and nearly backed out of getting married but I did not and went through with it and Daniel walked behind me and he was only nine months old. The day went reasonably well but there were was problems during the day for me but no one knew anything about them I kept them to myself and told no one. The wedding breakfast was very nice but were ever I went I was being followed and I found this very uncomfortable Isaac was there whenever I turned around he was there and it really got to me and upset me. It was not long before the evening reception started and all our friends were arriving but again I was feeling uncomfortable and my mum had too much to drink and was beginning to shout and embarrassing me she started shouting because I would not allow her to look after Daniel overnight and to pay for a room in her hotel for Adrian and I but I did not feel that this was appropriate for her to look after Daniel or us to be in the same hotel as her I did not feel safe so I refused her offer, and then she suddenly went quiet and Shouted she was leaving and not staying were she was not wanted and she was shouting at me and Shouting that I did not trust her to look after my son her grandson and she was right I did not and certainly not in the state she was in but more to the point I did not trust Isaac with my son. It was a relief when she left the celebrations and I began to relax somewhat and enjoy the evening I was still asking myself if I had done the right thing in getting married and was beginning to think that I had made a huge mistake but I felt that I was in a marriage now and there was no-way I could do anything about it and it was too late to change things now I was just going to have to put up with it and that I was going to have to make the best of it no matter what. We left the reception sometime around 12.30 am. I took Daniel and now husband back home and we travelled home by taxi with the compliments of where we had our reception, which was so nice of them. I put Daniel to bed and got change and went straight to bed and I laid on my side crying and when Adrian climbed into bed with me he thought that I was asleep and he just laid there with his arm around me unaware that I was crying. Our son woke us up somewhere around eight the next morning and We had to go back to the reception to pick up our gifts and take them home it was strange going back there and picking everything up it was hard to believe that day was over and we were now married once we had done that we were going to be going down to my in-laws for the day it really annoyed me that we were going down there but it was what we did every Sunday and this Sunday was no different and it was expected of us to go down. We did not have a honeymoon. I had just over a week in the flat with my family without my dad being there, which was not that long really but it was all I was going to get for a while. Time down the in-laws was hard for me and I felt an outsider when I was there but then again I always did even before I got married but it was something that I was going to have to put up with and accept that this was going to happen and there was nothing I could do to change this it was just something else that I was going to have to put up with for the rest of our marriage.

I felt frightened being married it felt like I could not make any decisions for myself anymore and I was being controlled again, I had to ask permission to go out or go and see a friend and I felt I had to ask permission to breathe I did not like this at all but something I was not going to change or had the confidence to change either. I had to make the best of a situation that I was now in and I regretted not going with my instincts on the wedding day and not getting married at all.

Daniel's first birthday soon came round and all my in-laws were round for his birthday and again I felt like an outsider in my home.

Postnatal depression was still hitting me hard and I was still on medication for this and was told that I would be on them for a while. I did not want to stay on them for that long as I wanted more children and I knew that this sort of medication could harm an unborn child and that is something I did not want to have to happen so I began talking to my GP and discussing about coming off them he told me I could but I am not ready to come off them yet but because I wanted another child it was agreed that I would come off them in six months time and cut them back in the mean time. So this is what I did when I was finally off them my

GP warned me that I would end up back on them when I have another child because I am not ready to have been taken off them yet and that it could be much worse for me next time and I was still very depressed and tearful.

At about a month after coming of the medication I discovered I was expecting my second child. Seven weeks into my pregnancy I missed carried and I was devastated about losing another child however it was not long before I was expecting again but again several times I threaten to miscarry again but fortunately for me I did not and give birth to a daughter almost three weeks and three days late I delivered her on my own and it was the special time that I had with her and I feel it give me a bond with her that I had not got with my first child. Adrian and Daniel came to visit me sometime early in the morning and Daniel was delighted to have a baby sister and my husband was also delighted and it was not long before all his family was there visiting and I just wanted to scream and tell them all to leave me alone and give me some peace but that was not to happen when one of the midwives came round during visiting hours they asked everyone to leave the ward for awhile whilst she checked me over and it was such a relief when they had left the bed and the ward for while and she did check me over and discovered that my womb had collapsed within in itself and they was going to put me on me on strict rest and I had to have several injections throughout the day and massage to help stimulate the uterus to go down normally and the next few days to stop this happening if she had not found this I would not have been able to have any more children and I would have had to have surgery on top of delivery my daughter and my visitors were asked to limit their visiting for the next few days which did not go down very well with the in-laws or Adrian and he started to have ago at me because they were on restricted visiting for twenty four hours he was so angry with me and was shouting at me and get very aggressive towards me when the midwife came down and told him that it was nothing to do with me but the medical teams decision and I need to have plenty of rest. He was not having any of it in the end they asked him to leave to calm down which he did and stormed out of the ward taking his family with him he would not even let me say goodbye to Daniel which hurt me terribly and after he left I was crying and I cried for ages but then the midwife came round and gave me the injection straight into the womb

224

through the top of my stomach and it hurt like hell and she said it would only hurt a little how wrong she was. It hurt more than a little it hurt a lot and I cried with the pain but she said it would soon feel numb and she was right it did but I was also given some pain killers to help make me much more comfortable. I cried for a long time after they had all gone and it was noted on my records that I was beginning to get baby blues and postnatal depression and was being looked after and kept an eye extra close eye on.

The Next day Adrian and Daniel came to visit us early on in the morning and around mid morning all his family was back and they stayed for the rest of the day with the exception to them popping out for something to eat and drink and the occasional cigarette which I could smell when they came back and it turned my stomach with the smell.

It was a very tiring day and I was feeling very overwhelmed by having everyone there all day and I could not get any rest and I was still on regular injections to which made me feel very drowsy and sleepy but I had that days to go through and that was all I was going to need at least that is what I hope that I would not need anymore

Shortly after the injection I began to cry and I was told that I was being soft and a baby and to pull myself together and grow up. I was so mad with the midwife that in the end I screamed at them to leave me alone and go away which brought several midwives running to see what was going off and they saw how upset I was and asked everyone to leave and they suggested that they come in small numbers and only two around the bed at any one time in the future.

They didn't like it but they accepted it but I knew I was not going to hear the last of it when I got back home I knew I would get a grilling about it. They just could not understand that I needed the rest and I didn't need all the visitors at once, my mother in-law looked very embarrassed and very angry and I had seen that look in her before and I knew that there would be consequences from this for me.

I was glad when they all had gone and left me in peace and just as I dosed off a doctor came round to examine me to see how the injections were doing and he seemed very happy about how I was doing and said

I should be able to go home tomorrow if I wanted to. I did but I was scared and the condition was that I got plenty of rest once I was at home and warned me what to look for just in case things were not as settled as they had hoped and that it could still collapse so I was suppose to be extra careful

I was so pleased when the next day had arrived that I was able to go home which meant I was going to be home for my birthday, which was the following day. Adrian and Daniel came to visit me not knowing that I was able to go home and they were so pleased to hear that I could go home but I would be kept a close eye on for several weeks to make sure everything was as it should be. I was waiting my paper work for me to be discharged and I was taken downstairs in a wheelchair I felt so embarrassed about going in a wheelchair to the car park. Meanwhile once I got back home everything started to go wrong for me I was had a go at for not stopping the nursing staff from asking them all to leave and that they had a right to be there and getting to know our daughter and was told that they are all coming back up later and will be staying till very late and I was expected to cook a meal for everyone when they got here, I did not want his and a certainly did not feel like having a load of visitors and cooking for them I felt that this was so unfair.

I was in considerable amount of pain and discomfort and so far some of the things that I was told that should happen so far had not happened as yet but this pain I was in was nothing like I was in whilst in hospital I doubled over in pain and Adrian told me not to be so soft and he wanted sex with me that night and that was the last thing that I wanted and so soon after delivering. One of the things the hospital warned me to look out for was clots and large ones more particularly and I was supposed to contact them if anything like this happened I felt I was in labour all over again and I was screaming with pain and I kept getting told to be quiet and stop being mardy, a few moments later there was a knock on the door and I thought that the in-laws and everyone was arriving but it was not it was a midwife checking that I was ok and she demanded that Adrian helped her to get me on our bed as she wanted to examine me to make sure I was ok which was obvious that I was not and on examination she discovered the clot that was coming away and told me this is why they give me the injections in hospital to prevent this and she had to give me another injection to release this clot and she had to take it away from examination for the hospital laboratories and it came back that I got an infection. When the midwife left Adrian told me that I had to get up and do what was expected for me I felt I could not make any decisions of my own anymore and felt I had to ask permission to do anything including going to the bathroom. I felt exhausted and very uncomfortable and in unbearable pain.

It was not long before his family was arriving and I had been crying and they told me to pull myself together and stop be so childish I have only had a baby and was reminded that it was a good job that I was not around during the war as parents back then, had a baby and got on with things regardless of what happened. I was then asked what I was doing for tea and I told them I don't know what you are all having but I am having a chicken, which did not go down very well at all. It was gone eight in the evening when everyone left and I felt exhausted and in a lot of pain and my daughter Robin had been feeding a lot during the day which had not gone down very well as it meant that she was not being passed from person to person all day long and it did not help that they were all smokers and I felt very chesty when they left and it took ages to get rid of the smell of smoke after they gone and this is one thing I had words about with Adrian that he should ask his family not to smoke in our home and the reply was they would smoke were ever they wanted and would not speak with his parents especially about this which made me so mad.

We had eaten late that evening I bath my children and got them ready for bed and read a story to Daniel whilst I was feeding Robin which was nice for all of us and give me quality time with both my children my son as usual fell asleep cuddling up to me. I finished feeding my daughter and put both my children to bed and went and had a relaxing bath myself and went to bed and I was intending to be asleep before my husband came to bed I was afraid that he was going to force the issue of what he wanted and I was not ready to give him what he wanted and it was only four days since I had delivered Robin and did not want anything else at this stage which he could not understand that all he could think of was what he wanted and not what anyone else wanted. I was crying silently and letting the tears run down my face and onto my pillow and I felt

Adrian climb into bed next to me but I laid there very still and afraid to move and I was hoping that he would have left me alone thinking I was asleep but that did not happen unfortunately for me. He pulled me into him and I could feel that he was aroused and I knew what he wanted but I was not ready for that yet I needed time to recover from giving birth to Robin and I did not feel that the time was right to be doing this. Unfortunate for me, Adrian felt and thought differently and what he wanted he was determined to get regardless how I felt or what I wanted. I did not fight him as much as I should have done and the discomfort and pain I was already was made worse with what he was doing to me he kept telling me to relax and calm down and enjoy what he was giving me I felt he was taking something from me that I did not want to give at this time and I asked him to stop on a number of occasions but he said it was his right to have this and he was not going to stop until he had release and had ejaculated once he got off me I got up and went to the bathroom and started to scrub myself clean I felt so violated and very scared and I was bleeding very heavy now and I was not before. I climbed back into bed and rolled on my side. I faced away from him and began to cry but not loudly just silent tears and I hated him for what he had just done to me and I felt I would never escape from my childhood or this but this was something I now had to put up with, as I did not believe I could leave or divorce Adrian I wanted to be different to my parents and make this work were they had failed I wanted to succeed if that was ever going to be possible and I hoped and prayed that it was. At this moment I was not so sure that it was possible but I was determined to give it my best and give everything into my marriage and this relationship regardless of what this would cost me personally.

It took me a long time to recover from having my daughter and I was very down and constantly in tears and three months later my next child was on the way it was not a straight forward pregnancy and another child that I lost in the very early days and once again I was told that I would not be able to have any more children but I was determined to prove them wrong once again It was not long before I was expecting again, I was scared about being pregnant again and I was scared that I was going to lose another child and a few months later I lost another child which I was devastated about. It was not long before I was expecting again though and I was terrified of losing another child and I did not want anyone to know at first that I was expecting again I just could not cope with their pity if I lost another child. It was a difficult time for me and I had threaten to mis-carry four times during the pregnancy but thankfully for me I did not and in April a day after I was due I was frightened when I saw that I was bleeding I looked out of our kitchen window and saw that the midwives were still in the building behind my flat and I went round to get their attention it took me awhile but I was persistent with my knocking on the window that one of them heard me and told me to come in and asked me what the problem was. I told them that I was due yesterday and that I was bleeding they quickly checked me over and was concerned that the placenta was beginning to detach it's self and sent me home and told me to get my case and a few extra bits and that they would send an ambulance for me and I had just got back into my flat and to tell Adrian what was happening and there was a knock on the door I was surprised it was the ambulance crew they got there very quickly, they tried to reassure me that I would be ok and not to worry but the more I was told everything would be ok the more I worried.

Once at the hospital I was put on a number of monitors and was examined a number of times by different doctors and they all came to the same conclusion that my placenta was detaching so as I was due they decided that the best intervention for me would be to induce labour. It was a long labour and longer than any of my previous two labours it would not have been as long if my baby did had not pulled its head back and rested it on my pubic bone where she got it stuck and that is where it stayed for the next thirty hours. I was worried as they were constantly checking my baby's oxygen levels and they were dropping rapidly I was warned that if they dropped any lower they would have to take me theatre and perform a caesarean section on me if it dropped any more they did a further two test within the half hour and it dropped in each one of them so it was decided that I would have to have a caesarean and I was taken into theatre a short while later I was terrified of losing another child and felt that this was a high possibility. Adrian had gone home with Daniel and Robin and it left my in-laws there to stay with me I was not to pleased with that one and the mother-in-law was in theatre with me when my child was born and as soon as they pulled her out she began to cry and that made me cry, the surgeon told me that I had got a fighter there and I smiled, I was shown my daughter very soon and I felt overwhelmed and love for her. I was not allowed to hold her straight away but I did about ten minutes later. I was soon on the ward and being made comfortable and given extra advice on how to feed my daughter easier and more comfortable for me. It was not long before Adrian, Daniel and Robin was coming to see me and I was so pleased to see my children and my children climbed onto the bed to cuddle me but I winced as they got on my bed as I was in so much discomfort. However it was good to have them in my arms again and they were delighted that they had got a little sister. They had done a drawing for me before they came to see me and it was a picture they had drawn with me, them and the new baby on it. I saw this and it made me cry.

Adrian was having a go at me I was getting use to this now but it did not make it any easier to take it from him. I was in hospital for over five days with my daughter Jade and by the time it came for me to go home I was glad to be going home and being in my own surroundings.

As the weeks went by I was getting further and further depressed and more tearful and feeling unable to cope and felt that I was a useless mother and not worthy to have my wonderful children here or deserved to have them I felt unworthy to be a mum and felt that I had already let them down. I did not feel worthy as a person or as a wife. We were also moving out of the flat and into a house now that the third child has been born and for weeks after her birth I was packing up the flat and moving home and it took it out of me as I could not do half the things that I needed to do but I was having to be careful in how much I did and I was trying to feed my daughter and move house at the same time as well as recovering from surgery. We almost moved from the flat to the house in the same day there was a few things we had to get on the Sunday but apart for a few things we had moved in the day and it took us hours and I was exhausted and in a lot of pain and discomfort I knew I had already done it but I did not know to what extent I had until I sat down for a few minutes and I put my hand across my lower stomach and discovered that I was bleeding very badly I had torn my scar and opened the wound up again I just cleaned it up and put one of the dressings that I had from the hospital and I planned to go and see the GP in out of hours the next day but I did not go and see him I got them out to see me in the end he told me that I would be ok and I needed to have plenty of rest and asked if I had a first aid kit which I had and asked if I had got any steri-strips in it I said I was not sure if I had or not but I had and he put them across my wound and told me to keep a dressing on it for a few days and give me a prescription for some anti-bio tics and more dressings which I collected the next morning or rather I did not I got Adrian to collect them because I could hardly move. However during that evening after the doctor had left he started having a right go at me telling me that I was so stupid for doing as much as I did and he slapped me round the face and walked out of the room for awhile I just sat down on the sofa and cried and hugged my children and fed Jade. In the middle of feeding my daughter I got my other children ready for bed and they sat either side of me and snuggled next to me whilst I continued feeding Jade it was lovely having all my children with me and being so close to me as they were at this time all of a sudden one of children got up off the sofa and went to fetch a book and asked me to read it and I said ok but not for too long as mummy is very tired but I knew that they would not be long before they went to sleep once I started to read to them it never took them long to fall to sleep with story and I was right it did not take them long and I only read a few pages to them to. Adrian came back in the room at this time and took our children up to bed and I continued feeding my baby. I was surprised how long I had been feeding her for and it was longer than I thought it was too but I was hoping that the move would not upset her sleeping pattern too much and she had been sleeping through since a few days old. I was lucky on that one. It was not long before I was putting my daughter in her carry cot and settling her down for the night by now it was gone ten in the evening and I was shattered and I was going up to bed in a little while and I was hoping for a peaceful nights rest and Jade was not unsettled in the new place or any of my children for that matter. It was not my children who had an unsettled night but me and what was going on in my room and I was not sure what to do I was feeling very frightened and unsettled and Adrian was not helping matters he hit me that night and raped me on more than one occasion that night he kept telling me that it was my duty and his martial right to have what he wanted from me and the more I struggled and fought him the worse it was for me including being hit I was very sore from having my daughter and still got the stitches in from having the caesarean and I was scared that I was going to have further injuries from what he was doing to me and I would have further complications. When he finally finished having his "so called marital rights" I rolled onto my side with my back to him I let tears go whilst I was holding Jade's hand as she was laying beside me I could not believe that Adrian would do this to me and I did not know what to do as I loved Adrian so much and I always said that I would honour my marriage vows forever and I would never leave him or get divorced as I did not want to be like my parents well that is what I believed and thought anyway. The next morning when I awoke the first feed which was around five thirty that morning and my daughter soon went back to sleep and so did I. I was later awoken with breakfast and a cup of tea and a smile from Adrian and an apology and a promise that he would never do anything like that again I was not so sure that he would not but I loved him and I forgave him but I was now starting to fear him and felt that history was repeating itself again and that it was something about me that made people do this to me.

When Jade was six weeks old we moved from the flat into a house which was hectic in itself but with three young children it was not very easy at all and it took ages to pack and move but somehow we managed to do all this in one day and began sorting things out at our new place which it was starting to look like home well as much as it could be in the short space of time but it was the best we could do in such a short time. It was good to be in a house and having some space to move around instead of being cramped up so much like we were in the flat. I was looking forward to our new home and I hoped that it would be a complete new start for us and what had happened we could now put it all behind us well that is what I hoped anyway I was soon proved wrong on this one and things were just as bad for us as they were before.

Jade was not four months old now and was moving about a little and was a happy child and was always laughing. However this did not stop me crying and being very depressed and wanted nothing more but to kill myself and that I did not belong in this world but I knew that my children were very dependent on me.

At this time my in-laws step mum had just had a stroke and was very ill and she was now being nursed at home by my in laws and by me when I was down there and that seemed to be more often than not at the moment to give them a break it was hard work looking after her and getting her in and out of bed and changing her and cleaning her up it was not very nice job to do but it made her feel comfortable and I was feeling very tired and I was still having to look after two young children as well as a baby. It was something that I said I would help with but I did not expect it to be to the extent that it was or how much I was doing either. I was so tired when I was back at home and found it hard looking after my children and I was very depressed and very emotional, as the weeks went by my in-laws step mum got sicker and became even more frail and more dependent on us than she already was and she kept asking me to help her end her life and to stop this suffering and it ripped me apart and upset me every time she asked me but I did not and just prayed that the Lord would take her soon and stop her suffering and give her peace, two weeks before Christmas she died in her sleep and I knew when I left that night that she would not be with us the next day I don't know how I did but before I left that night I prayed almost begging the Lord to take her away and stop this suffering and I knew when I left that this particular nights prayers were going to be answered and it felt somewhat relief for me as I left my in-laws that night.

The next morning my father-in-law came to the house to tell me that their step mum had died that morning. I burst into tears and felt guilty for asking this and asking God to take her and I knew I had nothing to feel guilty about but I did. I had to then phone Adrian at work and tell him and he came out of work as soon as he could. We all went down to my in-laws and there was a lot of work to do to sort out the room that she was in and it was hard for me to go into that room and not see her in there. It felt strange to be going in her room I kept expecting her still to be there but I know that she was not.

A week later was her funeral and it was very hard for me and felt like I had lost my Grandma all over again and the memories of losing my Grandma came flooding back to me and it left me feeling very raw and ripped me apart and I still missed my Grandma so much. Later back at the in-laws I threw myself into serving drinks and the food I felt I needed to keep busy I did not feel I had a right to grieve for someone else's family when I still had not grieved for my own Grandma like I should have done all those years ago but I still had not done that I was

233

never allowed to do that.

Once we got back to our place after the day I had with my two children it was a relief to get back home and just be sitting quietly in my front room. I sat down and cried and my children came up to me and give me a cuddle and told me not to cry gave me a kiss and a cuddle and told me everything would be ok. Adrian told me not to be so soft and to stop being so stupid and I got a slap around the face for being upset. Which just made me feel worse and cry more than I was doing?

The following days were hard for me and I was sinking further into depression and my health visitor also picked this up and was starting to ask a lot of questions and questions I did not want to answer at this time but I knew she would not leave it there she was not the sort of person to do that. She got me through postnatal depression but I was still very depressed and she was still asking questions but I still did not want to answer the questions she was asking I was too scared to. I knew though that she would not give up on this one and would keep asking me questions she would when the opportunity arose again and she would make the opportunity to speak with me about this once again and she did many times before I said anything to her.

Three months after Jade was born I discovered I was expecting again at first I was pleased then I started to think about that night Adrian demanded his marital rights and rape me and I was then angry that I was expecting again but I was going to keep my child and love it as I do my other children. When I discovered I was eight weeks pregnant I was horrified that I was pregnant from being raped but I was prepared to carry our child after all I did love Adrian a few weeks later I slipped on the top step and fell all the way down the stairs and Adrian came running down the stairs and alls he kept saying was he was sorry he did not mean to but I thought that I had slipped and then all of a sudden there was this unbearable pain and then I felt something happening and then I realised I was bleeding heavily and I was losing my child I was so angry and so upset that I was losing my child I was just grateful that we had not yet told anyone that I was expecting again my GP was called and he came fairly quickly and told me that I had just miscarried my baby and he said he was so sorry and that he would arrange for me to go into hospital do a D & C which he did and I was in that night ready for the next morning and no-one knew that I was in hospital but Jade had to come with me as I was feeding her. I was only in twenty-four hours and was soon home again with Jade.

My health visitor was making regular visits to me but then that was no different to what she was already doing anyway. She was keeping a close eye on me and did for such a long time.

The year of my daughter being born was a very long and hard year for us all I was feeling guilty that I had lost yet another child I felt I was being punished but for what I could not understand what I could be being punished for.

Just six months before Christmas my health visitor started to ask more specific questions about my childhood and I kept telling her it was nothing to do with her and there was nothing to talk about. She told me that she was there for me if I wanted to talk about anything I thanked her but said there is nothing I want to talk about. We were still decorating in the summer and she came round for a visit and asked me to go up to clinic to see her as it was not possible to talk to me whilst others were there I said that would be fine so it was arranged for the following week at clinic and we went in to one of the offices and we talked but I would not sit down at first she told me that I was depressed but not because of having a baby but it is deeper than that and she told me that it was something to do with my past at first I did not answer her then she repeated the question and I then said what do you mean she told me that I knew what she meant and I stood there for a minute then sat down and said I was abused terribly as a child and her reply was she thought so I was in tears and she put her arms around me and she was the first person outside my family that knew apart from those who knew at the time I was going through the abuse and then her next reply was what did I want to do about it my immediate reply was what can I do about it as happened and I have got to live with it somehow but I did not know how to deal with this or how to live my life and how I could even start to put this behind me. Then she told me that there is specially trained people to help me deal with this sort of thing and there is help there for me if I want to take it but she would not force this one on me but wanted to give me the options so I could make a decision about what I wanted to do she also told me she knew I had been abused a long time ago and wanted to help me I could not understand how anyone would know because I did not tell anyone outside my own little family as I did not want it to be used against me which I thought that it would have been and I was terrified of losing my kids because of something that had happened to me as a child and I asked her are you going to take my children from me she told me there was no reason to take them from me. I was not convinced that she would not do this but I had to trust her that she was there for me and this was very hard for me to do this.

She told me to think about what she said and that she was only a phone call away if I wanted to talk to her.

I had still not made any decisions about going to talk to someone and I did not feel that it would do me any good talking to someone and going over things how could it do me any good to talk about what others had done to me it would not make it go away. However it did play on mind throughout Christmas and at the beginning of the new year I was thinking more and more about seeking help and in the end I decided to give it ago and see what happens she told me that she would not do the referral if I was not sure but I told her to go ahead with it but I was so scared and why would anyone believe me now they would not at the time. I still was not sure but I felt I should was not sure what I was going to say once I got to see someone or what would be expected of me.

Six weeks later I was expecting my eighth child and I was hoping that this one I would not miscarry I was terrified of having another miscarriage. I was happy to be expecting again and so far everything was going ok I was going on for ten weeks when I started to bleed heavily and I was in a right state and I just kept saying please not again I was taken into hospital and checked over and everything was checked out and an early scan was done and the baby was doing fine but the bleed was from the placenta it was detached slightly so I was to have complete bed rest for the next few days even weeks and they were giving me regular injections to stop it detaching any further a few days later the scan was repeated and there was still the same detachment but no more had occurred and the bleeding had stopped so I was allowed to go home as long as I took it easy me taking it easy that was the impossible for me at least that is what I thought. I was warned if I did not for at least the next six weeks I would lose my child and that was the last thing I wanted to happen.

As the weeks went by it was decided that we would go away for a couple of weeks and my in-laws came with us it was a hard couple of weeks and my in-laws were heavy smokers at the time to but I decided that they would have the bedroom at the back of the caravan so hopefully that would keep the smoke away from me and my children and during the day we were not in much anyway and it worked to a point to. I was so tired for most of the holiday but when I could I rested in the children's room where it was peaceful. However my–in-laws kept complaining that I was sleeping too much and Adrian had to keep reminding them that I was expecting as they forgot as I was not as big as they expected me to be and they thought that I should have much more energy than I had but they had forgot that I had threaten to mis-carry again. Whilst we were away I felt my baby move for the first time which was very reassuring for me and I started to cry and I got told off for crying and was told that I have nothing to cry about and I should be happy but these were happy tears. I was relieved that my baby was ok.

Later that day we all had gone out for awhile, and my in-laws went off on their own and Adrian and I were with the children went on our own suppose to have been some quality time together and unfortunately that was not the case. I was had a go at because I was crying and I should not be crying and when I told him that I had just felt our child move he had another go at me that I had not told him that I felt my baby move and he wanted to feel it move. I was hoping that it would have been a pleasant time together but it was not and I was relieved to be back were my in-laws were at least he did not have a go at me well not as much as he did when we were alone. I was glad when that holiday was over and we were going back home but we had problems with the car and we had a split petrol line and the fumes in the car were fairly bad and I felt ill on the way home and we had to stop several times because I was being ill and I was being complained at for being ill but I just kept saying that it is all part of being an expectant mum.

It took several hours more than it should have done for us to get home because of the amounts of stops we had to make. Which did not go down very well at all and I was constantly being shouted at for having to stop and this also upset the kids and I was told to sort them out and calm them down and get them to settle again but I could only do so much in the car and then I shouted at him if he was not shouting at me then our children would not be upset which only made matters worse and I was glad when we did finally get home and away from those petrol fumes and back into the house and able to breathe and sit comfortably just for a change.

My health visitor was still coming round on a regular basis and was concerned that I had not heard anything from her referral for me and she was chasing them up constantly. I got a letter to apologise about the time it has taken to get me an appointment and as soon as there was a slot for me that I would get the next available appointment and I hoped that I would do as I was beginning to change my mind and have doubts about going to see someone, and all the time I was questioning myself if this was the right thing to be doing and the serious second thoughts about it I was not even sure that it was the right thing for me to do but wanted to see what would come of it. The time for me seeing someone was a very long wait and I finally got to see someone in the October 1993 and was asked a lot of questions and asked how much there is to deal with at first I said there was only four months to deal with and I was asked if I was sure that is all I wanted to deal with and I said it was. I was now in counselling and was not sure what to expect and what I would achieve from this but I was prepared to give it a go and see what happens. It was frightening time for me and there was a lot of uncertainty around for me and never sure what to say and I did not trust my counsellor and I knew that took time for me to trust anyone and I did not think that I would trust anyone again, but I was not sure that I would have the time to be able to trust her enough to talk to her and I was over seven months pregnant now and was not sure if this was for me and how I was going to manage with seeing a counsellor once I had my child. At first we talked about things in general and nothing in depth I was not ready for that one anyway I was not really sure that I would be ready to talk about what had happened to me it was just too difficult to talk to anyone and I was so scared.

As the weeks went by I did start to open up a little but I was still not so sure that this was the right thing to do but I had to give it ago for my sake and I was scared of letting anyone down. When I was in a counselling session my unborn baby became very active and moving constantly as if to say it would be ok and my child was here it was a strange feeling but a nice one to My counsellor was watching my every move and the movement of baby and how I was responding to her it made me feel very uncomfortable. I found it hard going to counselling without any support or anyone coming with me I was facing this on my own. Going home after a counselling session was getting harder and harder to do. I was staying longer and longer after a session because I could not cope with what had been said and I was getting more and more frightened about going home and how little I felt that Adrian cared for me and how little comfort he gave me when I got back in I was constantly told to pull myself together and stop being so stupid it is not that bad but how the hell did he know what it was like for me and what it was like re-living your past and all the abuse you have gone through, he knew what I had been through and how bad it was he just kept telling me that it can't be as bad this time it just made me so angry and so upset I could not understand his reaction and his responses to me what I was doing was so hard and so emotional and it drained me so much each time I went but hoped that I would be able to get through this and it will become easier as time went on. I was booked in for weekly sessions and for at least an hour each week but that was a minimum of an hour each week my sessions were beginning to get longer and longer as the weeks went by. I had still had about three weeks to go before I was due to have my baby I just wanted my baby to arrive I was getting fed up of the discomfort that I was getting and it seemed to be a very long pregnancy but it was not as long as my other pregnancies and I knew that I was not going to go over with this one as the hospital had already set a date for me to go in and have my baby and they had only done that because of the complications that I had with Jade and I feared the same happening again and I certainly did not want to go over like I had my previous three pregnancies and it was in a way nice to know when I was going to have my child.

In the mean time to the run up to having my child, I was going for regular counselling sessions but not opening up as much as I could do I did not trust my counsellor enough at this stage to trust her but I was trying to do but it was not happening as yet something else I had to give it time, time was the answer to everything I kept getting told but I was not sure that time would resolve this. However I did keep going but it was hard going and I was looking forward to having my baby in a few weeks time but I kept doubting myself that I was fit enough to be a mum and capable of looking after four children I began to panic and feel frightened about having this child I was scared that I would have failed all of my children and I would let them down and that they would hate me I did not feel good enough to be a mum or a partner or a wife I did not feel worthy to be any of these. It was coming round to quick for me and nearer to the date it got the more frightened I became. I was having a caesarean, which was planned after the last pregnancy I was frightened of coming close to losing another child, which I had almost lost my daughter but thankfully I did not. The day was soon here for me to go into hospital ready to have my baby and I was admitted the night before and I was so frightened and I hated being away from my children and it upset me more being away from them than it was upsetting me being in hospital.

I had decided that I did not want any more children after this one I just could not cope with threatening to lose another child or cope with anymore at this time especially under the current circumstances and I knew we could not afford to have any more children so I decided to be sterilised after having my baby which was another reason why I was having a caesarean. I was glad when my son was born that I did not go for a normal delivery and he was a big baby he weighed in at 10lbs 2oz and I was surprised at that one but he was healthy, which is all I ever wanted and hoped for that my baby would be healthy. Adrian did not seem too pleased that I did not want any more children and he told me time and time again that I should not have took his right away to have more children. He constantly told me that I was being unfair to him and accusing me of taking his rights to have more children and we agreed before I had this child that we would not have anymore but now he had changed his mind and now it was too late for us to have any many children any way I felt four children was enough to cope with for the time being and I said if you really want any more children we could always adopt of foster them which of course he was not to keen on but this was something I had always wanted to do and would do in time and when the time was right.

I stayed in hospital for three days and I dreaded going home to him but looked forward to going home to see my other children and being with them. Adrian brought Daniel, Robin and Jade to see us and they were delighted to see their baby brother Brendon and it was special time for me having all my children round me and all of us cuddling up to each other it was such a special time and I felt so much love from some that was so young something I knew only a mother could feel I was overwhelmed with love from them to me and me to them. It was hard when it was time for them to leave and I wanted to go with them but could not just yet but would be doing soon on the third day of being in hospital I asked if I could go home and I was allowed to do as I had been through this before and it was felt that I would recover better at home with my family around me. I was so pleased to be going home with my family. I just not anticipated how difficult it would have been for me and I was nowhere near prepared for looking after all my children it was a bit of a shock for me but I soon adapted and wanted to be the best mum that I could be but not sure that I was but I knew that all I could do was my best as long as I did that then I could not do anymore for them. However I did not feel that my best was good enough for them.

The first weeks at home were hard especially preparing for Christmas which was only a few weeks away it was hard work the lead up to Christmas with having a small baby it is that time of year anyway but it felt like everything was such a struggle for me and so much effort for me to do anything and I was in a lot of pain to which did not help matters or help how I was feeling. Adrian did not help matters by telling me that I was useless all the time and I was always in tears and told me that I was not fit to look after my children and was no good to him whilst I was like this and he was getting very angry and aggressive with me.

Christmas soon came round and most of it was a blare for me I blocked most of the day out. I also had my in-laws round for Christmas dinner that was a regular thing same routine every year and because I wanted to break it for one year it did not go down very well. I was accused of rejecting his family and not loving them and not wanting them there at Christmas of all days. I was being unfair to them and him and he told me that was the least I could do for him by having his family around for Christmas and do the decent thing but when I protested he called me selfish, uncaring and unloving and the only person I thought about was myself I told him that was not true but I got a slap for it so thought it was better not to say anymore and just accept it and let him have what he wanted and have his Parents over again for Christmas. I was not happy about it but what else could I do? Once they had left on Boxing Day he had a go at me and slapped me round the face for not making his family feel welcome and he accused me of being an unfit parent and that I was deliberately not making his family feel welcome and trying to upset and hurt them and him. He never let me forget it either.

I was glad when the New Year was over and done with and the kids were going back to school at least that give me a break to some degree. At this time Adrian was not working and but expected everything done for him and he was not helping me very much.

I was due to go back to see my counsellor the week after the children had gone back to school I was glad of that as it give me an opportunity to get out of the house for longer than half a hour in the morning and the same for the evening rest of the time I was expected to be in the house at my husband's beck and call and if I was not I was in trouble and I would get the third degree where have you been? Who have you been talking to? Why as it took you so long? And he would continue with this all day and I would not get any peace from him. My depression was getting deeper and I was struggling to keep going and I was hoping that others would not pick up on it so easily and would not realise things were so hard for me I kept putting a shield up and was telling people that I was ok but just very tired not sure people believed me but I was not bothered if they did or not.

When it came to going to see my counsellor and taking Brendon with me I would again get the third degree how long is it going to be today? And when will you be back? What are you going to do for our meals today? I often told him that I will be as long as it takes and he was quite capable of sorting a meal out for himself after all he was a chef so it was not if he could not cook because he could he just expected me to do everything for him. I found it so frustrating at times.

Two years later I was still in counselling and Adrian had now started a new job which meant he was out from under my feet and I was not being constantly had ago at all day every day which was a good thing for me. I was frightened of him and I dreaded him coming home from work and what he was going to do next.

Whilst I was in therapy I was asked if I would like to bring Charges against my step-father and my dad but I could not do a statement against my dad again I just did not feel that I could do both so decided to go and do the statement against my step father and I was very unsure of this and was not sure that it was the right thing for me to do but I thought about and this long and hard and finally I came to my decision and decided to go for it and see where it would lead, my counsellor arrange for a police officer to come and to talk to me and have a informal chat and give me some of the information to help me with my decision and left me to think once again about things but I had decided that is what I was going to do and so I did go ahead I made my statement about him which took me hours and it was very painful for me to do this especially going into some of the details that I was now having to go through and it felt like I was reliving everything and I had to go into precise detail it was very emotional and a scary time for me and I felt that I was facing this alone without any support from anyone I know my counsellor and the police officer was giving me lots of support but apart from them I was on my own and Adrian was not happy that I was getting this support and he kept telling me that they are watching me and they are going to take my kids off me if I am not careful I kept telling him that they would not but he would not accept that and he was becoming increasingly aggressive towards me and making me feel that I was not worth anything and that I was unable to look after my children he was very cruel to me.

As the weeks went by I was becoming increasingly scared of what was going to happen my step father had been interviewed and he denied everything which was expected the wait now was what crime prosecution service was going to do if it was done were I was living now then it would have gone to court but because this had taken place in Leicestershire they had different rules, and they did not like to take old cases unless there was more than a eighty to ninety percent chance of prosecution they decided mine was only about sixty to seventy five percent chance so they decide that they would not be prosecuting I was so angry and felt what I had gone through all this for nothing and it was a waste of time but I was reassured that it was not and I had done the right thing but it did not feel like I felt betrayed and let down again I felt he had got away with it and that he could do it again I could not believe that nothing was being done we tried to appeal to the crime prosecution service but they would not move on their decision. I had to accept that decision but I was not happy about it and I was very angry about it. It took me a long time to accept and I don't really think that I did ever accept it properly. My counsellor and I discussed this at length for several weeks and she was apologising to me because she was the one that had encouraged me to do this in the first place and she was sorry that it was not the outcome that we had hoped for and wanted. I had to accept this and move on but it took me awhile to accept and come to terms with but deep down I had not accepted this I just buried these feelings deep down.

As the months went by therapy got harder and more difficult for me I kept denying that there was something else and would not talk about it and there was something else that had happened by another person I could not face anything else at the moment but somehow my counsellor got something out of me and I started to talk about what had gone off with my dad and I was still talking about things with my step father it was very hard and distressing for me and it was getting harder for me to talk about what had happen and I was still hiding my feelings and would not let the emotions go either and my therapy often said to me that it was ok for me to cry and I told her no it is not only weak people cry she replied to me that it is not weak people that cry and showing your emotions is not weak but a natural thing to do but I could not accept that it was natural to cry I felt that it was a weakness and weakness would not be forgiven.

A few weeks before Christmas I got a telephone call from the British Embassy in Milan in the Philippines. They was dealing with my brother and needed him out of there very quickly and needed my help to get him out of there it was hard for me hearing from him after all these years and it felt strange hearing from him but it was nice to but I was not sure how I was going to get him out of there as I had not got money that was needed to fly him home I had been searching for Mark for many years but never felt that I would hear or speak to him again let alone going to be seeing him, somehow I managed it through a special fund that was available that could be tapped into in special circumstances but you had to meet the criteria to get it and lucky for me I met all the criteria and got the air fare to get him home and he was to live with us he arrived late or should I say in the early hours of the morning it was a wet cold morning and it felt strange being in the centre of town at such early hours of the morning it was gone two thirty in the morning and I was shattered and the bus was already twenty minutes late I was beginning to panic and felt that he may have had second thoughts and not come home, and I did not feel like spending the night in the bus station waiting for the bus to arrive but unfortunately I had to. I was nervous and excited about seeing my brother and I had not seen him since I been taken into care all those years ago and I knew what he looked like when I saw him last I knew he would have changed and he was much older now but I was frightened of how things would go and I was not sure if we would even get on or if I would recognise him or him me. We were sat in the car waiting for the coach to come in and I was beginning to feel that it was not going to arrive but it did some forty minutes later a coach pulled in and I got out the car and stood staring at the couch in anticipation of meeting my brother for the first time in nearly fifteen years, whilst I was standing there in the rain looking out for him I felt scared and my stomach was doing summersaults and then a young man got off the coach at first I just stood there staring at him then I called his name Mark, Mark he looked towards me and came running to me as I ran to meet him I recognised my brother immediately he looked like his dad and the love that I felt from him and me to him was spontaneously. I was stood holding him and he me with tears rolling down my face and we were getting wet as it was now raining quite heavily so we ran back to the car and we were shortly arriving back at my home and the first time in years I felt I had family and alive. Adrian did not wait up to meet Mark he decided he was not worth meeting and was not overly happy that he would be staying with us. However he had agreed to this before he came over but now he was here and now he is being awkward about Mark being here I felt that he saw Mark as a threat why I don't know. I felt it was ok to have his family here whenever they felt like it but I was not allowed my family round me I felt very cut off and felt that things were very unfair. It was two weeks to Christmas when Mark arrived and I was looking forward to Christmas for the first time in years and I had a member of my family with me I know had my children and they were my family but someone that was my family felt so special to me, It did not take Mark long to find work it was only bar work but at least it was better than nothing and I was proud of him for doing this so quickly after returning back into this country it just meant that he would be working on Christmas day I did not mind that as long as he would be with us for Christmas dinner even if it meant doing the meal later which I did and my in-laws was going to be there then again they was always there and I was happy that Mark was with me but I was very depressed to and very emotional it was extremely hard for me that Christmas I felt I had to please everyone but no-one was prepared to help me or please me. I felt that I was being treated unfairly but no one else could see that they said it was my duty to do what I was doing for them at Christmas time. I was not sure that was the case but I carried on doing what I was doing and at the same time I started having a drink of wine and continued drinking for best part of the day and through our meal I just wanted to feel nothing, I did not want to feel the pain that I was feeling at this time and I felt I did not feel I belonged here or anywhere for that matter. So I was determined to block out as much as possible as far as possible but at the same time I had my children to care for which somehow I still managed to do how I did I don't know. Once my children were in bed I could relax a little but not by much as soon as I sat down I was asked if I could get them this and get them that I was fetching and carrying for them all evening and I was getting very irritable with them but the more irritable that I got the more I was had a go at. I decided to bring myself a bottle of wine in with me and a glass and sat down and started drinking it I did manage to finish the whole bottle and I was asked by Adrian to get him something and I snapped back why don't you get it yourself as I am not your slave he shouted back at me if you know what is good for you, you will do what you are told but I still refused to get what he wanted I was fed up of running around after them and It would not hurt him to get a drink for himself or his family it did not go down very well and I was told that I would be dealt with later I just laughed at him and did not expect him to do anything to me even though he had not been kind to me before I did not expect him to be completely cruel to me. His parents left not long afterwards which I was glad of when they left at least now my home would feel much more like home even though Mark was there it was still home.

I went into the kitchen and Adrian followed me into the kitchen and as I went through the kitchen door Adrian grabbed my hair and pulled me backwards then he pushed me forwards and I fell onto the floor he was stood over me laughing at me. Then he was shouting at me to get up off the floor and was calling me names he called me a slut and told me that I was a ho and I was useless and that I deserved everything that had happened to me as a child, he was then dragging me around the house with my hair and shouting at me he kicked me in the stomach and told me that I would not insult his family again and in future when they were here I would get them everything they want but I was no-one's slave but according to him I was. He was still holding my hair and he pulled me up with my hair and knocked me backwards in to the kitchen and I landed flat on my back he was soon into the kitchen and on top of me and told me there is nothing I can do to stop him before I knew it he was pulling my underwear to one side and he was penetrating me, he was hurting me he would not get off me and told me that he would do anything he wanted to me and there was nothing I can do about it I was fighting him but that just got me slapped around my face for that. He told me that I had a lot to make up to him and this was just the start of what I had to do to make up to him. As he withdrew from me Mark came into the kitchen and he said something to Adrian and then Adrian got up and went for Mark and told him to keep his nose out of it and mind his own business otherwise he would not have anywhere to live. Whilst Mark and Adrian were arguing I noticed that I was bleeding heavily and I was frightened by this and was worried that there was further damage done. I was crying and this got me a punch in the chest and in the face. After awhile Adrian went to bed and I just sat there in the kitchen on the cold floor for what seems ages and I was crying no I was sobering I could not believe what had just happened and my stomach and face was hurting and so was my chest. Mark came and sat beside me and gave me a hug and tried to comfort me and I was calming down when Adrian came down and he accused us of sleeping together and I told him he was sick this was my brother and that is not what happens between siblings he was just comforting me and making sure I was ok he replied that he was the only one that was allowed to comfort me and touch me in any form he again dragged me around with my hair and he dragged me upstairs with my hair I was crying and it was hurting me he told me to stop being so mardy and to shut up and I was getting what I deserved. He dragged me into our room where he became even more violent to me he again raped me and told me that he would put me in my place one way or another and he would have his marital rights if I was to give it to him freely or if he take it by force.

The next day my in-laws were coming around again and I was expected to look after them and make sure that they had everything they need and that they enjoyed themselves. I felt so angry and so alone and isolated and very scared and I was not sure what they would think of me but I was also in a lot of discomfort from the night before and when I went into the bathroom I discovered that I had got a bruise on my face that was only just coming out and it was bigger than I had expected and darker than I had expected it to be to. I was hoping that there was nothing there but unfortunately for me there was and I was not sure how we were going to explain that one and I was not going to say anything about what had gone on I felt violated and very scared and I felt very dirty and that I had deserved what I had and that I could not do anything about what had happened. As expected there was a lot of questions and questions that I did not want to answer and I did not answer it was Adrian who answered them and he told everyone that I fell down the stairs last night and I banged my face on the side of the wall at the bottom of the stairs and I got that look that said if you say anything to the contrary I would pay the price and worse than I did last night so I went along with what he was saying because I did not want any more of what I got last night and I was frightened of saying something out of line and I felt shattered and in a lot of pain I was already on strong pain killers as I was in a lot of pain and in a lot of discomfort but that did not seem to matter to Adrian. I had a bad bruise on my face and it covered all down my right side of my face and I also had a bruise across my stomach, which was very painful. I was very quiet throughout the day and spent a lot of time sitting at the back of the room doing what I wanted I even started on a jigsaw so that I did not have to talk to them all and it kept me occupied for several hours and it was the only bit of space and peace that I got throughout the day. It was not long before they were wanting this and that and I was expected to get whatever they wanted and I was also banned from having anything alcoholic to drink but it was ok for them to have some to drink. However I did have the odd glass of wine without him knowing I did not see why I should not.

The pain I was in was getting worse and the pain killers were not helping and I knew I would be going back to the doctor the next day and I knew that I had to because this pain was becoming unbearable for me I was trying hard to hide it from everyone.

Chapter 10

THE NEXT DAY WHEN I WENT TO THE doctors I had a long wait to see the doctor but I did not mind that at least I was being seen and I went alone which meant that I got some peace and some space for me even if it was only for a short while but was told to get back within the hour otherwise I would be in trouble, a hour later I was still sitting in the doctors waiting room I was beginning to feel frightened but I was determined to sit there and wait for the GP to see me but I was becoming increasingly scared and panicked with all the time I was having to wait to see the GP but more worried about what was going to be said and happen when I got back home. About another fifteen minutes I finally got in to see the doctor, she asked me the usual question what can we do for you today I told her that I was in a lot of pain and the pain killers she had given me were not working and the pain was now unbearable and I asked her if there was anything else she could do for me she told me that she would after to exam me first to see how things are I was dreading her asking me where I got the bruises from and I knew at some point that she would do I was waiting for it with bated breath and finally after she examined me and I was sitting back in the chair next to her she asked me what had happened and were did I get them from I told her I can't talk about it she asked me if someone had done this to me I replied yes and then she asked me if it was someone close to me and at home I told her that it was, I was then informed that I could do something about it and there was help out there if I wanted it I thanked her and said no I can't do that. She told me that I don't have to do anything now but if I do they can support me to do something. I told her I don't want this going any further at this time but the option was there if I so wanted to do. She then gave me a prescription for further pain killers and she also give me some additional pain killers she gave me some pethadine she gave me enough for the next two weeks and she wanted to review me in two weeks time. I thanked her and went to get my prescription from the chemist and again I was asked what had happened and I said nothing apart from too one of my friends and at first I told her nothing but she knew me better and asked me who hit me and I told her Adrian had done that and whilst we were talking Adrian came into the chemist and shouting at me and saying what do you think you're doing in here still I told you to be home within a hour I told him I had only just got in here as I had to wait so long at the doctors he told me that he did not believe however one of the pharmacist told him that I had only just arrived as there was a delay in the doctors he told them to keep their noses out of other people's business. They apologised but were only saying what had happened I was grateful for them for standing up for me but were worried about the consequences that I would now get once we got back home.

Meanwhile back at home he was screaming and shouting at me and raising his hand at me as if he is going to hit me again thankfully for me he did not I just glared at him but at the same time I felt panicked and scared.

I started taking the pethadine and felt woozy at first and very spaced out but at least they killed the pain even if it was just a short while it was better than not touching it at all but I did feel strange about it and I felt very sleepy with them and I laid down on the settee and started to fall asleep he was there again shouting at me and telling me he wanted me to do this and that for him and if I did not do it I would get more of the same so I got up and did what he wanted it was better than getting another belting. After I had done what he wanted he went upstairs to our room then he called me upstairs so I went to see what he wanted, on entering my room I saw him laying on our bed naked and very aroused he told me that he wanted me and he was not taking no for an answer and I had to do what he wanted I looked at him straight in the eye and said no thank-you and went to turn and leave our room. He was off our bed very quickly and dragged me back into the room with my hair; my head was already sore from a few days ago. He was pulling my hair hard and had wrapped it around his hand to pull me backwards into our room and then he kicked the door to. I was crying and begging him not to do anything to me but I knew that he would not listen to me and that he would do what he wanted to me with or without my consent and it was without my consent he raped me and I hated him from that day and I told myself that he will never do anything like that again to me well at least that is what I thought. After he finally withdrew from me I felt so angry but so spaced out from the medication I was on but what my so called husband had done to me I felt that he did not care or love me and all he wanted me for was to beat me and rape me I still loved him but why I did I do not know.

New years eve soon came round that year and I was doing a party and it was the first party I had with Mark there but unfortunately things did not go to plan and Mark tried to kill himself and we spent the night down at Accident and Emergency department it was a great way to bring the new year in and not the way I wanted to bring the New Year in and not the way I envisage bringing it in. I felt hurt and so disappointed by this but there was nothing that I can do about this I just had to accept that this is how it was going to be and these things happen but why did these things always happen to me? Why was it my entire fault? What could I have done to change this? I asked myself these questions over and over again but never coming up with any answers.

Several weeks later I was back at the doctors and I was still in a lot of a pain and she referred me to accident and emergency for a second opinion and for a full assessment which I did go down and they sent me for a scan and they discovered that I had numerous goldstones and it was no wonder that I was in pain they admitted me on to one of the wards and this was one of the old wards and I hated it but I was in so much pain I did not really care where I was Adrian was not very happy that I was being kept in and he was more concerned about who and how I am going to manage my children whilst I was in hospital I told him that he was there and he was more than capable of looking after our children and it was not going to be for long I was only supposed to be in for a few nights at this stage and he was not happy about that one little bit at all.

I felt guilty that I was being kept in but there was nothing that I could do about it, one of the nurses brought some morphine for me to have an injection to help the pain but it did that but it knocked me out for several hours and when I awoke he was pacing the floor with clenched fists. I stared at him what seem ages but it was probably only for a few minutes but it seemed a lot longer. He saw me looking at him and had a go at me for starring at him and told me that I had better be going today otherwise I would pay the price for staying in hospital but I could not do anything about that if they wanted to keep me in which they did I was in over night to see how I was during the night I had a rough night and I was been given a lot of morphine during the night to ease the pain and the next morning I was allowed a light breakfast then they were sending me home until they could bring me in to operate on me which they said would not be too long. I hoped that I would not be in this pain for too long it was wearing me down I was already very depressed and my counsellor had noticed how much I had gone down and was asking a lot of questions especially when she saw some of the bruising that I was now getting however I did not tell her straight away when and where and how I got them. I was frightened that I would lose my children because of what was happening and that was something that I did not want to happen my children mean the world to me and I was terrified of losing them. It did not matter how much I was reassured that this would not happen I never lost the fear of losing my children. In turn I found it difficult to trust people and those that I did trust it took me a long time in getting there. I was always frightened of this being broken.

Mark decided to make a statement to the police about what our step dad had done to him and I supported him all of the way it was hard for me to do this because I knew the outcome would probably be the same as it was for me and I could not go through that once again it ripped me apart watching Mark do this and how he felt and how he was afterwards but there was nothing I could do to help him accept be there for him and give him the support that I was doing at least he had someone there for him unlike when I did my statement there was no-one there for me I went through it on my own and that was so hard physically, emotionally to it drained me completely and it took me time to get over the trauma of doing that.

Several weeks later I was admitted into hospital to have my gall bladder removed, my husband came with me on the day I was admitted and brought our children with us it was hard for me having my children there as I knew it would rip me apart when they had to leave. However when they did leave I was not aware that they had gone as they waited till I went into theatre before they left and when I came round I was not really aware that they had gone until sometime later I had expect Adrian to come back later that day but he did not. That upset me so much that he had not come back to see if I was ok and he did not even ring the ward to see if I was ok. Mark came up later that evening to see if I was ok and that I had come through the operation ok I was still somewhat groggy when he was there but he did not mind that at least he came to see me unlike my husband.

The next day no-one came to see me till well after seven in the evening which did not give long for visiting and Adrian had a go at me for still being in hospital and he said he needed me at home to look after my children and they needed me to look after them he told me that I better be home the next day or they would be trouble, I could not say when I was going to be going home I wanted to be at home but I could only go home when the medical staff said it was ok for me to go home but he did not care about that all he was bothered about was that I was at home looking after my children and running around after him and then of course there was Mark that I was looking after too I felt that no-one else was able or capable of doing what I do every day of the week but I knew that Adrian was more than capable of looking after them but he just did not want to.

The next day I was allowed home and I was glad of that but not glad to be going home as I knew that there would be more hassle for me and I knew deep down the only reason he wanted me home apart from running around after him he wanted his martial rights as he put it. I also knew that one way or another he would get them but I knew that was the last thing that I was up to doing but he did not care about that as long as he was happy. I was dreading going home for that reason. It was late in the afternoon that I finally got home and when we did Mark had locked the door and gone to sleep on the settee and it took some waking him up. When Mark finally opened the door Adrian had a go at him and told him that he knew I was coming home to day so why the hell did you lock the door he replied that he had done it for security and that way it was safe for him to go to sleep but we have a dog and he would not let anyone in and he would have barked if anyone was there he passed a comment he did not think about that and the next thing I knew they were both arguing and there was a number of punches exchanged between then something I did not need or want just coming out of hospital. I was surprised that my kids were not there when I got in and I was told that they were at their grandparents to give me time to get in and settle before they were climbing all over me and they would be back sometime around five that evening and my husband was going back down to his parents for a couple of hours and then he would bring my kids back with him. It was the longest few hours for me and it was much more than a few hours to but I was so please to see my kids once he brought them back and as he walked in the door with my children Mark left the house rather quickly but then again I am not surprised that he did that as we had not long had words.

As soon as my children knew I was at home they came running up to me and just cuddled me and kissed me as I did to them I was crying with joy at seeing my children it was the best feeling I could have and having my children home and having them in my arms again and seeing the looks on their little faces when they saw that I was home I will never forget that. A pure expression of love between mother and child that you would not get if there was not this bond between mother and child and child and mother I just felt so special seeing that expression on my children's faces and so loved by them.

As the weeks went by after my operation things at home were getting out of control and unbearable Mark and Adrian were constantly sniping at each other and trying to get me to take their sides which was hard to remain impartial but I tried but it was one of those situations were whatever I did I was wrong. It was hard for me as it was for them but I felt trapped between family and my husband and I did not like it at all.

A few weeks later whilst my husband was at work and one of the rare occasions that Mark was in and up at a reasonable hour I was talking to him and asking him why he was being like he was and trying to destroy everything I had and why was he so jealous that his sister was in a relationship and got a family and he just told me that what I have given my children it is all he ever wanted as a child and could not understand how I had managed to be so different from our mum in a lot of ways I was not sure how to answer him and in the end I just said to him that I wanted to be better than our mum and give my children the love and care that we never got as children I wanted my children to always know that I love them no matter what. He was shocked about that and he then told me that the only person who had shown him love as a child was me and it was my turn to be shocked but I thought that his grandparents shown him love but not as much as I thought they had done. Then again he did see them much more than me. Even so I was surprised when he said this as they always seemed to be very loving to me and showed a lot of love to both of us and thought the world of us both so I was surprised and confused why he did not feel he was loved by them I know he was maybe it was a mother's love that he was missing and wanted so much and we both did but knew we were never going to get the love of a parent a mother's love. Something both of us was going to have to accept sooner or later our mother was not a very loving person and especially not to her own children other people's children she always seemed to show them love and affection but not her own and as a child that was hard to take and understand and now when you are older and you got a family of your own it is harder still to understand and accept that your own mother did not give or show any love and affection to you as a child. It is hard on you as a child and as you go into adulthood it does have an effect on you and it goes deeper than even I realised and it hurts so much to.

Mark and I had been talking for sometime about a number of things and I started to cry he was sitting next to me and he put his arms around me and give me a very brotherly hug but he didn't leave it at that and tried to kiss me not on my cheeks but on my lips and he was trying to get me to respond to him and his hand went up my skirt and I had already pushed him away but he was back at my side trying to kiss me again this time I got up and slapped him around his face and told him to leave me alone and stay away from me I screamed at him you're my brother for crying out loud a brotherly hug is fine anything else is a no go area but he turned round on me and said he wanted to give me something that

Adrian was not giving me and I asked him to leave the house and go and cool off and only return if you were going to behave and treat me as your sister and nothing else he stormed out of the house and I felt dirty and shocked by what he thought he could do and get away with it just made me more angry I also realised that he needed some sort of counselling for what he had suffered but he seemed somewhat disturbed to me but could not think or explain in what way I felt this. I just felt it deep down and knew he would need some sort of help but not sure if he would be willing to do it and he could see that I was in counselling and the benefit I gained from that but then I had been going for awhile I was in my fifth year now and was still talking about things and I was surprised how much I had said but I did not feel that I had dealt with the feelings that went with what happened just the incidents of what happened the feeling somehow seemed to be separate but not sure how they were to me one went with the other but in counselling they did not seem to be together they seemed to be separate in some way.

The police finally came back with the outcome to Mark's statement and again they said that they would not be taking things any further it is what I expected but I hoped that it was going to be different this time but the outcome was the same they did not feel that they could go ahead with this as there was still not enough to guarantee a conviction which just infuriated me even more and felt once again that my step father had got away with it. Mark took this information very hard and he became very angry and very threatening to everyone but I knew he was only like this because he was angry and that he felt helpless because nothing was going to be done about what had happened to the both of us. I knew that the outcome was unlikely to change from when I did my statement because of the historic nature of the case and that there was not more than a sixty per cent chance of conviction I knew that crime prosecution wanted and liked well over seventy per cent chance of conviction and I knew it was only around fifty five percent for Mark and they would not take it to court and even with my statement did it raise the odds that much and in a way I was relieved that it was not going to court especially now and I knew if it had done then I would have been in therapy even longer than I was already. Somehow we both just had to accept that he had got away with it for the time being because I believed that everyone gets their comeuppance at some point. I knew and believed that but I knew that it would take awhile before that happens but I was not sure how or how that would happen but I knew I may never know that this has happened but I know in my heart that they would know that it has happened and I believed that they would get their just deserves at some point and they would be answerable to someone else. In the meantime I had to accept that nothing was going to happen to them not now, not in the near future and maybe not for a long time but I know that one day they will do.

I was talking to my therapist about Mark and said it sounds like he needs to be in therapy to but how would I feel about that I said if that is what he needs then it is what he needs and then she ask me how I would feel if he came to the same place as me I told her that would be ok but I had my doubts and she knew it but I did not feel comfortable about Mark seeing someone in the same building and I certainly did not want him to have the same therapist as me and I did not want to be there at the same time as Mark because I felt that this would not have done me any good and I would be worried how he was getting on and not about what I had to do and I knew that it would mean that I would be in therapy for even longer but it was agreed that he would go there but seeing someone else which I was grateful for and even the first appointment I went along with him just to give him some support but I was not comfortable doing this at all Lucky the first appointment was only for half a hour so I was not there for that long but it confused my therapist as she thought that we had an appointment and she had not put it in her diary I told her no we did not have an appointment but I was waiting for Mark and I did not feel comfortable about being there at all she told me that they had almost finished now and he would be down in a moment which I was relieved about. It was the only appointment that I went with him as I could not go with him for any more but made a point of asking how he was and everything went once he got home and tried to make sure that he was ok and I also give him the space that he would need when he got in and I was there for him when he was talking to me about how he felt even though it was hard for me I knew this was the only way I could help him and knew I was doing the right thing.

My therapy was still intense and some days it was unbearable and difficult to deal with it was not just about saying that this had happened

259

but the feeling s that you got afterwards and the emotions that went with it that was not dealt with in therapy just the incidents and it left me feeling very raw and angry and very upset however it was becoming easier for me and it was not so hard to talk about what had happened which was a good thing or maybe I was just getting use to talking to my therapist and talking about the abuse or maybe it was because I wanted to finish therapy and that I had done enough of therapy.

A few months later I went to the doctors without telling anyone what was wrong I was frightened to tell anyone why I was going to the doctors I was frightened of what Adrian would say and what he would do. I had discovered a large lump on my right breast and it had been there for a number of months but I just thought that it was probably a block milk duck but it was becoming very painful and was getting bigger. My GP was kind and gentle and when he examined me he told me that I would be referred to the hospital as a matter of urgency but at the same time he was giving me reassurance that everything will be done to sort this out I asked him what was wrong and what it was he told me that he did not want to make that diagnose until I had seen a specialist so I enquired what specialist I would be seeing and he told me one that deals with lumps that could be cancerous I was terrified and I was so young and I had a young family he told me that I had to wait in the waiting room whilst he phoned the hospital and he got me an appointment for the day next and I was to go there first thing in the morning I was crying when he told me this and I knew that it was serious and I was scared and I knew I would have to tell Adrian and he told me that it is going to be ok but I am going to have face this on my own. I was crying and he was being so cold towards me and I asked why you being like this with me. He told me that is only what I deserve.

The next morning I went to the hospital and I was terrified of what they were going to do to me, I arrived at the hospital in plenty of time for the nine o clock appointment I was shown to some cubicles and asked to put a hospital gown on and then asked to take a seat along the corridor in the seats provided I was sitting there and I was shaking and for the first time in a long time I prayed I was not sure why I felt that I should now but I did. I was taken into a large room what I thought was an x-ray room and thought that it was going to be an x ray but I was told that the monogram is the best way to look at the breast and I was so scared I was shaking and crying. It was painful having this done and I felt that it was never going to end she told me that a doctor would see me immediately after leaving that room. I was sitting in the corridor again waiting to be seen I was only there a few minutes but it felt a lot longer than it was and I was still crying, he told me that the lump need looking at further and he was hoping that it would be nothing for me to worry about but that did not reassure me at all if they are only hoping then what chance have I got he told me that he would bring me in as a day case and that afterwards breast feeding would be painful but worth continuing with if I could my next question was I am able to bring my baby with me I was told that I could but I was going to have to express my milk for at least one feed if not two and knowing how hungry my baby was I knew that what I expressed for what they say was two feeds would only be enough for one feed.

I was to go into the day care unit in the morning and be prepared to stay overnight if necessary but that was the one thing I did not want to happen was to stay overnight well not if I could help it I would not be. I took a slow walk back home pushing my baby in his pram and trying not to think about what lay ahead but as I was walking I was thinking about what am I going to do how would I tell my children and if the worse was to happen to me how would my children cope without their mum?

I could not answer these questions and people was walking passed me and several of them asked me if I was ok I told them that I was but they said are you sure that you are ok I told them that I was and then someone said to me if you are ok why are you crying I was not aware that I was crying I just felt numb and very scared and the thought of what I was going to have done and what it could be I was so frightened and felt alone. I could not say to this person why I was crying I was too scared to say anything to anyone then she said to me that I should pray and go and sit somewhere quiet to do this maybe that this would help and then she turned round and said you can always go into a church and sit there and pray or even talk to someone there I politely said to her no thank-you I can't do that and she said to me that she would leave me be and hope that I was going to be ok and she said that she would pray for me as we parted I could not understand why a stranger would be so kind to me and be so gentle and caring to someone she did not know.

I felt calmer as I walked away and I had actually stopped crying and I looked back and so this lady and she turned round after a split second that I had done and we both waved and smiled it felt strange to feel this but I suddenly felt some internal peace I cannot explain this feeling to anyone if I was asked to but it was so calming and so peaceful feeling.

As I walked the rest of the way home my baby started to cry and I knew it was getting near to Brendon's feeding time and I was hoping that I could get home before I had to feed him, I gave him his dummy till I got home and I was not that far from getting home as it was maybe ten minutes left to walk if that. As soon as I got home I was bombarded with questions where have you been. I told him that I had been to the hospital to have some test because the doctor was worried about something and he wanted me to get checked out at this point I had not got Brendon out of his pram but he had just started to cry again. Adrian was shouting at me and telling me I had no right to go and see the GP without telling him I told him that I had every right to consult my doctor if I so wished to do so and I don't have to tell you anything. Then he surprised me with what he said next and I could not believe he would think so little of me to say what he did he turned round to me and asked me if I was having an affair I told him no I was not I would not do that sort of thing and he knew I could not either. He then slapped me around the face and I just got angry and I shouted back at him if you must know where I was I was at the hospital having test and I have to go in tomorrow as a day case to have a lump removed he then replied to me that he did not believe me even with all the letters and information that I got back from the hospital he still did not believe me and it got me another slap around my face and I was shocked by his reaction. Brendon was starting to cry constantly now so I knew that I had to give him my attention and feed him but I felt too uptight to feed but I knew I had to. It was hard to feel calm to feed your child whilst you were so upset. Holding my son in my arms somehow I felt warmth and love for him more than I had ever done for him before this day it was as if he was being a distraction for me and I was glad that he was whilst I was feeding him I was crying and my other children came to sit next to me as they often did when I was feeding Brendon it felt so nice having my children with me at this time and I kept thinking what if this is the last time I can do this but I knew that the consultant was hopefully but it did not stop me feeling panicked and scared and with no support at home it was very hard.

Meanwhile later that night after I had settled all my children into bed and they were fast asleep I went and had a soak in the bath and Adrian came into the bathroom and he was much calmer with me now and told me that he wanted to have sex with me and I would not let him I was not in the mood for that and I was tired he told me that it was my duty to give him what he wanted and it would prove to him that I loved him and that there was no-one else and because I told him whilst I was in the bath that I did not want this he again accused me of sleeping with someone else and he demanded to know who it was and where he lived I repeated myself that there was no-one else and I was not having an affair just because I did not want to make love to him did not mean that I was having an affair. However he saw it differently he was getting very angry with me and he said to me he would be making love to me one way or another I was determined he would not be doing and I told him that he was not having his so called martial rights and not tonight I was too worried about what I was going to be facing the next day and what they would find and were this would leave me and my family and if it was about to leave my children without their mum. Having sex was the last thing I wanted and I was too scared about what lay ahead of me the next day.

Sometime later I was getting into bed and I had not long heard the front door opened and I went to look out of the window and saw no-one had left the house and I thought then Mark was home and I was right he was as I heard Adrian and Mark talking but it did not sound to pleasant. I decided that I was not going to go down stairs and see what was going off I decided to get comfortable and try to go to sleep if that was at all possible. The argument that was occurring downstairs was beginning to sound very heated but I wanted to keep out of it I was to scared to get involved with their argument if I did I knew that it would have been me that paid for getting involved and no-one else. After all I had to go to the hospital the next day and this was not something I was looking forward to having done and I was scared stiff about it. The night was along and very unsettled night for me and I felt lonely and afraid Adrian had finally come to bed and was trying to demand his so called martial rights but I was not giving him an inch on this one I did not see why I should do if I did not want to have sex with him why should I just because he wanted to with me, when he got into bed I laid there still and pretended to be a sleep and I hope that he would soon go to asleep and leave me alone and I was surprised that he did leave me alone for the time being and let me asleep it was not long afterwards that he soon fell asleep himself and I hoped that he would stay that way for the rest of the night. When I knew he was asleep I felt my body relax and calm a fair bit which I was pleased about but I could not sleep as I was thinking about what laid ahead for me the very next day. The minutes, seconds and hours seemed to go by very slowly as I lay in bed watching the clock. Tears were streaming down my face I felt very alone and very isolated and very vulnerable and terrified. The more I tried to go to sleep the more I seemed to stay awake. After several hours I decided to go down stairs and get myself a warm drink with the hope that it would help me to sleep and calm down a bit so I made my way downstairs and into the kitchen to have a hot drink made with milk so that is what I did and decided to take it back up to bed with me. I was part way through drinking it when my husband woke up and asked me how come he could smell chocolate I told him that I was having a hot chocolate with milk and it was very relaxing he asked me "how come I was having a hot chocolate at this time hour" I replied to him" that I could not sleep and thought this would help" he seemed to accept it and rolled over and went back to sleep I was thankful that he did and hoped that he would stay that way and go back to sleep. I was now beginning to feel calmer and relaxed it was not long before I had finished my drink and was settling down in my bed again I had just got comfortable and my eyelids were starting to get heavy and I could feel myself drifting off to sleep.

When all of a sudden I felt something tight on my arm and pulling me onto my back it was Adrian and he was not being very gentle at all and I knew what he wanted but I did not want to or wanted him to have sex with me but he had other ideas on that one. I had said to him on a number of occasions that under no uncertain terms that I did not want this. Adrian would not listen and he wanted sex and it did not matter to him how much he hurt me as long as he got what he wanted in the end even if he had to take me by force he would have done as he did that night and he was very rough with me and when he squeezed my breast it hurt and the pain was unbearable and blood was expressed out as he did this along with some milk to which was not very pleasant or very comfortable but he did not care as long as he got what he wanted and he did even though I said to him no I don't want to and he was hurting me he carried on regardless to my feelings and my request or how much he hurt me I was beginning to feel that I would never get away from all this hurt and all the abuse I had suffered, maybe I did deserve this, why I did I do not know why I deserved this. So why did people who were supposed to love me want to hurt me so much.

I had a very unsettled night and I did not sleep to good and I was scared and worried sick about going into hospital the next day I seem to spend the night watching the clock and crying and wondering what would happen next. The minutes, hours and seconds throughout the night seemed to go very slowly and seemed a long night it was around three in the morning when it started to rain it was light at first and getting heavier as the night went on then in the distance I could hear the rumbling of thunder then there was a flash of lightning and this made me jump which in turn woke Adrian up and give him the opportunity to have a go at me for waking him up and he told me that I was selfish for jumping when the flash of lightning stroke then there was another one and this time he jumped but nothing was allowed to be said when he jumped he just told me to shut up and say nothing a few seconds later there was a huge clap of thunder and it sounded right above our heads it was one of the worse thunder storms we had in such a long time and one that lasted for several hours to. I had not been sleeping before the storm came and I certainly was not sleeping now and did not expect to sleep again that night it was gone five in the morning when the storm finally went away and I was to be up at half past six so did not think that there was any point in going back to sleep but decided to just lay were I was in my bed just in case I could drop off for awhile and my alarm was already set for six thirty however I did not need the alarm as Brendon always woke up before the alarm went off so he was my alarm really but decided that I should continue to set it just in case he wakes up late one of these mornings. I was pleased that he had slept through the storm and did not stir but I was surprised that he did but then again my children were use to noise and could sleep through almost anything I was lucky that way.

The night had dragged for me and I was terrified on what was going to happen today and what they would find and I was facing this on my own is was a frightening time for me and a very anxious time unfortunately it was one of those occurrences that I was going to have to face on my own but I felt angry that I was facing this on my own I felt I should have been facing this with Adrian but that was not going to happen I was up and showered long before my son woke up for his feed which was unusual for him he was normally awake as I got into the shower but not this morning and he was not my alarm clock that morning I started to panic and wondering if he was alright but he seemed alright when I felt him before I got in the shower but I rushed from the bathroom and into our bedroom and I looked into his crib and he was not there I thought that was strange I got myself dried off and went down stairs and I saw that Adrian had got him in arms and I was surprised to see him with our son in his arms this early in the morning I looked at him and asked how long had he been awake he informed me that he been awake since I got into the shower and thought that I would like my shower first instead of me rushing around like I usually did in the mornings it was nice of him to do this then I thought to myself why can't he do this every morning but I felt that was too much to ask maybe I was pushing it if I had done and was going to make the most of him doing this today. Even thought it was not what he normally did I felt that there was still hope yet and maybe he would do this more often. I thought to myself it would be nice if this did happen on a regular basis but only time will tell on this one I suppose. I was getting nervous about going into the hospital I had to be there for as close to eight as I could be but they told me not to worry if I was later but I could not be later than eight thirty otherwise I would not be able to have the surgery. I was terrified about this operation and that I would not make it as everything had happened so quickly and that is what scared me the most. I was getting ready to go to the hospital my children were ready for school and waiting to go. As I was getting dressed a single tear trickled down my face then another followed by another and before I knew I was overwhelmed with tears. I continued to get ready to go to the hospital and face whatever was going to happen and Brendon was ready to go to and was sleeping in his pram I was relieved that he was asleep which give me the time to sort myself out and try and pull myself together. I was finally ready to go some twenty minutes later, I moved down the stairs very slowly still crying but knew I had to do this and I knew that the walk to the hospital was going to be a lonely walk for me. I seem to take me ages to get to the hospital but it was only about thirty five minute's walk and when I got to the hospital Brendon had woken up and wanting another feed I was not sure if I would have time to feed him before I was going to be taken into theatre but I hope and prayed that I would have time and I was frightened that this would be the last time I would be able to feed and hold my son. It was so special having my son in my arms and him being that close to me, and my son suckling on my breast but the right side was painful for me to feed him on but I preserved with it for my sons sake. I was hoping that after this feed he wouldn't need another one for some time well I hoped that he would not need another feed but I had expressed several bottles just in case he did need another feed but we were trying to timing it perfectly between feeds and I was not going to be having a full anaesthetic so was hoping that I would not be to groggy afterwards but I was told to be prepared to have a full anaesthetic if it came to it I told them I was prepared for what was necessary but I wanted it to be avoided as much as possible and they told me that they would do their best to avoid that if they could. I did have a lot of local anaesthetic though. They made a small incision round the nipple area and went in from that and they discovered the lump that was there and they told me instantly that it was a begin growth as it was a cysts and a large cysts and they were going to remove it after they removed it they said hang on a minute there is something behind the cysts and there was another lump and this needed to be removed immediately and they now had no choice but to put me to sleep because they needed to have a proper look at what was going on. I was in theatre longer than I was expected to be but I knew that this was necessary for them to find out what was going on and what this lump was.

I was coming round in recovery sometime later and I could hear a baby crying at first I did not realise it was my baby that was crying then I did and I asked for my baby and he needed me, the nursing staff had been trying to get him to feed from the ex-pressed milk that I had left for them but he would not take it he just wanted his mummy and I asked was it possible for me to be able to feed him myself as yet they said I could do but I had to be careful but I could not feed on the right side for the time being but I was worried that the effects of the anaesthetic would have on him and I was told that he would probably have some of the effects that I was having but he would be ok. So I fed my son what seemed to be hours and it was a long feed but he soon settled and went to sleep at this point he was put back in his pram and the surgeon came to see me and told me that I had a benign cysts but there was another lump under that which they had managed to completely remove and as now gone off for testing but he felt that it would also be benign. I hoped and prayed that he was right. I was slowly allowed up and moving but I had to take it easy for the time being I was offered something to eat and drink several hours later, which I accepted. I was still hoping to be going home on the same day and it was looking very likely that this would be happening that I would be going home.

After several hours later the consultant and nursing staff told me that I would be able to go as soon as I was ready to go and they asked me how I was going to be getting home I told them the same way I got here I was going to be walking no way am I walking on my own after having surgery I would be going in a taxi I told them I could not afford to go in a taxi and they told me that the hospital will be paying for it. I thanked them for the kindness and they called me a taxi and I went home.

When I arrived home I felt sick and frightened and not sure what sort of reception I was going to get once I got home as the taxi got closer to the house I felt fear and I was crying and shaking. I didn't want to go back in to the house I did not want to see my husband I wanted to see my other children but not my husband but I knew that to see my children I had to see my husband.

By the time I got home my children was getting in from school and wanting my attention I was feeling tired and very sore and did not feel very well and all I wanted to do was to sleep but I knew that was not going to be possible for a while but I was finding it hard to keep awake and give them the time they need. Somehow I knew that I would have to do but I was not sure how I was going to do this. I had been in about fifteen to twenty minutes before my husband realize I was in and then he started on me and asked me where the hell have you been all day and how come I could afford to get a taxi when I told him that the hospital had paid for it he told me that I was a liar and he did not think hospitals provided taxi's to patients so I got him to phone the taxi company up and asked them who paid for it and when they told him that the hospital are paying for it he thanked them and hung the phone up. He then started on me and telling me that I should not have accepted this taxi and I Should have walked home instead and the way I was feeling I am glad that I did not as I was feeling very woozy and feeling very sick and very shaky and tired he was then demanding that I made his and our children's tea. I asked him to do it and he got quite agitated with me and he dragged me up with my hair and slapped me around the face. I was crying and hurting and in a lot of pain.

Adrian didn't show much understand at first to how I was feeling and when his family was round he showed a lot of understanding and caring and after they left as they did not wish to stay very long as they did not want me to feel swamped by people and two many visitors it is was nice to have them there as they were talking to me and spending time with our children and keeping them occupied for awhile which was so nice to have at this time they ended up staying for about an hour but that soon went but I felt exhausted after they had gone and was drifting to sleep whilst they were there which is when they decided to leave and let me rest as they went out of the door they told me that if there was anything they could do to help we only had to let them know and they would be there I thought that they were really sweet in saying that.

After a short while after they had gone I had fell asleep with Brendon in my arms and two of my other children curled up around my legs and around each other all wanting to be close to me I was so warm and comfortable it was such a nice feeling and I felt so much love from my children and care it was so nice having them this close to me. I also discovered that also my eldest child had curled up on the floor curled up asleep leaning on the settee with his hand on mine it was a feeling of love that cannot be easily be described but it was a feeling and warmth that I never expected to feel from my children but it was wonderful feeling.

As I awoke Adrian started to speak to me and was being very kind to me and was offering me a drink and something to eat and for a change he was being so caring towards me. I had to ask him to take my baby and put him in his carrycot and I hoped that he would remain asleep once he had been put down in his carrycot and thankfully he did. I slowly moved to get up and trying not to disturb my other sleeping children at this moment and hoped I could get up without doing this and I did manage to do this but it was not easy moving two children off me without waking them up. All this just to go to the bathroom, I was feeling very light headed and sick from the anaesthetic which I was warned this could happen. It seemed to take me ages to go upstairs and every step took it out of me but this was something I had to do and it was not as if someone could go to the bathroom for me.

On my way back down the stairs I slipped on the stairs and slipped down a couple but I felt every single bang go right through me but I was ok as far as I could tell it was not till I got back into the front room that my husband asked were was that blood coming from on your top I said to him that I don't know but immediately checked the operation sight and that was where it was coming from and I had come home with extra dressings as I had to change the dressing on a regular basis and in case it seeped through like it was doing at this moment. I sat down and slowly removed the dressing and I was shocked how much it was bleeding but not the incision it was much smaller than I was expecting it to be. I was expecting it to be a large in incision but it was very small to what I was expecting to see. However I know that I would have to clean this up and get the bleeding under control and fast to. I had some sterile wipes to clean which is what I was now using and once I cleaned it up it did not look to bad and it had now stopped bleeding which I was pleased about I was worried about all this blood that I had lost but I still had to redress the wound with the dressing that was provided for me. I began to feel very faint and sick I still had my children to sort out for bed yet to and to get them ready whilst they were asleep just made them heavy than they would have been if they were awake. And I knew it was going to be a strain for me to do this and I knew it was going to hurt me to move them and to try and lift them whilst they were asleep in the end I did not lift them somehow I managed to get them undressed and in their night clothes without moving them too much and most importantly without hurting myself much I did feel some twinges for me whilst I did this but I knew it could have been a lot worse than it had been. I could not understand why my husband would not do this and why he had not done this or even offered to help me why did he want me to struggle

270

like this? Eventually my husband stopped watching me and came to help he had to carry our children upstairs to bed as there was no way I could have done it on my own I was beginning to get some discomfort. It was time for me to take some pain killers my husband that evening was kinder and more caring than I had known him to be in such a long time. It was good to see this side of him and I liked what I saw and hoped that this would continue for some time yet and would stay like this as this was the husband I fell in love with many years ago and this was a side in him that I had not seen in such a long time and the side of him I wanted to see more often it was this man I loved and married.

It was a few days later I got a call from the doctors and they had been contacted by the hospital to contact me and to give me the results of the test and I was to go into the surgery as soon as possible to get my results I was terrified of facing this and I was crying, Adrian looked at me and asked me what was wrong and I told him I have to go round to the doctors surgery to get my results and he said he was coming with me and I was taken aback that he was coming with me and he was being so kind and caring and I liked this and hoped that this would continue for some time yet.

I was also surprised that I was going to the doctors surgery rather than the hospital to get these results but maybe the consultant decided it was quicker for me to go there than to go to hospital. I was sitting in the waiting room at the doctors for what seemed hours but I knew that it was only a few minutes or so but it felt hours, when the doctor finally called me in at first I was going in on my own and she said that it would be best for my husband to come in with me, I sat down in the chair next to my doctor and I was shaking and tears were starting to roll down my face I just wanted to know what was going off and what was wrong I was beginning to think the worse, she looked at the notes she had in front of her told me that my consultant had been in touched and had been asked to tell me the results I just wanted her to get on with telling me what they had found. She told me not to worry everything is going to be ok then it was Adrian that got angry and said will you just tell her what is wrong this is so unfair on her, she told me that what they found they had found early enough and had removed all of it so there was no further treatment required so I asked her what it was, she told me that there was a large cysts which I knew but the lump behind that was benign but if I had left this any longer then it would have been malignant, I did not know if to cry or laugh at this point, I felt numb which is why my GP had given me the results but I still had to go back to the hospital in a few days time for a check up and given the full results of what they had found which was arranged for three days later but they wanted me to know as soon as possible what they had found.

Adrian was not too pleased that they had called me in to the surgery to give me part results but I said that they had called me in to tell me that I was going to be ok and that I had not got cancer I felt that it was good of them to do this but he did not think that it was.

It was a hard few days for me but I knew I did not have cancer and that was important to me that I was still going to be here for my children and they were not going to lose their mum which to me was important and meant I would still be here to see my kids grow up and be there for them.

The day soon came for me to go and see the consultant at the hospital and Adrian decided to come with me but I had asked the receptionist to ask the consultant not to give me the in depth results with my husband being there and she made a note on my notes to say this, the consultant was very sensitive and good to me and took me into the exam room to check the wound and to check that it was healing ok and there was no seeping and the stitches were ready to come out and they were so he decided to remove them there and then which was a little uncomfortable but it was much more comfortable once they were out, he also asked me some questions that I was not expecting and he asked me if I was being hit and treated roughly as the lump behind the cysts was caused by a lot of pressure on the breast but it has caused me a lot of problems and could cause me further problems in the future. He told me the look on my face told him what he had asked me was true he warned me to be careful and said there was support out there that could help me if I wanted this but I was so scared to say anymore about this and to do anything as I knew Adrian would have flipped if he knew what was being said and I was relieved that I had asked for him to tell me on my own.

However once we had gone back into the main room Adrian asked what is the results and if there was anything to worry about he reassured us that there was nothing to worry about and that it was just a nasty cysts and it would heal in time and that the wound was healing very nicely but he give us some advice that gentleness is far better than roughness we thanked him and left shortly afterwards and I felt angry that it was caused due to the pressure that had been put on me and now I was scared what was going to happen to me now and I knew Adrian was furious with what he had been told and he accused me of telling the consultant of what was going on and what he had done he would not have listened to me that I had not said anything to anyone. He told me I would pay for this but I kept telling him that I did not do anything or say anything to anyone.

I began to feel panic as I was going home and I began to cry I was scared of what was going to happen next and when we were back in our home. We were in the house a short while and I was just settling in and getting comfortable with Brendon and getting ready to feed him it was still painful to feed him on the right side but I knew I had to otherwise I knew that my milk would dry up and that is the last thing I wanted to happen, we were nice and comfortable and relaxing and just starting the feed when Adrian came in and started having a go at me and making accusations at me and told me that I had said something to the consultant which is why he said what he had done but I told him again and again that I had not said anything and it was just what they found when they did the surgery but he would not accept that and he was screaming at me and Brendon was becoming upset and refusing his feed but I told Adrian to shut up and leave me alone and he slapped me round the face and walked out of the room for awhile well long enough for me to feed Brendon well only just enough time to feed him and I still felt that he wanted more but Adrian told me that he had enough but I knew differently so I carried on with his feed which did not please Adrian at all. About half a hour later I finished feeding my son and he was now settled in his carrycot and I hoped that it would be that he would be settled and asleep for awhile Brendon was a contended child as all my children were. I was sitting back on the settee and just trying to remain calm and to relax when Adrian went for me and started slapping me and told me I knew what he wanted and I was going to give it to him without any fight or problems and he would be gentle if I let him I told him that in no uncertain words that he was not going to have what he wanted and I had every right to refuse him and when I said this to him he just got angrier and angrier at me and began to get very rough with me and in the end he got what he wanted yet again he raped me and hit me and each time afterwards he promised me he would not do this to me again but he never kept his promised to me. I knew that he would do it again but I felt trapped and could not do anything about it and I felt that I could not do this on my own and bring up four children on my own I was scared and very vulnerable.

I was crying a lot and still very depressed and not getting any better and I was still in therapy and knew I would be for awhile yet but I was working through things a bit at a time it was getting easier for me to talk about what I had been through well the things that I choose to talk about and that was it. There were something's that I never talked about and probably never would have done it was just too painful for me and I was not yet ready to deal with things that were going on at home I do not think that I would ever say to anyone about this as I believed that this was my punishment and this had to be hidden from everyone I was too scared to tell anyone about what I was suffering behind closed doors. I felt trapped in a life, in a marriage that I did not want to be in anymore but to scared to get out of it and with that being the case I knew I had to put up with it and leave things as they were or change it and get me and the kids out of there that did seem an option to me as I took my vows seriously the day I made them and I stood by them still to that day and I believed that I would always feel like this.

The months after my surgery things were still no better and Mark was still living with us and still trying to come between husband and sister and he felt he had more right over me than my husband did and he kept talking to me and trying to persuade me to go off with him and take the children with us and be a family I often asked him what he meant by this and he told me I knew what he meant but I would not accept what he wanted and would not go with him I felt my place was with Adrian and the children that was the family not with him in the way he wanted me to be with him. My refusal to go with Mark just made him angry which caused even more friction in the home and Adrian and Mark were constantly arguing over me both saying that they knew what was best for me when I knew none of them knew what was and is best for me but I did not want to get involved in their constant arguments I hoped and prayed that they would sort things out between their-selves in time well that is what I hoped anyway.

Mark and I spent a lot of time alone and talking and I was wary of keeping my distance from him when we were alone I was scared that he would try something on again if he got the opportunity and I was not sure how I would handle this if he did. However there was a time a few weeks later when we were alone and I was crying he came and sat beside me and put his arm around me and I leant my head on his shoulder and cried it was nice having someone comforting me whilst I was upset but I did not ask him to do anything else or did I want him to do anything else he was my brother and that was all as far as I was concerned I loved him as my brother and I cared for him after all he was the only family I got apart from my children. As I went to stand up after I stopped crying he stopped me and kissed me hard on my lips and I pushed him away and he told me not to do that as he said he knew that I wanted him to do this as I had wanted it from him as I had done from everyone else I told him he got that all wrong and I did not want what had happened to me to happen and I certainly did not want this from him. He told me that he had resisted for long enough and it was time I gave him what he wanted and what I had given to everyone else including Adrian so why should he be no different. I told him you are different your my brother your family but he would not accept this and wanted what he wanted and no-one was going to stop him.

I felt panicked and very scared and felt that I could trust no-one not even my own family my own brother. I felt very uncomfortable that Mark was acting in this way towards me and feared what was going to happen next even though I knew what he had in mind I did not want this and I was not sure I could stop him but I knew I had to try and stop him I did not need another person in my life who wanted me for their own ends or to rape me I had enough of people doing this to me and why did everyone feel that they had a right to do this to me? Why did everyone think and feel that I had no choice in what they did to me, why did I not have a choice in what happened to me what give these people the right to think they had more rights over me and what I wanted rather than what they wanted. Why was it so unfair on me? What did I do that was so wrong? Was I such a bad person and an evil person? I began to believe that I was.

Mark was increasingly coming onto me and told me that this is what I really wanted a proper man I felt nothing but disgust for him and at this minute I wanted to kill him and get away from him but he had such a grip on my leg and arm that I could not get away from him and I was scared and I never expected for him to commit incest against me but that was something else that I was wrong about. I felt so humiliated and violated and scared and I could not fight him anymore he had got me in such a difficult position that I could not get out of and I stood no chance of getting away from him and I knew that to. I was scared of being hurt and being raped again and certainly not by another member of my family. Mark committed incest against me and I hated him from this moment forwards and I feared him. I was quieter than usual when Adrian came home and he asked me what was wrong I told that nothing was wrong and I was just tired and feeling washed out from everything that I had been through in the last few months and weeks, he was surprisingly kind to me and told me to go and have a relaxing bath and he would keep an eye on our children and start on tea something he did not offer to do very often and I was not going to look a gift horse in the mouth and I did not have to be told twice to go and have a soak in the bath and relax for awhile and I was going to have a bath anyway I felt I needed to scrub myself clean and get rid of the feeling of being violated. I was in the bathroom for ages I took some candles in with me just to help me relax and feel calm and it was working for me to the point that I almost fell asleep in the bath which was not good for me to be falling asleep in the bath. About half a hour later I was getting out of the bath and getting dressed when Adrian came into our room with a nice cup of hot chocolate and I felt totally spoilt and I did not know why I was being spoilt but I was going to enjoy this whilst it lasted I just felt that he was feeling guilty with all the hurt he had caused me and everything he had put me through over the years. I did not feel it was right to question why he was being so nice all of a sudden but I was going to make the most of this whilst it lasted as it had been such a long time since I was treated so nicely and kindly. I felt scared about this but I was trying to accept this for what it was and that it was for anything else and hoped there was nothing going on underneath the surface. Adrian was pleasant to me throughout the evening and helped me with our children I was suspicious of his actions but was relieved to have this but was wary and scared about how he was now treating me I hoped and prayed that this would last.

Later that night once all our children was settled in bed and we were in our bed he asked me again what was wrong and what had happened during the day I told that I was tired and still in a fair bit of discomfort and that Mark and I had words that afternoon but I told him it was over nothing and I have sorted it out he seem to accept this and lay next to me and put his arm across me and just lay there and cuddle me it felt so nice and I felt loved and cared for once again and this felt more like the man I loved and married.

A few weeks after the incident with Mark I had woke my children up for school and my son was sitting on the settee on the edge next to Mark's feet and Mark did not take kindly to this and he had already been woken up but had gone back to sleep and he awoke and started taking it out on Daniel he sat up and belted my son for sitting on the settee and this upset my son so much and he was crying in my arms I sent him upstairs to wash his face and do his teeth for school, my other children followed Daniel upstairs to do their teeth and something deep inside me snapped and I saw red. I went up to Mark and dragged him off the settee and I was screaming at him how dare you lay your hands on my child what give the dam God right to touch him and before he could answer I told him that you have got ten minutes to get your things together and get out of my home and I never want to see you ever again. He tried to argue with me that I was being unfair to him and that I was not being -very supported of him and he had no-where to go and I just said to him that I do not care if you had to sleep in the gutter or on the rubbish dump just get out of my house and now. He looked shocked at me and was taken by surprise with my reaction and he never expected me respond to him like this but he did leave and it was such a relief when he was gone and he did try and come back many times but I stood firm and would not let him back in my home ever again. I even had to get the police involved on a number of occasions to get him to keep away and stop harassing me it ended up with us changing our phone number just so we could have some peace from him and the late night phone calls.

About eighteen months later there was a knock on our front door in the early hours of the morning with the police knocking on the door and telling me that Mark had been in an accident and it was possibly an hit and run but I suggested that it was more likely that he owed someone some money and they were getting it from him if he did not pay they made him pay and I was right he did owe someone money and he had not got it and they were giving him a bit of what he would get if he did not pay up. I was not pleased that they had come to tell me but he asked them to let me know and he wanted my help and I told them that in no uncertain words that I wanted anything to do with him and I was not interested in what had happened to him but the police asked me to contact the hospital so they could record his injuries on their records just in case anything happened to him. I did contact the hospital and was told that he was in intensive care and was in a bad way my next question was as he been drinking and when they said he had my only reply was that he has got was due to him and he has only got his-self to blame. I know that was cold hearted but it was how I felt I did not care and I did not want anything to do with him ever again and as far as I was concerned Mark and all my family were dead and in my eyes they were and it was easier for me to deal with things whilst I felt this.

Adrian and I had a good couple of years were things were not right but things were running much more smoothly between us and we seemed happier than we had been in such a long time and I felt that maybe things had now settled between Adrian and I and that maybe we had a chance of making our marriage work but I still had doubts and was still scared of him and frightened that he would hit me and rape me once again. It was always at the back of my mind but tried not to let it show so much, and I was feeling fairly happy and settled for the time being and I hoped and prayed that this lasted for some time to come yet.

By now all of my children was going to school and it felt strange not having them around during the day and I missed them dearly when they were not around and I felt lost and felt that something was missing in my life so I started to work as a volunteer at my children's school I just wanted to be near them but not with them I wanted to do something that would help others and do something that maybe I could enjoy and do something worthwhile for a change and at the same time it got me out of the house for awhile which could only have been good for me and healthier for the whole family, I spoke with Adrian about this and he felt that it was a good idea so I spoke with the school and they were grateful of the extra help and I enjoyed being round adults and children I felt human again felt that my life was worth something once again. My children loved it that their mum was in school and they were all proud of me being there and after a while they forgot that I was at school and looked at me as another member of staff which was nice for me and for them but it also give me and my children a closer relationship and that is all I wanted to be close to my children and to love them unconditionally and them to love me and I had got that which made me feel so proud.

The last couple of years were fairly good between Adrian and I and I hoped that they would stay like this now but what I hoped for and what happened was no different to what had happened before, Adrian became very jealous of me and was always accusing me of having affairs he could not accept that I was not just his wife and the mother of his children I was a person in my own right but he felt that I should be at his and our children's beck and call all the time and not have to time for me or for me to meet new people and have a life of my own. I felt great meeting all these different people but I was afraid to get close to any of them and to be overly friendly with them as Adrian got so jealous he saw everything I did as a threat to him I do not know why he felt this I was always loyal and faithfully to him he was my life and the one I loved so much. I just wanted the same back from him but that never seem to happen.

I had been in the school all day on this particular day and he had forgotten that I was in school all day and when I walked in with our children he started having a go at me and demanding who and where I had been all day and why was I not at home for when he got in, when I told him that I had been in school all day and been busy he did not like it one little bit he called me a liar and said there was no way I had been in school until the children said yes mummy as she was with me this morning and went into year two later on and into year three for a bit this afternoon he shut up then and stopped shouting at me whilst the children was around, he only did that because he knew that he was wrong once again. However it did not stop Adrian having a go a me once the children had gone to bed and I began to feel that things were now back to how they were a few years ago and I was now terrified of what would happen now and what I was about to go through once again. He was screaming at me and telling me that I would do what he wanted and what I was told, and now he wanted me to go to bed with him but I was not ready to go to bed and I certainly did not want to have sex with him. When I told him that I had things to do before I went to bed and get things ready for our children for in the morning he pulled me by my hair and dragged me upstairs and I was crying and begging him not to do this and that he was hurting me. When we got to the top of the stairs he punched me in my back and as I stood up he slapped me around my face and told me not to be such a softie, I wanted to scream at him but I did not dare do this I knew it would have only made things much worse for me. Once he got me in our room he started to hit me and strip my clothes off me and he told me that I would do what he wanted me to do otherwise or would suffer and he kept reminding me that I had let others do what he was going to do me so why should he be any different I found the courage to scream at him your suppose to love me and your my husband you're not suppose to treat me like this. We are suppose to have a caring loving relationship but this was far from that and I was scared and I was beginning to tell myself that it was time that I got out of this marriage but the problem was I was to scared to do anything about it as I knew that he would never let me go that easily well not yet anyway which meant that I had to put up with what he was doing to me until I had the courage to get out and be safe and I was not sure that this was ever going to be possible. Whilst in our room and I was stripped naked he was now starting to get undressed and he raped me in multiple ways he did not care how much he hurt me or what he did to me as long as he got what he wanted and many times he would say to me if I can let my dad and step dad do what they did to me when I was growing up then I can let him do whatever he wants to me now but I could not understand why someone who was suppose to love me do this to me and why Adrian wanted to use what others had done to me as a way for him to used that to get what he wanted from me.

I was becoming more and more frightened of him and was spending more and more time at school just to be out of the way. The next few years were no different from this and I was wondering how I was going to get out of this mess but I could not see any way out and I was too scared to do anything about what I was going through at this time.

I was horrified when I found another lump this time under my right arm and I was scared that this would be something more serious again and I was frightened of going to the doctors but I knew I had to go for my own sake and I booked in as soon as there was an appointment and did not tell a soul that I was going or what I was worried about. I just wanted it to go away but I knew it was not going to do, fortunately for me my GP could take the lump off in the surgery for me and send it off for checking and the wait for the results was a horrible wait but one I had done before and probably would do again but not something that I wanted to keep facing but it was better to get this checked out than be sorry.

A few days later my GP contacted me herself to give me the results over the phone and it was another begnin lump and I was relieved but I was told that it was good that I was noticing these things and doing something about it.

Sex between Ardain and I was becoming unbearable and I was in so much pain when sex took place and penetration was becoming uncomfortable and I was scared and I was getting depressed and was not sure what the doctor could do if I went to see them and Adrian was still demanding his marital rights as often as he wanted and when I told him no he raped me again and again and was told that he would have his marital rights at any time of day anytime he wanted to have them regardless of what my wishes were. The pain was becoming unbearable for me and I felt that it was time I went to see my GP but I felt embarrassed going to see them with me being in such pain and I felt that it was something wrong with me that penetration was so difficult for me and felt that it was because of something that I was doing rather than anything else I was also wondering if this was because of everything that had happened to me and maybe there was damage that was done to me that I did not know about. I was scared what they were going to ask me and what they would have to do to me. I was sat nervously in the doctors waiting room and was watching people come and go and I still had not gone into the doctor I began to panic and cry I got up to leave the waiting room and as I was about to walk past the receptionist the doctor came out and called me in to the doctors room and the usual questions were asked what can we do for you today and at first I said nothing and said it does not matter and apologised for wasting her time but she was quick enough to realise that there was something wrong otherwise I would not have come to see them. I sat back down and started to cry and she told me that whatever I am about to tell her it is nothing that she had not heard a thousand times before I knew that but I was just so embarrassed to say but in the end I told her what the problem was and she asked me if it was ok to examine and give me an internal examination and if I wanted the receptionist to come and be in the room whilst she did the examination I told her that this was difficult enough for me as it was and I certainly did not want anyone else in the room whilst I was having this examination and she promised that she would be as gentle as she could be but it is likely that it would still hurt. She was not wrong there it did hurt and she told me that she felt a number of lumps in my uterus but felt that there was nothing to worry about at this stage but I just panicked and was crying and she felt that the best action to take was for me to go and have a full scan which she arranged very quickly for me which I was pleased about but I was so scared of going and finding out that there was something very wrong with me and I was scared that I was going to die. I was not even sure how I was going to break this one to Adrian or my children and I was not sure that I wanted to do at this stage.

I had my scan a week later and I discovered that I had fibroids and I did not have a clue what these were or how they would be treated but I knew that it was nothing serious but would settle in time so I was told, I went back to see my doctor and she give me the information about fibroids and referred me to a gynaecologist to see what plan o f action they wanted to take if any at this stage.

Whilst I was waiting for the appointment to the gynaecologist Adrian was being his usually obnoxious self and still being very cruel to me and all the time I was keeping all this to myself and trying to keep it from them what was going on between me and their father I felt that I had kept a lot from them it was easy whilst they were younger but as they got older it was getting harder and harder to hide things from them

I did not want them to know what their mum was going through and what their dad was doing to me.

It took months before I got an appointment to go and see the gynaecologist and he repeated my scans and confirmed that there were a number of fibroids and of different sizes but they should cause me to many problems for the time being. He asked me a lot of questions about my life and my childhood and he felt that the pain I was now in was due to the trauma of what I went through as a child and felt that it was best to leave things as they were for now but he would see me in three months time to see if anything had changed and in the meantime I was to try different medications in hope that it would help me including some very strong pain killers.

As the weeks and months went by I was getting increasingly amount of pain and penetration was becoming increasingly difficult and when Adrian did penetrate me I was in so much pain and was crying with pain but that did not stop him having his martial rights and he insisted on this more and more why did he want to do this and why when I was obviously in so much pain. I could not understand why he wanted to hurt me the way he did.

Adrian started to go to his cousins a lot more and leaving me alone to tend to our children at first I did not mind but then it became that he was going up every weekend and several times in the week to he was often not back till the early morning and when he came in you could smell cigarette smoke on him even though he did not smoke himself his cousins and visitors did.

There was one particular evening he told me he was going up to his cousins that I invited one of my friends round with her kids and we were having a good evening until her daughter came down stairs and told me that Daniel had tried to kiss her and had pinned her down and she did not like it and understandably very upset it was not long before my friend left after that I felt that she was blaming me for that but she would not talk to me for ages after that day. After they left I called Daniel downstairs to talk to him rationally and calmly to see what had actually happened and he told me that he wanted to kiss her but he wanted to hurt her I found this very confusing then I was filled with panic I asked what he wanted to hurt her for and is simple reply was that it is all because of your dad, I was shocked for quiet sometime but I realised what he was referring to I immediately contacted Adrian and he told me to stop fussing and everything would be fine on asking if he was coming home he told me that he was enjoying himself and I can deal with the situation and he would be home when he is home and not before. I slammed the phone down on him and I was furious with him, I made the decision to contact the out of hours team for advice and it meant that I was going to be have to totally honest with them and tell that I had suffered by what my son was saying what had happened they reassured me and told me not to worry when they realised that I had been in counselling they contacted my counsellor who confirmed what I had told them and in turn she contacted me which I was very grateful of her doing this and she was very supportive of me and told me not to worry and I had not done anything wrong it was others that had done the wrong not me. However I felt so guilty that I had failed to protect my kids from what I had gone through and I knew when this had happened to Daniel to and the only time it could have happened was when my dad was living with us at the flat but I was surprised that he had even remembered anything from that time, I was also encouraged to explain to my kids a bit of what I had gone through and now was the right time apparently. I was not sure that it was but I did talk with my children I had them all cuddled up next to me on the settee and I started to talk to them I was terrified of what they were going to say and more to the point what I was going to say to them but I knew that this had to come from me and no-one else, I took a deep breath and started to talk to my children it was so difficult sharing what I was about to share with them, I started off by saying that you know mummy loves you and always would do, my children were silent and so still, and that you know mummy does not have anything to do with her dad my children said yes we know that mummy but why don't you have anything to do with your dad and I felt a lump come into my throat and I wanted to run out of the room but I did not and stayed composed and talking to my children and I told them that my dad did things to my body that a daddy should not have done to his daughter and he hurt me and touched me where he should not have done, I am telling you this now so you know that if you see him you know not to trust him and you cannot do this unless you know something, them one of my children asked me what he did and were he hurt me and all I could answer to this was he hurt my body in a way he should not have done and this was very painful for me, then one of my daughters turned round to me and said "that it does not matter what someone else did to you we still love you" that was it I was in tears a child so sweet and so innocent to say that just made me cry. I felt so much love that day and felt that the bond between mother and child had just grown so much more stronger.

I slipped back into depression and started to take anti-depressants once again I did not feel that my life was worth living and on a number of occasions I had taken a number of tablets that I knew would have caused me problems including ones that would effect my asthma and possible trigger that off but fortunately for me it did not, after I had took them I went to bed and I hoped and prayed that I would not wake up the next morning but I did and my life just continued in the cycle for many years but I did come off medication for a while.

The next couple of years soon went by and I was still suffering and still in the same amount of pain the gynaecologist said they had tried everything and nothing was helping me and I was getting worse by the day and he was talking about me having to have a hysterectomy but did not want to do it yet as I was still so young and did not want me to make any rash decisions but this had already been going on for almost four years now and I had enough of the pain and the discomfort and the suffering and by now I was having to take a lot of pain killers which was making me feel drowsy and I did not feel that I existed and my life was not worth living. I was having to go to the doctors on a much more regular basis and having to take to many pain killers and these were not touching me anymore so my doctor was adding more and more pain killers for me to take I was beginning to feel very zombiefied but that was no surprise with the amount of pain killers I was having to take. I was still going to see the gynaecologist on a regular basis and he was seriously considering operating on me but he was still not happy about doing the surgery he was not convinced that this would solve my pain however what convinced him was when he repeated the scan and saw that the fibroids had grown in size and there were so many more now to what they were on the last scan so he decided to operate and do the hysterectomy that I knew I would have to have almost three and a half years ago. The day for surgery was set and I was to be on holiday just before so I would be fairly relaxed when I went into surgery but they were worried how I was going to cope with the surgery and the anticipated that my recover time would be slow and the risk of complications were high for me as far as I was concerned the risk outweighed the pain I was in and it was worth it and I know that this was the best decision for me and I did not regret it one little bit and I know that it was the best decision for me, I knew that this is what I needed to have done and after all I had all my children and did not want anymore and if I did decided to have more children I could always adopt and foster which has always been my intention to do and I hoped that one day this would happen for me.

The day soon came round for me to have the surgery and I was scared but I knew that it was for the best for me, I had requested to be the first down into theatre but I was second but I did not mind that one I was in surgery longer than expected and it was a complete success and all I had to do now was recover and I knew that was going to take time to do. Adrian and the children visited me in hospital but they never stayed long Adrian said that they had lots to do and not got much time to do anything I felt lonely, scared and very isolated but I was on the mend and no longer in pain apart from the discomfort from surgery otherwise I was doing ok I was only in hospital for a couple of days and was soon going home and it was a relief to be going home but was not sure what I was going to face once I got back home, I had missed my children's first day at school of the new school year and new school's but I was there when they got home and they had no idea that I was going to be home as they were expecting me to be into hospital for over ten days well the consultant was expecting me to have a number of complications so therefore my stay would have been longer but luckily for me I did not have any complications and everything went straight forward I was pleased to say.

I had been home for a number of days when I received a letter in the post from my dad it was out of the blue and totally unexpected and he was asking me to put the past behind us and move on and that he had heard that I was being cared for by Adrian and was worried when he heard that I was ill and thought that it was something serious I felt that he was trying to lose some of the guilt from his own conscious from what he had done to me. However I was so angry that he had got in touch with me and I wanted to know who had told him as I felt that they had no right to do that and if I wanted him to know I would have told him myself which of course I did not want him to know. Amongst his address he had and e-mail address so I sat at my computer and I sent him an e-mail demanding to know how he found out and what had given him the right to contact me as he knew that he was not allowed to do that so I wanted answers however I did not think that I would have got a response or the answers but I did get a response and apparently it was someone who Adrian delivered post to had told him. What I also told him what I had done and told him that I was fine and did not need anything from him and he had no right to contact me. He replied again and asking me to let the past go and move on, I was furious by now how dare he ask me to put the past behind us after all he should not have done what he did to me and I did not think why I should put it behind us for his sake I did not care what he wanted all I know is that I wanted him to stay out of my life and not contact me again.

I was soon back on my feet but I was still tired and recovering from surgery but was moving around a bit more comfortable and getting out and about a little bit more and Christmas was fast approaching and I was nowhere near ready for Christmas and it was another year that I did not want the in-laws round and at first Adrian agreed to this as I had such major surgery I had been back to see the consultant in the last few weeks and got the results of my surgery and discovered that they did the operation just at the right time for me as the fibroids was beginning to show signs of change not that they gave me much more than that except that I would have be facing cancer if I had not been so persistent about the pain and if they had turned I would have been one of the few that it happened to so I was even more relieved to have had the surgery. As Christmas day drew closer he started putting pressure on me to let them come for Christmas as it was not fair to leave them on their own for Christmas and I told him that she as two other children why can't she go to one of them and is only reply to that was that they did not want them to have their parents round and it was our duty to do this, I told him no and dug my heals in with this I was determined that they were not going to be that Christmas but Adrian kept the pressure up and told me that if I loved him I would let his parents come for Christmas but I did not feel that it was fair so I kept saying no I knew in the end I would give in but I was determined to fight this one. However Adrian was keeping the pressure on me and was becoming increasingly aggressive to me once again and I was very frightened and was not sure what was going to happen next I never did but I knew to a point what would happen if I was not careful. In the end his parents did come to us at Christmas but I was not happy about it and I made my feeling s very clear including ignoring them, Adrian was furious with me but then maybe if he done what I had asked and not invited them then I would not have been like that with them. However it did not get me any favours just enough slap around the face and being dragged round the house with my hair he was very careful what he did to me when the children were around or awake but once they were out or asleep that was a different thing for me. I felt that I was not a person with feelings but just someone else's slave. Adrian continued to force himself on me and demand he got his marital rights and this just helped me pull away from him a little bit more each time and I knew in time this would completely destroy me or both of us.

In the year I had decided that I wanted to go back to driving lessons and I had not done that for such a long time and I now felt it was time to get my license but was not sure if I could do this and I was scared however I found a driving school and started lessons and I remembered plenty from previous lessons from years a go but some things had changed so much since the early lessons I had to adapt some things and learn new things. Everything did not go smoothly with this as Adrian was jealous that I was in another man's company well that is how he saw it not that I was learning to drive he was always accusing me of having affairs but I never did anything wrong and he knew that I was sure of it. Driving lessons were going ok and I was already booked in for my test not that I thought that I was ready to do there was still things that I was having problems with certain things but went for it anyway with the hope that I might just be lucky to get through this but I did not and neither did I the next time round and then I had to change instructors and my next instructor was amazed that I had test when it was obvious that I was not ready for it. Adrian however was happier that I had changed instructors and he no longer seemed to be threatened by him which I was pleased about which also meant that I was much more relaxed than what I was with the previous instructor however when it came to the test I panicked and convinced myself that I could not do this and that I was not good enough to do this come the autumn of that year I had decided that I had got one more test to do and then I was going to have to stop and I even got to the point that I was going to cancel the test but it was to late for me to do this by a day but thankfully I passed that time round and I was so pleased and it was a night for celebration and friends came round to celebrate with us. It was such a special day for me and I felt proud that after all this time I had finally passed my driving test. Friends and neighbours were congratulating me. I was working at a temporary employment agency and they phoned me to see if I had passed this time and they were delighted that I had passed and asked me how I felt about going up to Buxton at the university there I told them that I would give it ago on the condition that if it got to much for me that they would pull me out and find me something much more local for me and this was agreed.

Two days later I was driving up to Buxton on my own for the first time this was a very frightening experience for me and to be travelling so many miles a day just after passing my test everyone at work was surprised that I had just passed my test and doing this distance so soon if nothing else it tested my driving skills but I also gained so much from this early driving experience.

Two weeks later I was beginning to feel exhausted and it was taking so much out of me and I made the conscious decision to contact the agency and to get them to take me out of there I felt guilty for doing this but I had to do what was right for me but I did also say that I would stay until they had found someone else, I had not discussed this with my manager in work at this time but as soon as I had made the call to the agency and I was back in the office I went into the manager and asked if it was convenient for us to talk I was worried how she was going to take this news but when I told that it was becoming too much for me and I had spoken with the agency but was willing to stay till they found someone else she was so pleased that I went into tell her and understood why I had made the decision to go and supported me all of the way. I went back into the reception and told the ladies I had been working with and they said they were sorry to see me go but again understood why I was going. Whilst I was working in Buxton I applied for a post in the university in Derby but so far not heard anything from them on this one so did not think that I would have been successful. However the agency got me in to the university doing another post and this was much easier for me without the travelling time on top of my days work. Whilst I was working in this temporary post I heard from the post that I had applied for and to my amazement I was offered the interview and a short time later I was starting a new post for a temporary contract of six months and I was delighted with this. In December I started my new post with a days delay as I had an asthma attack whilst I was in the university the day before and I felt guilty letting my new employer down on my first day however they were understanding at the time but the very next day I started working in my new post but was taking it easy as I could and there was an understanding that if I wanted or needed to go home then I could do.

It was now one month to Christmas and I was almost ready for the first time in a few years and I was working now full time and starting to find my feet in my new post and was introduced to a lot of people including all the faith advisors and chaplains in the multi-faith centre not that I could remember all of the names but I knew I would do in time.

That Christmas the in-laws were there as usual and a friend of mine was joining us on boxing day and she was going to be staying over and I was looking forward to this and hopefully things would be calm at home whilst friends were there but that was not so. That night we all had a fair bit to drink and we were laughing and joking between the three of us and it was a pleasant evening when my friend and Adrian started flirting with each other and making passes at each other they were trying to be discreet but I had noticed which infuriated me I made my excuses and went to bed however this did not go down very well but I did not care I did not see why I should stay in the room whilst they were making passes at each other I had seen enough and I wanted to get out of the way and go to bed. Adrian followed me up to bed and was telling me that it was just a bit of fun and I should not take things so seriously but how else could I take it?

He got into bed at the side of me and wanted me to have sex with him but I refused and I rolled over and turned my back to him, He laid next to me for a very short while then he got up when he thought that I was asleep and went downstairs to where my friend was and it was some hours later when he returned back to our room and our bed. I felt him claim back in behind me and I was still facing with my back to him and I knew that once he got back into bed that he had sex with my friend I could smell it on him with the odour he was giving off and from that day onwards I started to pull further and further away from him and the love I had for him had now been completely destroyed.

Chapter 11

FOR MANY YEARS TO COME WHAT I HAD been through, effected me for a very long time until I was ready to face the past and at some point we all have to do this you got to face whatever as happened to you however there are still things that I am having trouble dealing with even now but this is an ongoing process and I need to deal with everything proper so that you can get on with your future. There are times that my past still haunts me and causes me problems and I am still dealing with a lot of things from my past and it does still cause me a problem but it is hard to deal with everything and for it to never bother you again. I know this is a part of whom I am and always will be.

Working at the multi-faith centre was very challenging for me and I was finding working and home life increasingly difficult and depression was beginning to hit me hard again but I was trying to hide it from everyone and keeping myself to myself as much as I could do and not talking to many people was my way of hiding a way from everyone and trying to deal with what I was feeling and what was going on for me I had seen my GP on a number of occasions about how depressed I was getting and how little I was sleeping I was afraid to sleep she put me on anti-depressants which also acted as night sedation just to try and get be back in to a routine but I was told that I had to be careful with them.

I was working very hard but I was not happy and I kept telling myself that I can do this and find a way to work through how I was feeling I just needed a bit of help and support however I was afraid to ask for help at first.

I just kept myself to myself and got on with my work but inside I was screaming for help it was only when I was chatting to someone that became a friend in time that I realised how bad I was and I knew I was already deep into depression and I felt that I had no way out and nowhere to turn but Anthony was trying to encourage me to speak with one of the chaplains but I did not feel that I could do and because of that we fast became close friend and he was one of the few people that knew how bad I was and where I was heading before long and I knew it to. However I discovered that I was not on my own but there were people and friends that were there to help me and would be there for me no matter what but at this stage I did not feel that there would be anyone to help me. Through my work I had become friendly with several people and one in particularly I was become close to and we were becoming very close friends and a bond had already developed between us and he watched me go further down there were several other people that had noticed how down I was and they often said to me that I was not my bubbly self like I was when I first started working in this office. I just smiled at their comments but I knew that they were right I had changed over the last couple of months.

I was upset a lot during the February and I was in constant communication with my vets as my old dog was losing his battle to survive well he was almost eighteen years and I knew the day was coming that I would lose him and I had him since he was baby and I was devastated that I was losing him but I knew it was going to happen sooner or later. I did not want to lose him yet. A few days later I knew that we were going to lose him but I was terrified of having him put to sleep but I knew I would have to make that decision sooner or later however it was going to be sooner rather than later and I did not want him to go but I knew that he had a good life and it was his time but it was still upsetting for us all, I was arranging for the vets to come to the house to put him to sleep but it was decided that it should be done at the vets so we took him down that evening and he was still fighting after all of the injections and when I said it is ok for you to go now he slipped away. After several moments we took him to bury him all the family was upset by this and

I said I would not have another dog again but I knew I would in time however I said I would not have another dog for a while, well that did not last for too long as within two weeks I was looking on the RSPCA's website and there was a number of dogs that I was interested in looking at and a friend of ours told me to go to just for dogs so I phoned them up to see when their viewing arrangements were and they advised me that if I wanted to come up today as it was an open day then I could do so. It was not long before we arrived at just for dogs I knew that there was a young dog there that had only been there for a week if I was interested in such a young dog. We worked left to right to look at the dogs and all the dogs on the left hand side was very large dogs and as I went passed this particular kennel there was a small white staffie cross and she just put her paw on me knee as I went passed and my heart just melted and I knew that she was the one for me. What I did not expect to be able to do was to take home straight away but we were able to do so and she was not the most confident of dogs but I was determined that she would soon come out of herself and be much more confident and I was prepared to give her the time and hope that she would become much more confident she was frightened of people to start with but I worked hard with her to the extent that Adrian accused me of caring for the dog more than I did him. I had a couple of people that I had become very close to and was beginning to confide in them. One of my friends I was very close to and I was speaking to him a lot and he was there for me when I was at work and at home he was always at the end of the phone to me or at the end of his pc as I was for him and we both often called onto each other the support we gave was different but meant just as much to the other.

I had gone very low and I could not see a way out and I was struggling to survive and I was regular having suicide thoughts and did not want to be on this earth any more it was just too hard for me to keep going but my friends somehow kept me going and supported me and remained there for me no matter what they were there for me.

I know my marriage was not easy and I was determined to work at it no matter but the last six months were extremely hard for me and were things changed for me and I found some things very hard for me to accept I could not believe that Adrian would have an affair and especially with my best friend at first I thought that it was just a one night stand but as time went on I knew that it was not and I started to lose the trust and care and finally love for him.

I had spoken to one of the faith advisers before mainly in passing but this particularly day I stopped at the door way to the office he was sitting in and made conversation with him I needed to talk but was scared at first to ask if it was ok, I was fighting tears constantly at this time I know whilst I was chatting tears were at the brim of overflowing but was scared to let them go but I know the odd tear seeped over and I was told if I wanted to talk then they were here for us, I then asked Clive if it was ok for us to talk and invited him to my office to talk and that morning I had been given some more anti-depressants. We talked for ages and I did let some of the tears go and after awhile we were interrupted by one of the receptionist and Clive made his excuses and left and popped back in to my office to give me one of his cards and said it was there if I needed it I discreetly put it in my pocket and thanked him. However after he left the receptionist asked me if everything was ok and I told her no and I do not want to talk about it. A few moments later Anthony came into the office to see if I was ok and if I had a good morning so far he knew how upset and depressed I was and was checking up on me to see if I was ok and if there was anything I needed and as it was lunch time he asked me if I wanted to go for a walk so we could have a chat but only if I wanted to do and as it was a nice enough day we did go for a walk he talked whilst I listened. He was having problems with one of his courses and asked me if I could give any input to how this could be resolved at the time I could not think of anything but then again I was not thinking that clearly and finally when we were on our own he asked me if I was really ok and I remained silent for a while and he knew by this I was not ok and he asked me to turn round and face him and when I did I was in tears and when we were walking he put his arm around my shoulder and told me that everything would be ok it was that day that I would that I cannot do this anymore and he noticed that I was even more withdrawn than I already was. He knew me well enough to know that I was not right and that I had gone further into depression and at one point I knew I was heading for a breakdown of some sort if things did not settle for me or if things did not change for me. Depression hit me hard and I began to feel I had no way to turn and I was completely on my own even though I had my friends I could not see why or what I had to live for.

If Anthony was not there for me and not giving me the support he was doing and for Clive I do not know what I would have done.

It was not long after Clive had come to my office for a chat that I was contacting him but I was having to be careful how I made contact with him as Adrian was being more aggressive and accusing me of all sorts of things including that I was having an affair or I was sleeping with every male that I came into contact with me, he shocked me at times with the things that he said to me but the more I denied that I was having an affair the more he accused me of it. When I made contact with Clive I mainly did this when I was in the house alone or via the phone when I was walking rose it was the only time I could do this safely and without being having a go at and I was scared that Adrian would accused me again. I was becoming increasingly scared of Adrian and I was dreading him coming home from work when the time came that he was due home I started to shake and physically shake to.

Anthony started to come for walks with me mainly so he could have a break from his studies which he started to do on a regular basis with me it was nice to have my friend with me on these walks and to listen and I listened to him to, and he was there for me as I was there for him and it was good to have this support but that support went both ways and we had developed a special bond a special friendship that I knew would not be broken. I never knew how close we would become and how much we would be there for each other but what I did not know this was a friendship that did not come along very often and I was determined to treasure this for always.

we would walk for hours and for miles and just talk and one evening we were talking and Adrian and been constantly phoning me asking how long I was going to be I told him not long but he would not wait for me to come home he came looking for me and he met us along the road and he was not happy at all and felt that he was right to tell me when to come home and he did not like that I was talking to another man even though this person was a very good friend, before he even turned up I said to Anthony that he will be down here in a moment as I had told him where I was as I had nothing to hide and the next second when I looked up he was standing over the other side of the road glaring at me and it was not long before Adrian stormed off back up the road towards our home, I began to panic and I was scared and I was shaking so much that my friend could see it, but when I got home he was not there so I phoned him to see where he was he then started shouting at me and accusing me of having an affair and shouting at me and I told him that we were not and that we were just good friends and If I was having an affair do you think I would have told you were I was of course I would not but he would not accept that and he got angrier and angrier with me and when he came in I was on my computer talking on msn to my friends including the friend that I had just had a walk with and he was worried that I was not ok I told him that I was ok but this is not the end of it yet and I would let you know if I was ok or not and we would speak soon. However we remained on msn for some time and so did my other friends to just chatting about day to day things and asking what we thought of this or that in the news it was a very civil conversation and when Adrian came back in my tone changed towards one of my friends and he knew why because I had pre warned him that I was going to do this. It was my signal to him that he was home and that I would talk to him in awhile he understood this and was worried for me.

Adrian came in and he was so angry with me and very threatening to me both verbally and physically and I was scared of him, I already knew my marriage was over but it was just the case of having the courage to end it as at this moment I did not feel I had the courage to do this but I knew for the sake of my family and me I had to do something it was either end my marriage or end my life that was the choice I had not much of a choice really.

After Adrian went to bed I told my friend that I was phoning him and he said that was ok and I called Anthony to let him know I was ok and it was as bad as things got for me and whilst I was on the phone to Anthony, Adrian came back downstairs and once again screaming at me he grabbed me by my hair and slapped me around my face I knew my phone was still connected to my dear friend and was wondering what he was now thinking and I suspect he was now very worried. Adrian dragged me upstairs and punched me in my back and raped me repeatedly and once he was a sleep I sent Anthony a text message saying sorry speak soon.

The next morning once Adrian had gone to work and I left at the same time I phoned Anthony and asked him if I could come round he said that I could do and he was pleased that I had gone round to and he saw the state that I was in and was glad to see me and that I was as ok as I could be but the state I was in was not very good at all. I phoned work to say that something had happened and I would not be in till much later but in the end I did not go in at all that day, Anthony and I talked all day about all sorts of things but the main topic of conversation was about what had happened the night before and if I was sure I was ok well I wasn't but it was the best I was going to be for awhile and I knew it to. When the time for me to go home came I was crying and shaking it did not feel like home to me, that had now been destroyed for me I was not safe there anymore I did not belong there anymore.

When I got back in the children were in from school and were watching television and doing their homework and they came up to me as I walked in the door and greeted me with a big smile and a big cuddle and a kiss from each of them that, my children were the only reason why I was going home and not for any other reason either. It was my children that I was going home for and not for any other if it was not for my children I would have probably just disappeared without a trace or I would have killed myself not sure which one either would have been a possibility for me but I had the children so disappearing was not an option at this time.

I was back at work the next day but my heart was no longer in it my heart was not in anything anymore the spirit of me had been knocked out of me and I was so low I did not care what happened to me. However my friends did care and they were concerned about me and was doing everything that they could to help me and support me but at this time none of my friends knew to that extent things were happening at home or how things were for me at work. I was too scared to say to anyone how bad things were for me at home but Anthony realised very quickly how bad things were for me at work and how much work I had to do to get this project completed and he even told me that there was no way that I would get it finished in time but I was pushing myself so hard at work just to try and get things done but by doing this I was rejecting myself and started not eating properly, I refused to take regular breaks and I was already mentally and emotionally pushed to the limit and now I was pushing myself physically to the limit and Anthony was getting increasingly concerned about me.

I was walking my dog one evening and talking to my friend about his studies and the problems he was having and making suggestions on what could be wrong and between us we thought of everything but could not think what was wrong with it. I looked towards the A38 and said to him that it would be so easy and no-one would miss me but he told me he would and he wanted his friend to stay here and I agreed with him for now but could not promise that I would not have these thoughts again. I had walked a fair way down the path and I said to Anthony that I don't feel to good and he told me that he had picked it up awhile back but was not sure until I said something to him we were still talking but I don't recall much of the conversation after that the next thing I knew I was on the floor and not very responsive at all and the next thing I remember Anthony was at my side on the path with one of his house mates. He was there several minutes before I came to and was responding to him he had called an ambulance for me as I was not very responsive and he was worried about me and I was so cold but it was not cold out. I was in and out of consciousness for some time and I was talking but not making any sense to anyone, I was dazed and confused but knew my friend and that he was there for me I was looking for my dog I could not see her and Anthony said it is ok his friend had got her and was keeping her occupied for the time being well that was until the paramedics arrived and she was not to please that someone who she did not know was near me and trying to look after me but she was kept under control. Anthony was very worried and was there for me and was relieved that I was not going to be in the house that evening and that I would be safe for at least one night well that is what he thought anyway. However the problem was that my dog had to be taken home and there was no way Anthony was going to be able to take her home and I must have looked worried or something as the paramedics said it was ok they would take her home in their car which I was relieved about, however as they tried to get me up on the trolley my legs buckled on me and down to the floor I went again and this time three paramedics picked me and Anthony helped, he give me that reassuring cuddle and look to tell me that everything would be ok. He looked very worried and I could see Anthony looked it to and a little scared maybe too.

Whilst I was in the ambulance I was put on all sorts of monitors they took my blood pressure well at least they tried to do but they could not get a good reading they checked my blood sugars and that was very low it was less than two and they were worried that both my blood pressure and sugar was very low. My temperature was also very low and again this was causing concern. They eventually took me down to accident and emergency department were I was seen quiet quickly but there was no infections which is what they had thought, whilst I was in accident and emergency Adrian came into to see me and he was not at all very pleasant he was fairly aggressive towards me and I pulled away when he touched me I did not want him anywhere near me I hated him but it was not till this point that I felt this. I was scared of being alone with him I did not want him there with me. A few hours later I was still being checked over and they could not find any reason for me to have collapsed so they sent me home but I did not feel that good and as I got off the trolley I went very dizzy and I felt woozy and faint but I was still discharged and home we went. However once back at home Adrian was not at all pleased and was having a go at me for being taken to hospital and that the paramedics had brought Rose home and he said that if I was not having all these affairs then maybe I would not be so exhausted I wanted to slap him but I did not see the point I just went up to bed and tried to get some sleep as I had work to do in the morning if I was up to going but I was determined to go to work if I stayed there that was another thing but I could not decide that till the morning and it was already gone three in the morning so half the night had already gone so I did not think that I was going to get much sleep anyway but I was going to try and get some sleep though even if it was not much.

A few hours later the alarm was going off and it was time to get up and get the children up for school I felt rough the next morning when I awoke but decided that I would attempt to go into work if I stayed there then that was another thing. I had texted Anthony to let him know that I was out and would be in work and if he wanted a lift in then I would pick him up. I went into work on my own and it was not long before Anthony was at my office asking me what I was doing at work and if I was really ok he did not like the way I looked and asked me if I should have been in work I told him probably not but I am here anyway, I stood up to get something off the shelf and almost fainted again and Anthony asked me again should I really be in work and of course I should not have been but wanted to keep busy as I could be. He left my office then for a few minutes and popped back in and came into the office just in time as I almost went down again and that was it he told me to sit down and not move the next thing he was doing was bringing me a drink and something to eat it was just a biscuit but it was something and the thought was lovely. A few hours later lunchtime arrived and I did not have anything to eat and I did not take a break. However the manager was coming up the corridor with a visitor and I interrupted her to ask if she minded if I went home for the afternoon as I was not feeling to good she said I could go home. However when Anthony came back into my office I was getting ready to go home and I asked if he had finished for the day and thankfully he had so I asked if he could come in the car with me as I was not feeling to good and he agreed to that I was relieved as I was worried about driving on my own, however I did not want to go home and I asked if he would mind if I could go back to his for awhile and he agreed that would be ok, we talked a lot that afternoon but I also slept a lot to but I felt guilty for sleeping but Anthony was great with me he just got on with what he needed to do and let me sleep and it was the most peaceful sleep that I had in such a long time well that is what I thought anyway but I was shouting out and having nightmares but Anthony was great he just sat quietly next to me and told me that everything would be ok and just offered me comfort and support which was great and eventually I had some peaceful and calm sleep and I felt loads better once I woke up. I felt guilty for sleeping but my dear friend did not mind that I had done and he understood that I needed this but at least I was safe whilst I was at his and no-one was going to hurt me whilst I was there I was totally safe. However I panicked when I awoke as the time was getting on and I needed to be home and soon otherwise I would be in even more trouble than I was already the last thing I needed was more trouble from Adrian. I manage to get into the house a few seconds before Adrian got in which was what I usually did and did not want him to accuse me of anything else well he had accused me of everything anyway so why not something else.

I got in and made a meal for all of us, I ate mine and went to take rose for a walk and of course my dear friend was going to be meeting for a walk. Before I left to take rose for her walk he started having a go at me and telling me that I had half a hour tonight to take her for a walk but I told him I would take her for as long as a walk as I wanted to do, the tension between us was mounting and I could not stand being in the same room as him and I wanted to be as far away from him as possible and for as long as possible. I had decided to take rose on the park that night to see how she was going to be with other dogs and to see if she was going to be as good as she always was with me and she was and she enjoyed the freedom of being off the lead we walked all round the park, it was a pleasant evening and it was still fairly warm but I could feel a chill in the air so I decided to head back. I enjoyed the walk but I enjoyed my friends company even more it was good to have a close friend who did not want to hurt me or do anything to hurt me I valued that so much it was a good strong friendship and Anthony had fast become one of my closet friends and these sorts of friendships don't come along very often and when they did you keep them special and treasure them for always but I did not expect to find two friends that was that special to me and in time came close to me.

As the time for Anthony and I to go our separate ways I started to feel panic well up inside of me I did not want to go back home well it was not home anymore then again I have never really had anywhere that I could really call home well not since I lost my Grandma was the last place that I really felt that I had a home to go back to, I knew I had to go back home soon but I was delaying it as much as possible and I was crying as I went back, Anthony give me a hug and told me that I would be ok and we would speak soon and I knew we would do. As I walked the last bit of the way home tears were rolling down my face, I felt physically sick I would rather have gone anywhere but back to there, the only reason I had to go back for was my children and because of them I went back, sometime I wished that I had not as no sooner I walked through the door I was being had a go at. Adrian was always having a go at me these days and I was getting more and more frightened of being in the same house as him I did not want to be in the house at all it just give me the creeps if it was not for my children I probably would not have gone back.

Adrian and I had a heated argument later that evening and he was demanding his martial rights as he always did but I was determined that he was not going to get anything that I did not want but I knew he had other ideas but not me. However much I was hurting inside and the silent tears that I often had, I was deeply hurt and very scared not sure where things were going to go from here on, I also no longer loved Adrian and I certainly did not trust him anymore, I felt numb, I was feeling and thinking more and more that I should not be in this world and maybe the time had come to get me out of it I could not cope with anymore and I was constantly shaking and trembling I was too scared to breathe without Adrian having a go at me. I could not go on my computer without being having a go at but it was ok for Adrian to go on my computer to talk with his friends and meet other people but not ok for me. However I let him use my computer without me asking him who he was talking to and without making accusations at him so why could he not show me the same respect I had showed him and trusted me, I did not trust him anymore and that started going back on Boxing Day but I never question him.

The next day at work when I went in I was asked into the manager's office and told to shut the door, I was told that my depression or whatever it is, is effecting everyone and it was felt better if I did not work there anymore however I was tied into a contract and the only way I could be released from this was to place me on garden leave with effect immediately I was divested and very upset and now I had lost one of the reasons why I got up in the morning s but in many ways I was angry about this but in other ways I was glad to be getting out of there the pressure that I was under was unbearable and it was just one more pressure that I did not need but at the time I did not see it like that, I was hurt and very upset. I sent Anthony a text and told that I am out of here and I told you so, as we arrived that morning I told him that I was finished here just got the feeling that I was, and he told me that I was wrong but I was not. In my text I told him where I was and when he had a break I would be still there I knew how long he was in university that day, he found me on the break and give me a hug and sat down and got me another drink and told me to calm down as by now I was wheezing and he was worried I was going to have another asthma attack. There were others coming up to speak with me to see how I was and to see if I was ok I was polite with them and smiled at them but inside I was screaming why can't you just leave me alone. Anthony had to go into another lecture for about half an hour and asked if I would be ok and he would be back as soon as he could be and he would then get me out of here and get me to calm down. I was still crying a little later when he came back and he said to me what you like I know he only said that to make me laugh and it usually worked but I was crying to this time, he laughed to but it was nice that I could still laugh with my friend. I was still wheezing when we got in the car but being so upset I was not surprised that I was wheezing, we headed towards Anthony's place he knew that I was in no state to be left alone and I also needed company he knew me well enough to know what I would allow and not and when I would not let him make any decisions he was lucky this day that I needed to be in company but I also needed some space to and he knew that space was what I needed but to have someone there if I wanted to talk. The friendship that had developed was a close and special friendship with trust, understanding and care. I felt like I had a brother in Anthony that was the sort of bond that we had between us and I felt that this would never be broken. It took me awhile to calm down once I got to Anthony's but I did and was washed out but mid afternoon and I was very quiet and I looked up and noticed that Anthony had dozed off on the settee, I learned back in the other settee and curled my feet up and I dozed to sleep it was not until one of his house mates came in that I woke up and by now it was going on for four in the afternoon, it had been a long and draining day.

I was also in touch with Clive through e-mail and I had left a couple of messages on his answer phone but not heard anything as yet but I had only done this that day so it was early days as yet.

That evening we were due to go to the local drama group which we were part of and had been for a few years now I had been longer than Adrian, but we all went including the children I was going up to help with some bits for the spring play and Adrian decided to come to, when my phone went off it was Clive but I had missed his call so I tried ringing him back but could not get through at first I did not recognise the number well not until he rang me back a few moments later, he was very supportive but unfortunately he was on holiday and would not be back for a couple more days we had a good conversation and we would arranged to meet once he was back from his holiday and I thanked him for calling me but I was glad that he had done and I was not doing so good at that time. I was even being careful what I said just in case Adrian came out and questioned me that was the last thing I needed further hassle from him. We kept the conversation brief as we could and Clive had rang me as I had left messages for him on his answer phone I appreciated that he took time out to contact me whilst he was away but also that my messages had been passed on to him I felt someone else was there for me.

We did not stay long at the drama group that night but there was no need to do either, once we got back home I made sure our children was getting ready for bed and going to bed they were tired and it made it a late night for them on a school night when we went to the drama group but it was only once a week that we went and our meeting night was a Wednesday it was just one of those things that it was mid week.

Once my children were settled into bed I went and checked my e-mails and see who was online I had a number of friends online including Anthony and I opened five conversations up that night and was managing fairly well to have a conversation with all of them until Adrian came down and raising his voice at me and telling me that I had no right to be on my computer now and he was angry but I had no idea why he was so angry but then I did not usual know why he was angry. He demanded that I went to bed with him right here and now and I told him that I would go to bed in a little while, well that was it, he grabbed me by my hair and dragged me onto the floor where he kicked me in my back and ripped my clothes off me and again raped me. I was crying with how he was treating me and what he was doing to me I felt disgusted with myself for not fighting him more. After he withdrew from me he punched me in the chest and walked calmly upstairs and went to bed for a while I followed upstairs to go into the bathroom were I cleaned myself up and got my dressing gown on and then went back downstairs to make a hot drink and continue talking to my friends, whilst I was talking to them most of them was now saying good night to me but Anthony and I just put the symbol of someone crying onto the msn conversation and said no more I did not have to my friend knew that something had happened as I had not replied to the conversation that we were having. I was just about to say goodnight to him when Adrian came down the stairs and shouting at me and telling me that I think more of my friends than I do him and at the point I did care more for my friends than I did him at least my friends did not hurt me like he was doing I did not expect them to do either.

The next morning I was talking to Anthony on msn and we were talking and I asked him if there is anything I can do to help he only had to ask and he asked me if I would proof read his dissertation for him to make sure that there were no un-foreseen errors and I agreed to do this gladly I asked him to e-mail it to me and I would start looking at it straight away for him he thanked me and sent it to me, It was good but there was a couple of errors but easy enough to correct or I saw something that could have been worded better it took us hours to go through this but it was worth it at the time but I also had to have some of background information to the topic so I had an understanding of what I was reading so I could make some sense of it and it worked quiet well having this information. After I had been reading it for a while I asked Anthony if he would like some company and have a break from his studies he said he would like a break for while, I asked him if he had eaten anything that day so far and when he informed that he had not I asked if he would like me to bring lunch down and if so what did he want we settled on a sandwich from birds and I took to him and as always when we met we always greeted each other with a hug, I gave him his lunch and made sure he ate it before I left as I knew what he was like he would leave it till later and not eat it but he also needed a bit of a break from study I stayed for just over a hour and went back home to continue reading through his dissertation and offering alternative ways to wording something's, it was why he asked me to look through it for him and I felt I was being too harsh with it but he told me that is what it needs and was pleased that he asked me and he knew I would tell him straight and I would be honest with him. He knew I always was.

Once it was done Anthony had made all the changes that needed to be done and it was ready to hand in, I was pleased that I was able to help my dear friend.

A few days later I was back down at Anthony's by mid morning and

307

when he greeted me with a hug a winced and I had not realised that I was in so much discomfort until I got this hug off Adrian and he asked me what was wrong and at first I told him nothing and the look on his face told me he did not believe me but I told him it is not for now there were others around and I was not about to let them know what was going on for me and I knew Anthony would not tell them either. I had been at Anthony's for a couple of hours when he asked me again what was wrong earlier and I just said to him would you mind if we talked privately he told me that was no problem so we went into his room and closed the door he asked me again what was wrong and I told him that my back is sore and would you mind looking at it for me he was nervous about doing this and he knew I was putting a lot of trust in him by asking him he was shaking because he was concerned about what he was going to find and when he saw the bruising on my back he asked me if I wanted him to take some photo's of the bruising for me and that he would keep them on his pc well hidden in case I ever wanted them or needed them for anything, I thanked him for what he had just done and then I was crying he sat next to me and held me can give me the comfort that I so badly needed and when he asked me when this happened and when I told him that it was the other night when I was not talking to you. He said that he knew something had happened. Then he asked me what I was going to do now I told him I did not know at this stage I was too scared to do anything but I would have to do something sooner or later. I knew that he was right to and I had considered contacting my solicitor and get some proper advice as I was not sure what I should or not do at this stage but I decided to think about it this some more before making this decision to go and seek legal advice. I was nowhere near ready for that one as yet. Anthony and I talked about a number of things and we had a laugh and Anthony told me it was nice to see me laughing and able to have a laugh with everything that was going off for me I could still manage to have the odd laugh with my friend it was days with my friend that helped me cope with things a little bit once I got home.

Once Clive got back from his holiday we were in touch at first through e-mail and also through phone calls I was glad of this extra support and it was not long before we were meeting up and talking about things but his kindness and care and friendship meant so much to me but I was wary of him at first but as my trust built up with Clive I was ok and I had to put a lot of trust in him to be able to open up a little bit to him I found this difficult at first but I knew I had to trust someone soon. However went me met up I did not tell Adrian that is what I was doing he thought I was going up to the drama group but I did not care what he thought anymore I knew I need to talk to someone and fast to. I knew I could not take much more on my own or cope with much more I was breaking down slowly but surely. Seeing my fiends was one of the few things that was helping me and keeping me going it was because of these two friends that I had the will to continue and to keep fighting even though it was difficult at times it was worth it at the time I did not see it this way I saw it as I had no way out and I had no way to turn well that is how it felt anyway.

I was talking to Clive and Anthony a lot and I was in constant contact with Anthony as he was with me things at home were getting worse and by now I had removed my wedding, engagement and eternity rings I did not feel that I should be wearing them anymore I did not feel married or loved anymore and I decided that there was nothing left in our marriage and now I wanted out, it was not long before I made the decision to go and seek legal advice and I was given some good advice but any correspondence from my solicitor was sent to Anthony's address because I feared what would happen if they went to my address and Adrian getting hold of them I was terrified of him knowing that I had done this and I certainly did not want to be hit again if I could avoid that situation then I was determined to do.

I was starting to feel I was losing my friend he was finishing university and going back home for awhile and then going into care force for a time but I was going to miss him dreadfully once he was gone. I was helping him pack his things up from his room and at times I would just sit quietly and cry or I would just be so quiet that I was in deep thought I was not ready to lose my friend just yet but I knew deep down I was not losing him things were just changing life was changing for him and for me. I felt scared and I was not sure how I was going to cope once he had gone and I did not know Clive that well as yet and I was scared. The day soon came for Anthony to say goodbye I originally said I would not go down on that last day I as I could not bear going to see him and saying goodbye it was hard for me to say goodbye to a close friend and I knew we would still be in touch but that was not the same but I would have to adapt to him not being around so much, but we were still there for each other at the same time his other house mates were moving on and I had got to know them all quite well to and I said goodbye to them and I promised myself that I would not cry when Anthony went and I was doing well until he started to cry and that was it just set me off and I was in tears Anthony is a special friend he is like a brother to me and that is the most special friendship that you can have but it did not half hurt when he left but I knew he had to go but I was going to miss him dearly. However as the weeks went by Anthony was noticing more and more bruising on me and often asked me where I got that one from and I had often not noticed or I chose not to notice that I had got bruising appearing it was often best not to notice this but Anthony had and he would not let me ignore them either he asked me how did you get that and when. Often the bruises were of finger marks or all hand marks and sometimes there were fist marks on me but I tried to hide as much as I could. Anthony also commented on the fact that I was no longer wearing my rings and when I told him they don't mean anything anymore it is over. He questioned me to see if I was sure but I was but it was doing something about it that was the scary part of it. I knew that now I had made this decision I had now got to find away to end my marriage but was not sure how I was going to do that and I was scared.

Anthony also helped me go on the motorway I was terrified of driving on the motorway and I asked him he was able to help me with this one and he said he would be delighted to help me so he got me on them at first he sat at the side of me and then a little while later I followed him onto the motorway and I panicked at first and nearly backed out but I did not and when we pulled off the motorway we pulled in for some lunch and Anthony treated me to say well done. However he told me that we could do with doing a longer run on the motorway and so we did I was so pleased to be able to do this and I was feeling confident that I could do this but that was thanks to a dear friend and his kindness and care that I was able to do that.

The day Anthony left was a reasonable day the sun had been shinning but now it was overcast and threatening to rain and I give Anthony a huge hug and we parted I wished him a good and safe journey home and for him to take care of himself, he promised me that we would be in touch very soon and he was.

When I got home after Anthony had left I was crying and very upset and Adrian knew I was going to say goodbye to a friend but it did not stop him having a go at me and accusing me of being in love with Anthony and I turned round to him then if loving and caring for someone like a brother then I am guilty but if you he was asking me if I was in love with him as in relationship then the answer was no I was not, I love Anthony as a brother and a special friend and nothing more. Adrian was furious with my answer he was hoping that I would say that I was in love with him and when I did not he was angry he thought he found the perfect excuse to have a go at me but he did not need an excuse he did it anyway. I was on my computer when an e-mail came in from Anthony telling me he arrived home safely and he thanked me for everything I had done to help him but I did not feel that I had done that much.

Chapter 12

I HAD NOT HAD A BREAK SINCE I had my operation but I was becoming desperate to get away but I knew that I could not get away whilst things were the way the at home.

From the time Anthony left to go back home the next few months went by very quickly. One Sunday morning Adrian and I were talking and he asked me if I still loved him and when I told him that I did not he told me he still loved me but I told him that he had a funny way of showing it to me with raping me and hitting me and now it was too late for me the love I had for him was now gone and had been destroyed by the way he had treated me and I certainly did not trust him anymore and I knew without trust there was no relationship. He asked me what I wanted him to do next and I could not answer that one I did not know myself but I was hoping that we could have built things back up again but I was not sure about that either so for the time being we carried on as we were knowing that I did not love him or trust him. The school holidays were fast approaching and I was not sure how I was going to handle that with all the stress I was under with my marriage breaking down I did not feel I could cope with that on top of everything else. I decided to take our children to Matlock for the day they love it there and so did I, even though it was busy it was peaceful and it was there that I made some from difficult decisions including that the time had come to end my marriage once and for all, I know my next action was cruel but it was the only way I could do this without there being anymore arguments without Adrian begging me just to give him one more chance I could not bear that one so I sent him a text and said I feel that the time has come for you to move out I was crying when I sent it after all we had been together eighteen years but enough was enough. I got a text back saying that I am cruel but ok but we need to talk before he left I knew that he was going to do that one I felt that it was another attempt to get me to let him stay for awhile longer. A few days later the children were at their grandparents and the discussion still had not been had and I was scared of this happening. I was on my computer when he came in from work and he asked me if we could talk and I told him we could and all he ask me was why did I tell him a text and when do I want him to go I told him the sooner the better but I was not going to be the one to tell our children I told him he had to do that and to my surprise he did that was the hardest thing to deal with telling my children that their parents were splitting up at first we thought that it may have only been temporary but I knew deep down that this was permanent I had had enough and I could not take anymore. We agreed on the date that he would move out and I was scared that he would not go and I would suffer even more.

That evening I went for a walk as usual with rose and I needed to be as far away as possible for a few hours I wanted time to think about what had been discussed and time out I also made two phone calls one to Anthony and one to Clive Anthony told me that he will make sure he is a round on the day that he goes. Clive was just as supportive of me but no-one could do anything now it was out of my hands and no-one could see what was going to happen in the future but I had two very special friends who were there for me and I valued their friendships so much and I always will do.

However before Adrian Left he was still demanding his martial rights and I would not give it to him but he took it from me by force, the next day I spoke with my old counsellor just for a general chat and to touch base a little bit and she told me that my marriage had been like this for years now and she was surprised that we had lasted as long as we did when I told her what had happened she asked me what I was going to do about it and when I said nothing she seemed surprised but I did not feel I could go through what I had done before I just could not cope with that. She understood and wished me well. I thanked her and wished her well.

The day soon came for Adrian to go and all day I was scared if he would go or not I hoped and prayed that he would go without any problems, when the time came for him to come back home from work I was on the phone to Clive I had told him my decision but not now the day had come I was scared and I was asking if I had done the right thing he told me if I had made a rash decision he would have been more concerned but because I had made the decision awhile ago he was not that concerned that I had made this decision and as Adrian came in from work I had to go and hang up I was terrified of him and what he was going to do even though he was going. I was still not sure he would go but the last few days he had been packing his things and he had packed his clothes and a few other bits and pieces that he wanted I did not care what he took as long as he was going I told myself not to cry but I knew I would do when the time came but he was delaying things and biding for time it was almost eight in the evening and he still had not gone and I was thinking that he would not be going and I began to panic he just did not want to leave but he did and as he left I started crying and part of me was screaming inside to tell him to stay but I stayed by my decision for him to go I knew I could not have carried on the way I was doing.

A sent a text to Anthony to let him know and it was not a clear text but a jumbled text and he called me but I was in tears and so were the kids so he decided to call me back later and give me some time to calm down and to give me some time with the children and give them the comfort they needed as this was a major change for them to and now things had changed so much so quickly and not just for me but for my children to. Adrian had made promises that he would come and see the kids everyday but he did not keep to his promises and in the end he came up on a Tuesday and a Thursday and the children went down to his parents on the Saturday were he was now living.

I had to go down and see him a few weeks later get some money from him and whilst I was down there he said that I owed him to give him what he wanted otherwise I would not get the money he had for me I told him to forget his money and I went to leave but he grabbed hold of me and pulled me back and told me that he was going to have what he wanted I was begging him not to do anything but he once again raped me and I felt that this was somehow my fault and I deserved this maybe I did. I went home and I was crying and felt so violated and scared and I sent Clive an e-mail and he asked me what had happened but to forget about it and move on but I did not tell him too much detail but enough.

The children was going away with the grandparents the following week and I was taking Daniel and his girlfriend camping for a few days I had been desperate to get away and had been for some time, the tent went up well and we got organised and rose had come with us I did not go anywhere without her she was the best company I could ask for I was also hoping that I would get some time on my own and time to think and reflect about the last few months I was relaxed whilst we were camping and it was good to be away for awhile and to have a break from everything that had been going on for me. However I was very low and very depressed but I was determined to enjoy these few days were I could. Daniel and Susan enjoyed theirsleves which was all I was bothered about. When the time came for us to go home I felt panic and scared I did not want to go back and face everyone back at home.

We got back later that afternoon and everything re-hit me once again and I just did not want to be here anymore, Susan had asked me to take her into Loughborough for something and I took her and whilst I was there I bought myself a bottle of Archer's and took it back home once back at home I felt I had nothing to live for and I had drank half a bottle in one go and sent Clive a text to say what I had done but there was nothing he could do about it at the time I was already in the car and driving I did not care if I came back or not but I got a text from Clive asking me to go back home and I know he was worried about me I did go back home after a short while, I drank the rest of the bottle and then texted Anthony and Clive, Clive was relived that I was back at home and at least I was safe Anthony could not understand the logic in me drinking and driving but I was no way thinking clearly at all and I just wanted out of this world. I was texting Clive and he was me, I asked for help and he asked me if he could get someone to talk to me would I agree to this and I did but things did not work out that way, but he was supposed to be going out that night but he came round to mine and when he arrived I was on my bed crying and the first thing he said to me was what are we going to do with you and I just shrugged my shoulders he sat on the edge of the bed towards the bottom of my bed and I sat up and I was crying even more I rested my head on his shoulder were I got a friendly hug. He asked me if I would talk to anyone if he could sort it I told him I would but when he contacted my Doctor and they put him through to NHS direct and until a doctor had seen me there was nothing anyone else could do. Daniel made Clive several cups of tea and Rose was all over Clive I was also threatening to take the paracetmols that I had bought but I had not done. Clive was with me until the very early hours of the morning and spoke with me several times during the next couple of days. Community Mental Health Team came out and accessed me and I was no longer any danger to myself so there was nothing else that they could do at this time as I was already on anti-depressants there was nothing much else they could do unless I got worse. This just infuriated me and Clive and our hands were tied with this one they had made their decision and that was final.

A few weeks later I was feeling much the same as I had been for a while now and not getting any better so I went and fetched the paracetamols out of my car and took them into my room and I contacted Clive and asked for his help and asked him to phone me and when he did he heard me taking the paracetmols out of the packet and had started taking them I had took eight so far when Clive phoned me he asked me what it was he could hear, he knew what it was he just wanted me to confirm it and somehow I promised that I would not take anymore and it was not long before our conversation ended and I was settling down to sleep.

The next morning Clive rang me to make sure I was ok and I could hear the relief in his voice that I was ok and he seemed pleased that I was he was a truly good friend to me and one that cared about me. I appreciated his concern and making sure I was ok not many people would have done what he had done for me.

I was meeting Clive on a regular basis and was beginning to open up to him about what I had gone through as a child and he felt humbled that I felt that I could share some of what I had gone through as a child but it was hard talking to him about what I had gone through but it helps but it was hard for me to do this but I felt that it was necessary for him to understand where I was at and why I asked the things I did and why

I was so frightened and why I did not trust people very easily. I wanted him to understand why I was the way I was and he did understand where I was at, he understood more than I expected him to do.

I asked Clive to act as next of kin for me as my eldest child was under eighteen and I did not feel that it was right for my child to be this and I was pleased when he agreed to this for me. When I had an asthma attack a few weeks later he was there for me but when I texted Adrian to collect Jade from the hospital he did so and had a go that I should be going home to look after our children and I expected him to stay and look after our children whilst I was in hospital and he had not stayed he had gone back to where he had come from which was Leanne's whom was my best friend but not anymore and he said he could not stay at my house it was not fair, Clive had seen me shake when I was contacting him and had not seen anything like it before and nothing so instantly as I was when I was contacting Adrian and that just showed him how bad things were between us he had known that they were bad before but that night the reality of it was clearly shown that night. Once they were going to admit me to the ward Clive decided that it was time to go home and get some rest himself I thanked him for his kindness and as always he told me that it was ok. He had been at the hospital a couple of times when I had an attack and I was glad that he was there.

At the same time I was still part of the drama group but I was finding this increasingly hard and the stress for me was unbearable, and it was hard, having to work so close to Adrian. I was having serious second thoughts about being involved in pantomime that year but for the time being I was going to persevere with this for the time being.

A few weeks later my feeling s and what I thought was going off still with Leanne was confirmed to me, Adrian came round to see my children and told me that he wanted a word with me and when he told me I was furious with him I knew what had happened back at boxing day and what I suspected was going on was confirmed that they were officially together I was livid with him and I was angry with her how could she betray her friend so much, I sent a text to him after he had gone and told me how the hell dare he accuse me of having affairs when he was doing it himself. As for Leanne she got a text to, basically saying that she was a slut and she was sleeping her way through everyone in the group and how dare she call herself a friend when she can go and do that. After Adrian had left I contacted the chairman of the drama group and asked him to contact me urgently and I was crying when I left the message and it was not long before he called me back and asked me what the problem was and when I told him that I do not think that I can continue with the group he asked me why and I told he was shocked and angry about what they had done and he was not surprised that I felt the way I did but asked me to think about it before I made any rash decisions and as I was away camping the following weekend he told me to think about it and get back to him when I got back I agreed to this. However once I got back I decided that they were not going to push me out of the group and that I would continue with the pantomime but he knew it would not be easy for me and was there to support me where he could and he acted as a go between so that things were as manageable as they could be. It was a stressful few months for me with being so closer involved with pantomime and the atmosphere there was unbearable and at times I wanted to go.

However in the mean time I had received an e-mail from my dad asking me if I was ok and that he heard that there were problems between Adrian and I and if I was ok I replied to him and told him that we had separated and he says he was sorry to hear that and he told me that he was there if I needed him to be but I had kept my distance from him for so long but something made me contact him and go and see him he seemed genuinely sorry for me and told me he knew how it feels. Whilst we were talking he also apologised for what he had done to me and said that he wanted to make amends for that and if there was anything he could do to help then I only had to say I did not want anything from him however he was being genuine when he said he was sorry. He invited me out one evening with him and my step mum and I went but I felt uncomfortable all evening and felt trapped and very scared and it left me feeling frightened and when I got back I did not want to live any more. I e-mailed Clive and told him how I was feeling and he told me that it was not worth it and I should not see my dad again if this was the reaction I was going to have and I knew he was right so the little contact I have with my dad the better and that is what I do have no contact with him it is safer and better for me to do this.

I was also asking Clive about me going to a church and if he felt that I was ready to go back into church and his reply to me was that it is important if I feel ready to go back to church I was but I was scared and scared of being betrayed again. We were discussing this at length then one day he informed that there was a service at his Chapel that evening and I would be welcome to come if I so wanted to do but I was not sure at first and I asked him what if it freaks me out and I cannot cope with this he told me I could just leave the service that was not a problem, then I said to him that is not allowed and I knew what was going to come back and he said who said it is not allowed he told me that I could come and go as I pleased. There was no pressure on me it was up to me. I told him I would see but I also asked how many would be there. What if I got upset what would people think? He then informed me that there is not many probably no more than ten and no one would think anything if I got upset because it was ok in the safety of their fellowship. I then made the decision to go to the Chapel that evening I knew if I thought about it some more I would not have gone but I went however once I got there I froze and could not go in but thankfully for me Clive came out to my car and tapped on my window and told me that I did not have to do this if I did not want to do but I told him that I did and he waited with me for a few minutes and took me inside were I met his wife but I could feel myself shaking he told me that I was ok and there was nothing that could harm me here and I was safe. Everyone started to arrive and I started to feel uncomfortable and panic raised through me I felt so scared but I could not go in to the Chapel properly for the service I sat outside the doors and felt panic but I was ok and I actually enjoyed that service even though I was not in with the rest of them I was there. However I felt guilty afterwards for not going in properly and I apologised to Clive and he told me that I am a lot closer to going in to what I was before that Sunday and what I had done was very brave thing for anyone to do but especially someone with my history even so it was very brave I did not feel brave I felt I had let my dear friend down even though he said I had not I felt that I had. I stayed till everyone had gone and I stepped into the chapel whilst it was still set up for the service it felt ok but frightening to me to be doing this but I felt safe.

For several service I could not go completely into the service and then one day I took the plunge I waited to Clive had gone into the chapel and I followed and went to sit down I sat furthest away from the door I knew that way I was less likely to run and I remained in the service for the full service and I do now for every service after that.

The day were to go live with the pantomime was getting closer by the minute and I was very anxious about this but I knew I had come through these last few months without two many problems but the stress was getting to me and I was getting fed up of being snipped at all of the time and I knew that it would not be long before one of us snapped.

During the first weekend of the live shows there was problems as I was back stage and cast manager a job that I had done for so many years and a job that I enjoyed especially with all the organization of everything I enjoyed it was tiring but I enjoyed it and during the first performance I was being constantly being undermined by Leanne in front of everyone and I took as much as I could and then I got upset and went to see Alex the chairman of the group and told him that is it I have enough and I was in tears, he took me off stage and found somewhere quiet for us to talk and he asked me what the problem was and when I told him he said he had noticed but was not interfering as long as I was ok but I was not and he had to have words with them and told them that if they had changed anything they should have had the decent to let me know I almost walked right in the middle of the performances and that would have meant they would have had to find someone else to play the parts I was doing and Alex told me that it would have been their own fault and they had brought it on their-selves and they should have thought about their actions before they did what they did and he was not pleased with them. However I decided for the sake of the group that I would continue but I made it clear that I was not there for them. All through the pantomime I wanted to scratch Leanne's eyes out how I did not I do not know how I showed such good control.

I was supposed to be having the after show party at my house and it had been arranged that they would be there but would go as soon as the speeches were over, however someone decided to interfere with this and approach Alex who spoke with me and said for the sake of the group someone else was going to do the party and when I told him that they were going as soon as the speeches were over he told me that it was just someone interfering were they did not have to do.

I was glad when the pantomime run was over but before I went to the party I spoke with Adrian and told him that if he shows any affection towards Leanne then I would have words with him he was not to show any affection in front of me or our children and he promised me that he would not do. However once at the party once everyone had arrived, I was seated on one of the settee's and Jade came in through the patio doors just as Adrian went to kiss Leanne, I saw the look on Jade face and she ran through the house and out of the front door and she was crying fortunately for me someone was after her and was with her comforting her I was pleased to see now I could deal with what had just happened. Adrian had gone into the kitchen to fetch himself and Leanne a drink and I followed him in and I just snapped I told him that I had asked you not to show affection towards Leanne so how the hell dare you go against your promise not to do this, how dare you upset our children even more than you have done already have you got no decency and at this moment I saw the glasses that was in his hands which were now full and my hands were at the right level to the glasses and I just knocked the contents all over him he was a bit red faced to say the least. However I was then asked to leave the party but Alex said to the people who were hosting the party that it was not my fault and that if I was having to go then so should they but they said no I had to go I was upset about this and was crying and Alex was holding me and I was crying for the first time in front of everyone and he told me to let it out it is ok he really felt for me. He told me that when I was ready that I should go home and get out of this gold fish bowl that I was in and had been in since the separation and he told me that he was proud of me and how I had handled the situation and he told me that I should be proud of myself they're the ones that should be ashamed not me.

I now go to a completely different type of church to what I went to as child but it is of my choice that I chose something different I wanted something different. However I am much more comfortable with then I ever was when I was a child. It has took me a lot to get where I am today and being part of the Chapel is so perfect for me now. I am glad that I have got this and that it is becoming special for me again. It has been hard to lose some of the power from the past but I am getting there and

I know that this will continue to improve for me as time goes by and this will become so much easier for me in time but that is what you have to do give yourself as in time you can get through this and overcome most things it is not easy at the time but you can get there in the end but it is not something that can be achieved over night but over a long time and I have got frustrated with things at time because I have not been able to do things when I have expected myself to be able to do things but over time I have got there and will continue to get there but I have to remember that these things take time.

It has took me a long time to be able to go into a church or a Chapel again but I was introduced to a lovely friendly Chapel through one of my dear friends just by Clive inviting me to a service but there was never any pressure on me to do this and I am so grateful to him for inviting me back into church but most importantly supporting me through this time and being there for me always and for being such a special friend to me and I enjoy the service and being back in church I never thought that I would have done again after everything that had happened and being betrayed by the church so badly as a child it has been hard but it has been worth it for me to be able to feel free and safe in a church building again and the Chapel I go to is perfect for me.

And so my life goes on.

Epilogue

MY FUTURE IS NOW LOOKING MUCH BETTER AND safer. I still have times were I am very down but thanks to Clive and Anthony I am still here today. I have discovered I have had a lot to live for and a lot to be thankful for. I want to say a huge thank-you to my close friends for everything that they have done for me and for being there for me and may do for in the future and for keeping me going through some very difficult times for me I am sure at times that it was not easy for them to see me as bad as I was, but they never gave up on me no matter what happened. I have also got someone very special in my life and I am going to treasure this for now and always, as I will do with my friendships. I am eternal grateful to these special friends for their understanding, kindness, and caring. I would also like to thank my counsellor for be patientence with me and for her understanding and care. I have suffered throughout my life and like so many others have, but my life is starting to turn around for me and my future looks brighter and I am happier than I have been for such a long time. I have got some very special people that I will always be grateful to and forever thankfully for.

I still miss my Grandma terribly but I will never forget her and she is always in my in heart and memories forever and always very close to me.

God bless

Lightning Source UK Ltd.
Milton Keynes UK
12 June 2010

155498UK00001B/56/P